ROUTLEDGE LIBRARY EDITIONS: LITERARY THEORY

Volume 3

E. M. FORSTER AS CRITIC

E. M. FORSTER AS CRITIC

RUKUN ADVANI

Routledge
Taylor & Francis Group
LONDON AND NEW YORK

First published in 1984 by Croom Helm Ltd

This edition first published in 2017
by Routledge
2 Park Square, Milton Park, Abingdon, Oxon OX14 4RN

and by Routledge
711 Third Avenue, New York, NY 10017

Routledge is an imprint of the Taylor & Francis Group, an informa business

© 1984 Rukun Advani

All rights reserved. No part of this book may be reprinted or reproduced or utilised in any form or by any electronic, mechanical, or other means, now known or hereafter invented, including photocopying and recording, or in any information storage or retrieval system, without permission in writing from the publishers.

Trademark notice: Product or corporate names may be trademarks or registered trademarks, and are used only for identification and explanation without intent to infringe.

British Library Cataloguing in Publication Data
A catalogue record for this book is available from the British Library

ISBN: 978-1-138-69377-7 (Set)
ISBN: 978-1-315-52921-9 (Set) (ebk)
ISBN: 978-1-138-68395-2 (Volume 3) (hbk)
ISBN: 978-1-138-68398-3 (Volume 3) (pbk)
ISBN: 978-1-315-54423-6 (Volume 3) (ebk)

Publisher's Note
The publisher has gone to great lengths to ensure the quality of this reprint but points out that some imperfections in the original copies may be apparent.

Disclaimer
The publisher has made every effort to trace copyright holders and would welcome correspondence from those they have been unable to trace.

E.M. FORSTER AS CRITIC

RUKUN ADVANI

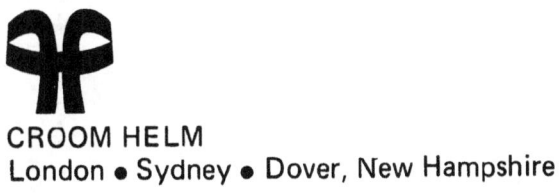

CROOM HELM
London • Sydney • Dover, New Hampshire

©1984 Rukun Advani
Croom Helm Ltd, Provident House, Burrell Row,
Beckenham, Kent BR3 1AT
Croom Helm Australia Pty Ltd, First Floor, 139 King St.,
Sydney, NSW 2001, Australia

British Library Cataloguing in Publication Data

Advani, Rukan
   E.M. Forster as critic.
   1. Forster, E.M. Knowledge – Literature
   I. Title
   801'.95'0924   PR6011.058Z
   ISBN 0-7099-0545-9

Croom Helm, 51 Washington Street, Dover,
New Hampshire 03820, USA

Library of Congress Catalog Card Number: 84-45981
Cataloging in Publication Data applied for.

Printed and bound in Great Britain

CONTENTS

PREFACE

LIST OF ABBREVIATIONS

INTRODUCTION: FORSTER AND THE LIBERAL DILEMMA.... 1

1. FORSTER'S VIEW OF THE NATURE OF MAN AND HUMAN EXISTENCE. 22
2. FORSTER'S VIEW OF SOCIAL ORDER 53
3. FORSTER'S VIEW OF RELIGION 72
4. FORSTER'S AESTHETICS 92
5. FORSTER'S VIEW OF THE NOVEL 123
6. FORSTER ON CRITICISM AND AS A CRITIC 152
7. FORSTER'S LITERARY CRITICISM 168

CONCLUSION 208

SELECT BIBLIOGRAPHY 213

INDEX 249

PREFACE

This book discusses an aspect of E.M. Forster which has hitherto received scant critical attention - the novelist's criticism of society and literature. No one can doubt that Forster's fiction, in particular Howards End and A Passage to India, is the real basis of his distinction, yet it has not been sufficiently noticed that he had interesting and valuable things to say about man, society, religion, aesthetics and literature.

The world after the First War decreasingly permitted the kind of fiction Forster wanted to and could write: the creation of aesthetic wholes in novels was simply too remote from the fragmented reality all around. This was an important reason which made Forster a socio-literary critic and propagandist of art. At one level Forster's criticism reflects the heterogeneous and unyoked world it comments on, for it was written over a long period and seems made up of disconnected and unconnectable bits and pieces. But I have tried to show, even while keeping history and chronology in view, that Forster's criticism is not a chaotic mass because loose thematic threads run through and unify much of it. Although written in the form of discrete essays, broadcasts, reviews, lectures and occasional notes over a period of fifty or so years, the most significant pieces within the body of Forster's critical writing contribute implicitly to ideas which revolve loosely around the author's conception of what constitutes order in human life. I have tried to show that Forster's post-Edwardian non-fiction, which focuses on literary and social subjects in an apparently random manner, is at a deeper level a search for and critique of order in four broad areas - the individual, society and politics, religion, and art.

After an Introduction where I outline a

PREFACE

historical and cultural context within which answers from liberal humanists to questions about the nature of order became imperative, and which in large measure made necessary Forster's transition from artist to critic, Chapters One to Four separately discuss each of these four areas. Chapter One discusses the order which Forster perceived within the individual. This emerges through analysis of Forster's engagement with assumptions about human nature in Marxism, Fascism and the scientific and mystical varieties of Socialism. Chapter Two shows how Forster's notion of the individual extends into his ideas about democracy, tolerance and spiritual aristocracy. The next chapter is an exposition of Forster on religion. Against the doctrinaire order demanded by Christianity, Hinduism and Islam, Forster asserts an alternative, eclectic humanism which, in my view, emerges most clearly and forcefully when seen in relation to what it argues against or rejects. Chapter Four analyses Forster's ideas about aesthetic order or art. I have tried to see Forster's aesthetics as a part of his concern to discover order in his universe and discussed why Forster saw art as the most perfect expression of order. In doing this I have also suggested that Forster's view of art is a via media between the extremes of aestheticism and moralism in literary theory. Chapter Five examines Forster's theory of the novel from the perspective that <u>Aspects of the Novel</u> represents its author's perception of the ways in which fictional universes may be made perfectly ordered. The idea of perfect fictional order is shown to have indubitable, even if tenuous, links with the ideas about order outlined in earlier chapters. The penultimate chapter is about Forster's view of criticism. His hostility to criticism is seen as fundamentally consistent with his view that because art represents spiritual order, criticism is unhelpful inasmuch as it breaks up such order with inappropriate logic and analysis. Forster's own methodology as a literary critic is also discussed here. The last chapter is a mixture of documentation and analysis which seeks to outline some of Forster's best literary criticism, as well as show how a peculiar and unusual world view make this criticism distinctive. This final chapter, as much as the earlier ones, tries to fulfil a major objective of this book - to give exposure to the large body of Forster's writing which is readable and valuable but which has remained mostly unpublished and undiscussed.

PREFACE

In an earlier form this book was a Ph.D. dissertation written at Cambridge between 1978-82. It was supervised by Iain Wright and my first debt is to him for his informality, warmth, personal interest and perceptive observations. I cherish memories of his friendly and unselfish encouragement. I am equally grateful to Dr. G.K. Das who suggested the subject of my research and who was (and continues) a spiritual mentor. Dr. Brijraj Singh and Dr. A.N. Kaul have helped in ways impossible to define. So have my closest friends - Ratan, R.K., Kade, Shalini and Thibaut. The Butlers, the Meyers, the Reeds, the Brews, Chris Reinking and the Kesavans all have a hidden hand in this.

I also wish to thank Dr. John Beer and Dr. Elizabeth Heine for reading an early draft of some portions and helping with several useful hints and insights. Dr. Michael Halls was always pleasant and accessible. The Inlaks Foundation gave the island of money on which this book is built. The Edwina Mountbatten Fund and Trinity Hall kept the waters out at crucial stages. The Provost and Fellows of King's College and the Society of Authors have been kind enough to grant permission to quote from the Forster manuscripts.

LIST OF ABBREVIATIONS

AH	*Abinger Harvest*
APTI	*A Passage to India*
Aspects	*Aspects of the Novel*
CB	*Commonplace Book*
GLD	*Goldsworthy Lowes Dickinson*
TCD	*Two Cheers for Democracy*
Thomson	*E.M. Forster: Albergo Empedocle & other writings*, ed. G.H. Thomson

For

S.K. and 3, HERRICK HOUSE

INTRODUCTION: FORSTER AND THE LIBERAL DILEMMA

Forster's last novel, A Passage to India (1924) ends on a pessimistic note with the breaking up of a personal relationship. Aziz and Fielding are parted because of social, political and cosmic forces over which they have no control. The last scene of the novel focuses upon two individuals who are dwarfed by a vaster world within which their own wills and personalities seem of little consequence:

> "Why can't we be friends now?" said the other holding him affectionately. "It's what I want. It's what you want." But the horses didn't want it - they swerved apart; the earth didn't want it, sending up rocks through which riders must pass single-file; the temple, the tank, the jail, the palace, the birds, the carrion, the Guest House that came into view as they issued from the gap and saw Mau beneath: they didn't want it, they said in their hundred voices, 'No, not yet,' and the sky said, 'No not there.' (1)

This I think may be read as a symbol of the fragmentation of a once ordered universe in which individuality, personal relationship and inner self-development were unthreatened. One of the reasons why A Passage to India is greater than Forster's earlier novels is because it recognizes the complex interplay of social, political and metaphysical forces which affect the lives of men. The England of Howards End (1910) is not a harmonious unity, but there the conflicts that mar a unified world are thought capable of resolution through individual effort. If only the empire-builders (Wilcoxes) and the aesthetes (Schlegels) get to understand each other and do something practical for the oppressed (Basts), there is hope for the socio-political future

INTRODUCTION

of England. In *A Passage to India*, however, although individuals are important in themselves, they are shown to be of less social and political significance than in the earlier novel. The conflicts that prevent the existence of a connected and coherent world are between systems, institutions and ideologies. Individuals may strive to transcend these barriers in an effort to resolve conflict, but in the ultimate analysis they are overwhelmed by the larger orders and rendered powerless to forge the rainbow bridges that will harmonize the world. Personal relationships enable only a purely temporary transcendence over differences of nationality, religion and socio-economic status. In the end everyone who believes in relationships Mrs. Moore, Adela, Aziz, Fielding - is disillusioned. The difference between the fictional universe of *Howards End* and *A Passage to India* is therefore that in the latter the world has expanded and split up. Everyone is forced back from the effort to create harmony through relationships into narrow, isolated cells - Mrs. Moore into nihilism, Adela into despair, Aziz into Islamic nationalism, Fielding into cynical scepticism and Godbole into solipsistic mysticism. The atmosphere, the general pattern and the conclusion of Forster's last novel suggest that it is a poetic symbol of the collapse of the liberal world which started in or around 1914. This collapse of the liberal order is the historical or sociological reason why Forster ceased writing novels after *A Passage to India*.(2)

Before looking at the post-Great War decline of liberalism adumbrated in *A Passage to India*, one could look briefly at Forster's other, personal reasons for abandoning fiction. These have been recounted by P.N. Furbank. According to Furbank there was a strong psychological reason, Forster being "one of those who, on realizing their dearest wishes, are afflicted and inhibited by superstitious fears - the fears in his case taking the form of a conviction of sterility." (3) Such fears had been occasioned by the success of *Howards End* earlier, but were confirmed after *A Passage to India*. A second reason was that as a homosexual, Forster was bored with structuring his fiction around man-woman relationships. The impossibility of publishing *Maurice* to some extent deterred him from undertaking another novel, and even the completion of the earlier abandoned *A Passage to India* required a considerable effort. (4) Third, Furbank feels that Forster had exhausted his inspiration. This is confirmed by

INTRODUCTION

Forster himself in his 1959 interview with David Jones, where he remarks - "I somehow dried up after Passage. I wanted to write but did not want to write novels." (5) This is understandable since Forster's novels are really variations on a few basic themes - the limitations of suburban existence, the desirability of a full and responsive life, the importance of relationship, the need to connect imagination and reason, the necessity of preserving the natural and aesthetic heritage of England. The re-formulation of such themes into another complex fictional structure probably required an effort which Forster did not feel up to. But while these reasons prevented further novels, the reason why Forster turned to criticism in later life is probably best explained by briefly surveying the altered social conditions in which the Edwardian liberal assumptions were no longer the dominant social features.

The word 'liberal' means different and often contradictory things through its evolution from the sixteenth century, but one broad strand of it which can be traced in the nineteenth century through the English Romantic poets, John Stuart Mill, Matthew Arnold, Leslie Stephen, G.E. Moore, Goldsworthy Lowes Dickinson and the Bloomsbury Group is of particular importance in understanding Forster. This tradition implies one very specific belief which is re-stated in varying forms in all that Forster writes. It implies that the supreme end of existence consists in the well-being of the inner life of the individual and in the development of the order of the mind. It sees society as an atomic aggregation of separate and unique individuals, and values socio-political order only to the extent that this enables a world made up of free individuals to develop their unique personalities. Tolerance and freedom from all but the minimal restraints necessary for general self-development are the social ideals of this liberalism, while enlightenment, human relations and art are the personal ideals which are believed to achieve the moral and spiritual order that constitutes well-being. The primary emphasis is upon freedom, individuality and moral order, for it is assumed that equality and improvements in society and economy will grow out of the morally developed personality.

This moral idealism was the basis of the political and cultural outlook of the Independent Review and the Nation, liberal journals which attracted the progressive-minded intelligentsia before World

INTRODUCTION

War I. (6) Forster's enthusiasm for the <u>Independent Review</u> is evident in his biography of Lowes Dickinson (7) and for the <u>Nation</u> in his frequent contributions to that journal (and its counterpart in outlook, the <u>Athenaeum</u>) after his return from Alexandria. Both Stone (8) and Crews (9) have provided excellent accounts of this 'new liberalism' which conceived of a social utopia to be created through gradual reform. Every individual in the world of its vision would have the liberty and the opportunity to develop what was best in him, and would accomplish this through literature, philosophy and human relationships. G.E. Moore's <u>Principia Ethica</u> (1903) had already established that the Good was a state of consciousness attained through the appreciation of beauty in Art, nature and human relationships. (10) In an indirect way this philosophy reinforced J.S. Mill's and Matthew Arnold's displacement of religion by culture as the method of human salvation, (11) and the effort of the <u>Independent Review</u> and <u>Nation</u> new liberals was to work towards the social conditions within which the Good could be more generally realized by humanity.

The assumptions of this outlook had been questioned in the nineteenth century by Marxism, which argued that the root cause of disorder and social conflict was an economic system which made it impossible for every individual to attain the freedom and enlightenment extolled by philosophical liberalism. Conflict was not a matter of individual differences between people who mysteriously failed to relate to each other, but of fundamental differences between the economically determined outlook of social classes. However, Marxism was never taken too seriously in England until the late twenties and early thirties period. Harold Laski points out that a gauge of the dominance of liberal ideals between 1870 and 1914 is "the failure of Marxism in this period to obtain any serious hold of the English mind. The typical English socialism was Fabian, a body of doctrine upon which the emphasis of J.S. Mill's ideas was far more profound than that of Marx." (12) Before the First War all socially progressive thinking people had a profoundly rationalistic belief in a gradual and peaceful transition of capitalism into socialism. Leonard Woolf recalls that "In the decade before the 1914 war there was a political and social movement in the world, and particularly in Europe and Britain, which seemed at the time wonderfully hopeful and exciting. It seemed that human beings might really be on the brink of

INTRODUCTION

becoming civilized... The forces of reaction and barbarism were still there, but they were in retreat." (13) Woolf's summary of the period after the First War is a stark contrast - "In the years 1918 to 1939 one impotently watched a series of events leading step by step to barbarism and war:the Versailles Treaty and the canker of reparations;the creation of Stalin's Russia, the iron curtain, and the cold war; the rise of fascism and nazism; the failure of the League of Nations; the menace of nuclear war; the Hitlerian Gotterdämmerung." (14) Forster reminisces in a similar vein in an unpublished talk. He remembers that around the turn of the century his generation believed in jingoism, the Boer War and Kipling. But within a few years people saw through the crudeness of imperialism and developed the idealistic view that...

> ... evolution speeded up here and there by the efforts of a few individuals, would gradually make the world better... At the beginning of the century they (relationships) were exalted into something political, and it was felt that if they were solved the problem of civilization would be solved too... the liberalism of those days hoped that by exalting the individual the community would be benefitted... in 1912... I thought that if the English would only behave more politely to the Indians, the difficulties between the two races would be solved. Good manners were to do the trick. I see now (i.e. 1939) how superficial my conclusion was. (15)

Fabians and advanced liberals could not believe that rational persuasion would scarcely compel capitalists to minimize profits in the interests of humanity, nor that legislation would be impeded or diluted so long as a moneyed aristocracy was firmly in control of the political structure. The emphasis upon social change brought about through education or alteration of the inner order of the mind was seriously undermined only by the First War and the socio-economic turbulence after it which led to the Second. It became much more overwhelmingly evident over this period that material conditions required political and economic solutions, and were unlikely to be substantially bettered only by education, civilization and the outward expansion of inner order.

Everything after 1914 pointed away from the liberal belief in order at the microcosmic, individ-

INTRODUCTION

ual level, towards the primary need for durable order at the macrocosmic level of society, economy and international relations. Personal moral idealism had obviously little relevance in practical politics since it was powerless to prevent a war in which millions died and in which individual distinction meant less than at any previous period in history. The First War, as well as a violent suppression of the struggle for independence in Ireland (Easter 1916) and India (Amritsar 1919), were some of the features which destroyed the liberal hope of private decency and the life symbolized by art, philosophy and relationships expanding outwards to gradually embrace mankind. It came as almost a shock that the inner life did little to contribute to international peace but depended entirely upon it. Forster's description of Dickinson's immense disillusionment with the world after 1914 is testimony of how deeply the liberal vision of the world had suffered. (16) Forster's sceptical temperament made him relatively immune from the kind of shock suffered by the idealistic Lowes Dickinson; nonetheless even the mildly idealistic could hardly have remained unaffected by the war, for it became obvious that militarism, patriotism, violence and propaganda made a mockery of discussion, aesthetic appreciation and the disinterested pursuit of truth. The moral centre of liberal meliorism had been severely damaged and its subsequent survival as a viable philosophy depended as much upon a recognition of the new imperatives - social equality, economic organization, international peace and justice - as upon belief in the necessity of individuality and creative self-development. That is why the belief in moral order achieved through personal relations found its logical extension in an ardent belief in the League of Nations. This was conceived of as a disinterestedly idealistic forum within which member nations would sort out their problems through civilized discussion. Liberal intellectuals in the twenties, led by Lowes Dickinson, Lord Bryce, Leonard Woolf and Gilbert Murray, united mainly around this assumed apotheosis of international sanity. This belief marked a short-lived resurrection of pre-war Independent Review liberalism.(17)

There were other features besides warfare which undermined liberalism. Michael Bentley points out that in the twenties the general feeling of the liberal intelligentsia was that "Liberalism was being crushed by the twin juggernauts of Unionism (with the Tories) or socialism." (18) The middle

INTRODUCTION

ground of British politics was slowly caving in. The conflict was sharpening into capital versus working class, these being represented politically by the Tory and Labour parties. Between 1910 and 1914 the Liberal Party lost most of the by-elections held, to Labour. (19) The 1918 election split the Liberal party between those who supported Lloyd George and those who supported Asquith, and though Lloyd George's coalition won a clear majority, most of his support depended upon Conservatives. The Labour Party gradually strengthened its parliamentary representation at the expense of the Liberals. In 1918 it improved from 42 to 63, in 1922 it jumped to 142, and in 1923 to 191. In these new conditions, Bentley points out, "It was a plausible argument for socialist propagandists that Liberalism and the Liberal Party had now parted company and that the true Liberalism lay in supporting the Labour Party and progress." (20) Most radical liberals became virtually indistinguishable from Labour. By 1922-3, says Leonard Woolf, "Massingham had become bitterly hostile to the Liberals, and Hammond, Hobson, Nevinson, like Brailsford, Noel and Charles Buxton, who before the war had been active and distinguished Liberal intellectuals, had all drifted into the Labour Party." (21) Forster's poem 'A Voter's Dilemma' (1923) suggests, by its dismissive attitude towards both the Liberal and the Conservative candidates, that Forster himself was by this time a Labour supporter. (22)

Alongside foreign affairs and party politics, attention also focussed on the economy. This went through four phases after the First War. Between 1918 and 1920 there was an inflationary boom when prices soared and fortunes were made. This was followed in 1921 and 1922 by a massive slump and unemployment. The third phase, 1923-9, showed partial recovery but the government followed a deflationary policy and unemployment never fell below the one million mark. The fourth phase started in 1929-30 after the collapse of the American stock market. This plunged Europe into an economic crisis of unparalleled proportions. (23)

But cutting across these upsurges and downturns in the economy was a basic stress on the necessity of increasing consumption, production and trade. Material well-being depended on these factors. Technology, mechanization, planning, commercialisation, advertising and propaganda were other words which assumed a new significance. Literature and the arts were affected by these economic changes. Books

INTRODUCTION

(pulp fiction) were churned out for consumption and immediate sensation (24) and the very nature of capitalism seemed to have necessitated a neo-Benthamist stress upon material well-being achieved through consumerism and acquisiton. Pushpin, in such circumstances, was more valuable than poetry because pushpins could be manufactured in a factory and thereby benefit the employment situation. Moreover, world-weariness and disillusionment with ideals led to what Forster, in his essay on Proust, describes as a detached curiosity about the future and a concomitant thirst for immediate and casual pleasure.(25) Forster prefers the detached curiosity of the twenties to the fanaticism of the thirties, but it became equally clear at this time that despair led logically towards the amusement and gimmickry being offered by the new entertainment industries and not towards the liberal hope of a social order in which art and intelligence would be generally cherished. The thirties and forties only accentuated the drift away from 'civilized' ideals.

Major transformations which undermined liberal idealism also occurred through the work of Freud and Einstein. With the passing of the politico-economic stability of the Edwardian era, there was less confidence in fixed ideas about right and wrong. In such an atmosphere, according to Noreen Branson,"the teachings of Freud began to assume a new significance... his works had made little impact in Britain before the War... Now the new psychoanalysis... it seemed, could provide the clue to the mysteries of human nature." (26) Freud seemed to have proved that the personality was not the solid entity it had been assumed to be, but that it was divided even within itself. The attempt to understand the complexities of human nature coincided with new ideas about the physical universe. Einstein's theory of relativity, completed in 1915, was comprehensively understood only by mathematicians, but its larger implication that everything is relative and nothing absolute filtered through to the average person. Alongside these revolutionary theories, ideas about world affairs also altered. Nationalism had been the basis of history taught in schools, but horizons gradually became international. The wireless, the motorcar, the cinema and the aeroplane enabled the individual to see himself in relation to a wider world. H.G. Wells's The <u>Outline of History</u> was a bestseller in the twenties and helped to broaden the intelligent man's vision of history. Some of these features are remarked upon by Forster -

INTRODUCTION

> ...since 1918 it (industrialization) has accelerated to an enormous speed, bringing all sorts of changes into national and personal life. It has meant organization and plans and the boosting of the community ... personally I hate it ... there has been a psychological movement, about which I am more enthusiastic... It has brought a great enrichment to the art of fiction... This psychology is not new, but it ... becomes general after 1918 - partly owing to Freud ... another factor ... is the shift in physics exemplified by the work of Einstein ... the idea of relativity has got into the air...(27)

This was the context confronting the liberal intellectual in the post-1914 world. The efficacy of the inner life as a means of gradual social improvement and order had been discredited. The question which posed itself as a corollary was whether the liberal stress upon self-development, moral individualism, enlightenment and the arts had any relevance even as an end in a world which required social, economic and international order - a context which seemed in fact to be rapidly eroding these values. Almost all of Forster's criticism may be seen as an answer to this central liberal dilemma. (28)

The War and its aftermath both challenged liberal principles, and by doing so, forced their concrete expression. Commonsense, fair-play, reason, moral values, the arts and the inner life were unthreatened and therefore implicit or obscurely defined values only so long as the socio-economic-international conditions permitted. MacCallum Scott, a Liberal, wrote in his diary - "Liberalism is not a programme, a formula, a formal and dogmatic creed. It is a spirit, a motive, an attitude towards the world" (29) and H.W. Massingham, liberal editor of the Nation from 1907 to 1922, also refused or was unable to define his personal political philosophy. (30) This is broadly characteristic of idealistic liberalism, a philosophy in which principles are stated with deliberate vagueness so that circumstances may be allowed to determine their specific implications. Theoretical consistency is not a liberal virtue - on the contrary it is consciously shunned. But under conditions of stress, and under assault by the challenges thrown up after 1914, the liberal intellectual was compelled to define his ideals more precisely and demonstrate their relevance

INTRODUCTION

amidst the new imperatives. Bentley has shown that the post-1914 writing of the liberal intelligentsia is framed in deceptively personal terms and that this may camouflage a larger concern with the character and relevance of liberalism and liberal values. This is certainly true of Forster's criticism, which is at one level a personal criticism of a variety of books and authors, but at a broader level defines more specifically the meaning and relevance of liberal humanist values (in particular the value of art) in the new economy.

Stone has pointed out the analogy between Coleridge's inability to write inspired poetry after the Dejection Ode and Forster's to write fiction after Passage. In both cases a Benthamite world which equated poetry and pushpin was spiritually starving its creative artists. (31) The personal experience of a cultural crisis which is seen to erode man's spiritual, transcendent and ahistorically 'human' self is a common phenomenon among nineteenth century poets. The springs of creativity dry up because the milieu which once nourished them is no longer amenable. Raymond Williams has shown how in the last century artists increasingly regarded the technological world with antipathy or horror because it was seen to collectively contain the forces responsible for dehumanization. (32) Emotional and spiritual fulfilment through the appreciation of beauty in art, nature and relationships is upheld in this context as the antidote to the materialism which debases humanity. When the feeling of socio-cultural crisis is specially acute, the creation of works of art may be both stultified and considered an insufficient step towards healing the crisis. After Coleridge, the most striking example of such a 'drying up' is Matthew Arnold who virtually abandoned poetry for literary, social and religious criticism. Arnold recognized that art can only have relevance in social conditions which permit creativity and appreciation. This general outlook is more or less duplicated if one looks at Forster's career, the second half of which is mainly an attempt to define and defend art, and the inner life of which art is a product and a symbol.

As an artist Forster could not care for the post-Edwardian world since the dominant emphasis had shifted from spiritual fulfilment for the individual to social equality for the masses, from the personal and aesthetic sphere to the political and economic. For someone like Forster who was born into the liberal intellectual aristocracy (33) and

INTRODUCTION

nourished in the liberal intellectual ethos of Lowes Dickinson and G.E. Moore, and who wrote novels about how the inner life of personal relations and art might harmonize society, the world after 1914 was increasingly becoming as vast, fragmented and disillusioning as the India discovered by Fielding, Adela and Mrs. Moore. It was, as Forster puts it in a review essay, "the world which failed to solidify after 1914." (34) It was not easily possible in this context to structure fiction around personal relationships, and in this respect Passage is a last effort which contains Forster's recognition of the relative marginalization of the inner life in a world overtaken by beliefs in new political, social, economic and psychological (or psycho-religious) theories. Stone points out that art for Forster "is the creation of wholes, the harmonizing of contrarieties. not the celebration of lonely and unmended division." (35) In a context where attention is focussed more and more upon forms of order larger than the individual (i.e. society, economy, politics, religion), a fictional universe which attaches supreme importance to the individual's spiritual connection with friends, with nature and with historical tradition is likely to be both anomalous and peripheral, and therefore difficult to conceive.

What, then, were the alternatives to fiction for Forster? For liberals generally, it was possible either to retire into an ivory tower or to be forward looking and adapt their old-world values to the new social reality. To take recourse to the first course of action would probably have meant increasing isolation, if not bitterness and cynicism. (36) Forster chose the other option. Without either abandoning his early beliefs in the uniqueness of personality and the value of art, or identifying with any of the new currents of belief - Marxism Christian Socialism, Scientific Socialism and Pacifist Mysticism - he chose to engage for the rest of his literary life in a polemic with some of the contemporary issues and ideologies. If the relevance of liberal-humanist values was to be driven home, more direct and hortative forms of discourse than the novel - such as the book-review, the broadcast, the critical essay - were likely to be effective. This is probably the reason why Forster turned to criticism. I am not suggesting that Forster's career was a consciously thought-out program - on the contrary it seems to have developed into one unconsciously - but that because of his failure to (in the words of Spender) "imagine in novels a world

INTRODUCTION

in which the values he supported had been defeated", (37) he turned to journalistic criticism where values could be spelled out and arguments for them offered before a new, wide-ranging audience.

The basic attempt of Forster's criticism is to heal the breach between the liberal stress on moral individualism and art on the one hand, and the anti-liberal stress on social order and mass civilization on the other. He does this through criticism of some of the trends and beliefs which characterize the post-1914 world. He tries to prove the relevance and necessity of individual distinction and art to a world which increasingly ignores them and which thereby severs a precious connection with its own human past. This does not entail the setting up of an opposition between individual and social good, for Forster tries to show that the new emphasis upon social good must be made compatible with the old emphasis upon individual good if it is to have any meaning. Against the dominant tendencies of his time, Forster reasserts a liberal definition of the word 'order' by focussing attention upon the spiritual needs of the individual and tries to demonstrate his view that true 'order' only exists at the microcosmic level of the individual and the work of art. He does not discount the necessity of some form of socio-economic order, but he is centrally concerned with arguing that no contemporary social order is viable unless it integrates within its structure the liberal - and in its widest connotation, the human - values of creative individualism and cultural tradition. Forster's contribution as a critic is to point out a definition of 'order' deriving from the traditions of philosophical liberalism and English Romanticism, and to distinguish between this definition of order and those contemporary doctrines which equate 'order' with external imposition, tyranny and the curtailment of creative individualism.

II

Forster's bibliographer, B.J. Kirkpatrick, lists 518 articles published in journals and another forty-two as introductions or other contributions to books by other authors. (38) The best of these were included by Forster in three anthologies - Pharos and Pharillon (1923) Abinger Harvest (1936) and Two Cheers for Democracy (1951). Alexandria: A History and a Guide (1922) and Aspects of the Novel (1927) are the two other important books in

INTRODUCTION

Forster's critical career. There are, in addition, the biographies - Goldsworthy Lowes Dickinson (1934) and Marianne Thornton (1956), the autobiographical The Hill of Devi (1953) and Commonplace Book (1978), and finally the unpublished essays and fragments of essays which exist in the Forster Archives at King's College, Cambridge. I will concentrate attention upon this material with a view to define Forster's conception of 'order' as it emerges from his comments on the individual, society, religion and art.

The list of journals to which Forster contributed runs into more than two dozen, but there are only nine or ten names of importance within this list. The first is the Independent Review, the nature and aims of which have already been commented upon. The second important journal is the Nation, the organ of the 'new liberalism' which, in a sense, succeeded the Independent Review. The group of writers who centred around this paper included J.L. Hammond (former editor of the Speaker), Henry Brailsford (who became editor of the New Leader in 1922), L.T. Hobhouse (the Liberal philosopher) and C.F.G. Masterman (Liberal M.P. and author of The Condition of England (1908) and The New Liberalism (1920)). (39) The Nation upheld liberal principles but was not a spokesman for the Liberal Party. Its editor, H.W. Massingham, was (according to his biographer) "given to distinguishing between Party philosophy and Party practice." (40) This is probably the reason why the paper also attracted advanced liberals and Fabians. During the war it advocated the Union of Democratic Control, agreeing with this body about the urgent need for a negotiated peace. It also published some of the anti-war poems of Sassoon and Owen. In 1918 it supported the League. Forster contributed seven articles to the Nation between 1919-21.

Keynes was part of a group of financiers who wrested the Nation from Massingham and merged it in 1922 with the most famous of the Victorian weeklies, the Athenaeum. It appeared between that year and 1930 as the Nation and Athenaeum, when Keynes was again instrumental in amalgamating it with the New Statesman. (41) The Athenaeum, the Nation and Athenaeum and the New Statesman were three other journals to which Forster contributed heavily. The first of these was revived in 1919 by Middleton Murry. It was, says Forster, a paper which cheered him and Lowes Dickinson after the War, because it "linked up literature and life." (42) He wrote 42 pieces for it between 1919-21. When it joined the

INTRODUCTION

Nation, Forster continued to write for it, contributing 25 articles to it (i.e. Nation and Athenaeum - it was edited by H.D. Henderson) between 1921-30. The New Statesman had been founded in 1913 by Bernard Shaw and the Webbs. Desmond MacCarthy was its literary editor and Leonard Woolf a regular contributor. In 1930 it appeared as the New Statesman and Nation with Kingsley Martin as its editor. Martin was a socialist, but according to Hyams his socialism "was not a party Socialism, although it entailed critical support of the Labour Party." (43) He reversed the imperialist and anti-Indian policies of his predecessor (Clifford Sharp) and championed Gandhi and Nehru in the thirties. He appointed Raymond Mortimer as its new literary editor and allowed the literary section of the paper to develop its own, Bloomsbury tone. Most of the old Nation writers came to write for the paper, which made it eclectic or pluralistic in outlook - there was in fact a noticeable division between the political and literary halves of the paper. (44) John Freeman, its editor after Martin, has said that the journal set out to be inquiring, sceptical, dissenting and non-conformist, and that its basic ideal was (and is)"to show men by analysis and reason how they may apply to public affairs and great issues the standards of personal morality and common sense which civilized men take for granted in their private dealings with one another." (45) This is an editorial policy with which Forster could only have been in complete agreement. Forster contributed 41 articles to this journal between 1930 and 1953.

    The other overtly left-wing paper to which Forster made a significant number of contributions (14 between 1919-20) is the Daily Herald. This first came out as a strike sheet in 1911 but was subsequently resurrected as a socialist daily. The outbreak of war forced it to become a weekly but it re-emerged in 1919 as a daily with George Lansbury of the Independent Labour Party as its editor. Sassoon was its literary editor and persuaded Forster to write for it. (46) According to Francis Williams, the paper was "gay, impudent, passionate, rebellious and unofficial." It collected around it a famous group of contributors - H.W. Nevinson, Walter de la Mare, Aldous Huxley, Rose Macauley, Robert Graves and Bernard Shaw - who left it in 1922 when it became an organ of the Labour Party.(47) Forster's reasons for writing for the Daily Herald were unlikely to have been passionately political, for over the same period he contributed 18 articles to the

INTRODUCTION

Liberal, pro-Asquith paper, the Daily News.
The Daily Herald and Daily News apart, most of Forster's essays of the twenties went to the Nation and Athenaeum. In the thirties the essays divide mainly between New Statesman and Nation, The Spectator and the The Listener.
Forster sent 42 contributions to The Spectator between 1930-60. Over the forties it is evident that he became more and more involved in broadcasting for the B.B.C. because there is a large increase in the number of his articles published in The Listener. The Listener was anti-Nazi but otherwise non-political. It had begun publication in 1929 and between 1934-39 its circulation was 50,000. By 1950 it had reached 150,000. Its first editor, R.S. Lambert, tried to make it a vehicle of general culture. (48) J.R. Ackerley became its literary editor in 1935 and got Forster to write for it as often as he could. (49) Forster contributed 113 articles to The Listener between 1930 and 1959.
Within this output a general trend is visible. Forster's literary career seems to develop steadily from fiction towards purely critical writing. The fiction (excluding short stories) culminates in 1924. This is followed by literary essays or literary criticism - Aspects and Abinger Harvest, and finally the socio-literary criticism comprising Two Cheers for Democracy. These are the three roughly separable stages in Forster's writing. The separation is made possible by the decline of the creative and the progress of the critical elements. While Forster's prose always retains its strong imaginative quality, over the years its proportion withers in favour of direct, undisguised critical analysis. The movement is visible both in terms of a slight shift of interest from literary to social issues, as well as an alteration in the method of analysis.
The broad shift of interest may be discerned merely by comparing the contents of Abinger Harvest and Two Cheers for Democracy. In the first anthology the literary interest is predominant. Essays such as 'Notes on the English Character', 'Liberty in England' and 'The Mind of the Indian Native State' which are directly concerned with social issues, punctuate the wider interest in art and artists mainly for their own sake. The interest is loosely, in civilization. In contrast, Two Cheers for Democracy is organized around Forster's growing social concern during the thirties and forties. The essays of its first section have a thematic unity because each in its own way focuses on the conflicting

INTRODUCTION

claims of Fascism and liberal democracy. This leads down to a central personal statement in the essay 'What I Believe', then to a detailed exposition of particular beliefs in the section 'Art in General', and finally to an application of personal values in the discussion of specific writers in the section 'The Arts in Action'. This last section corresponds to the one titled 'Books' in <u>Abinger Harvest</u>, but as its title suggests, Forster's later interest is more specifically on the action of art upon life.

This slight shift of emphasis from the exposition of art as something unquestionably delightful towards the more concrete examination of the relation between art and life also embodies a change in the nature of Forster's later essays. Whereas in <u>Abinger Harvest</u> Forster is more a Romantic essayist lighting upon random topics in the manner of Lamb and Hazlitt, in <u>Two Cheers for Democracy</u> his concern with values is primary, not incidental. It is stated overtly, not cloaked by a subject which has aroused the creative imagination. Forster's tone is forthright, urgent and compelling instead of discursive, impressionistic and dilettantish. This transition occurs in the early thirties alongside the rise of Fascism, so that although <u>Abinger Harvest</u> reveals Forster as the literary essayist, it also reflects his development from essayist to socio-literary critic. The essays within it were written between 1903 and 1936, which makes it a collection of two kinds of essay - the creative and the critical. In 'Macolnia Shops' (1903) values are presented obliquely during a narrative re-creation of history. The etchings on a Greek toilet case suggest to Forster that "when the body is feeble the soul is feeble; cherish the body and you will cherish the soul." (50) In contrast 'Roger Fry: An Obituary Note' (1934) and 'Liberty in England' (1935) belong more properly to <u>Two Cheers for Democracy</u> because they directly address an audience.

My examination of the values which unify Forster's criticism will centre first on the later essays and then select from the rest of his criticism those statements which help to define his personal credo. As my main concern is Forster's world-view as it emerges from and unifies his criticism as a whole, the procedure of analysis will not be strictly chronological. Although, as I have suggested, Forster shifts from creativity to criticism, his fundamental beliefs do not alter radically. Modifications in his views do occur with social change and these will be seen, but these in

INTRODUCTION

themselves do not preclude a more or less synchronic (rather than diachronic) Forsterian world-view. Furbank has said that his problem as a biographer was "how to make a narrative of the life of a man for whom time stood still... his contemporaries seem to have agreed he was exactly the same at twenty as he was at ninety..." (51) Stone also feels that "between the stories and *Passage* there is an evolution of the artist from almost a child's to a man's estate - but as regards his work after 1924 ... it can all be read as a single, continuing effort to enunciate a humanistic gospel..." (52) I broadly agree with these views for it seems generally true that Forster adapts his liberal humanism to a changed world without adopting any fundamentally new philosophy.

III

There are four main strands or themes to which Forster's ideas and values seem generally to contribute, and which provide an underlying structural unity to his criticism. These are - (1) Ideas about the nature of man and human existence. (2) A view of human society and the nature of social order. (3) A view of religious order which emerges from Forster's criticism of Christianity, Hinduism and Islam. (4) Ideas on aesthetic issues and an overarching view of art as a form of order. These four inter-connected themes will be the subject of the next four chapters. A special application of the idea of art as order will be seen in the fifth chapter which will discuss Forster's notion of order as it can be made to exist in the novel. The sixth and seventh chapters, which will discuss Forster's view of criticism, the chief principles of his own method as a critic, and selections from his criticism of other writers - will derive from and be clarified by the earlier chapters. These chapters, each dealing with one theme, will inevitably overlap with each other. Forster's criticism of the individual, society, religion, and artists or works of art is never itself presented within such divisions - on the contrary these themes are closely intertwined within it. Chapters, therefore, should only be taken to indicate the loose thematic divisions observable in the corpus of Forster's criticism.

NOTES

(1) *A Passage to India*, Abinger edn., ed. O. Stallybrass (London: Edward Arnold, 1978) p.312.

INTRODUCTION

(2) An interesting analysis of the desiccating effect of the First War upon Forster exists in Samuel Hynes, 'The Old Man at King's: Forster at 85', <u>Edwardian Occasions: Essays on English Writing in the Early Twentieth Century</u> (London: Routledge & Kegan Paul, 1972) pp. 104-11.

(3) <u>E.M. Forster: A Life</u>, (1978; rpt. London: Oxford University Press, 1979), vol. II, p.131.

(4) See Furbank II, p.132.

(5) 'E.M. Forster on his Life and his Books: An Interview Recorded for Television', <u>The Listener</u>, 1 January, 1959, vol. LXI, p.11.

(6) <u>The Independent Review</u> was published between 1903-1907. Between 1907-1908 it appeared as the <u>Albany Review</u>. The <u>Nation</u> grew out of the <u>Speaker</u> (established 1890) in 1907. It's editor was H.W. Massingham and its contributors included such other famous advanced liberals or Fabians as L.T. Hobhouse, H.G. Wells, H.W. Nevinson, Bernard Shaw, Roger Fry and Leonard Woolf (who became literary editor in 1924). Lowes Dickinson and Gilbert Murray were supporters. Virtually the whole <u>Independent Review</u> group migrated to the <u>Nation</u>. In 1921 this journal merged with the <u>Athenaeum</u> and carried on as the <u>Nation and Athenaeum</u>. This merged in 1930 with the <u>New Statesman</u> to form the <u>New Statesman and Nation</u>. See Alfred J. Havighurst, <u>Radical Journalist: H.W. Massingham 1860-1924</u> (Cambridge: Cambridge Univ. Press, 1974) pp. 146-149 and Edward Hyams, The <u>New Statesman - The History of the First Fifty Years 1913-1963</u> (London: Longmans, Green & Co., 1963) p.119.

(7) <u>Goldsworthy Lowes Dickinson</u>, Abinger edn., ed. O. Stallybrass (London: Edward Arnold, 1973) pp. 96-7.

(8) Wilfred Stone, <u>The Cave and the Mountain: A Study of E.M. Forster</u> (1966; rpt. Stanford: Stanford Univ. Press, 1969) pp. 50-60.

(9) Frederick Crews, <u>E.M. Forster: The Perils of Humanism</u> (Princeton: Princeton Univ. Press, 1962) pp. 29-36.

(10) A key passage in Moore's book reads: "By far the most valuable things, which we know or can imagine, are certain states of consciousness, which may be roughly described as the pleasures of human intercourse and the enjoyment of beautiful objects ... personal affection and the appreciation of what is beautiful in Art or Nature, are good in themselves ... worth

INTRODUCTION

  having purely for their own sakes ..." *Principia Ethica* (Cambridge: Cambridge Univ. Press, 1971) p.188.
(11) Mill criticized Bentham for ignoring "about half of the whole number of mental feelings which human beings are capable of, including all those of which the direct objects are states of their own minds." 'Bentham' in *Mill on Bentham and Coleridge*, Intro. F.R. Leavis (London: Chatto & Windus, 1962) p. 71. Arnold's faith in poetry as a substitute of religion in his essay 'The Study of Poetry' complements Mill's emphasis upon inner culture.
(12) *The Rise of European Liberalism*, (London: Allen & Unwin, 1936) p. 241. Dennis Dean provides a similar analysis in 'The Character of the Early Labour Party, 1900-1914' in *The Edwardian Age: Conflict and Stability - 1900-1914*, ed. Alan O'Day (London: Macmillan, 1979) pp. 97-112.
(13) *Beginning Again: An Autobiography of the Years 1911-1918* (London: Hogarth Press, 1964) p. 36.
(14) *Downhill All the Way: An Autobiography of the Years 1919-1939* (London: Hogarth Press, 1967) p.28.
(15) 'Three Generations', a paper delivered to a political discussion group at the University of Nottingham on 28 January 1939, *King's College* MS., vol. 16, pp. 180-213 (pp. 181, 184).
(16) See GLD, pp. 134-5. Keynes's 'My Early Beliefs' conveys the same feeling. See *Two Memoirs* (London: Hart Davis, 1949) pp. 75-103.
(17) See Noreen Branson, *Britain in the Nineteen Twenties* (London: Weidenfeld and Nicolson, 1975) p. 49 and Michael Bentley, *The Liberal Mind 1914-1929* (Cambridge: Cambridge Univ. Press, 1977) pp. 141-2.
(18) Bentley, p.119.
(19) See Bentley, pp. 119-128, and Chris Cook, *A Short History of the Liberal Party 1900-1976* (London: Macmillan, 1976) p.63 and passim.
(20) Bentley, p.121.
(21) *Downhill All the Way,* p.96.
(22) 'A Voter's Dilemma', *New Leader*, 30 November 1923, p.8. Rpt. in AH.
(23) See Noreen Branson, p.13 and passim.
(24) As demonstrated by Q.D. Leavis's *Fiction and The Reading Public* (London: Chatto & Windus, 1932). Mrs. Leavis, however, also tried to prove that pulp fiction was eroding an organic and harmonious community. This argument has

INTRODUCTION

       been refuted by Iain Wright's 'F.R. Leavis, the 'Scrutiny' Movement and the Crisis' in <u>Culture and Crisis in Britain in the Thirties</u>, ed. Jon Clark & others (London: Lawrence and Wishart, 1979) pp. 37-65.
- (25) 'Our Curiosity and Despair', <u>New York Herald Tribune</u>, 21 April 1929, Section II, Books, pp. 1, 6. Rpt. in AH, pp. 109-15.
- (26) Branson, p.97.
- (27) <u>The Development of English Prose Between 1918 and 1939</u> (Glasgow: Jackson, Son & Co., 1945) pp. 7-11. Rpt. TCD, pp. 267-9.
- (28) Pamela McCallum's 'The Cultural Theory of I.A. Richards, T.S. Eliot and F.R. Leavis' (Unpublished Ph.D. dissertation, Cambridge University 1978) and Iain Wright's essay (op.cit.) are fine analyses of the response of the major literary critics to the post-First War socio-cultural crisis.
- (29) <u>Diary</u>, 30 July 1926, Quoted in Bentley, p.219.
- (30) See Havighurst, p.177.
- (31) <u>The Cave and the Mountain</u>, p.8.
- (32) <u>Culture and Society 1780-1950</u> (1958; rpt. Harmondsworth: Penguin Books, 1976).
- (33) Defined by Noel Annan in <u>Leslie Stephen</u> (London: Macgibbon & Kee, 1951) pp. 3-7, and in his essay 'The Intellectual Aristocracy' in <u>Studies in Social History: A Tribute to G.M. Trevelyan</u>, ed. J.H. Plumb (London: Longmans, Green & Co.,1955) pp. 241-87.
- (34) 'An Indian on W.B. Yeats', <u>The Listener</u>, 24 Dec. 1942, p. 824 (p.824).
- (35) <u>The Cave and the Mountain</u>, p.18
- (36) Clive Bell was one of the 'Bloomsberries' who retreated from the new world. In the dedication to Virginia Woolf in his <u>Civilization</u> (1928) he says "...since the war, the Russian Revolution and the Italian <u>coup d'etat</u>,nothing has happened, and I have read nothing, seriously to alter my conception of civilization or of the means by which it might be attained." <u>Civilization: An Essay</u> (London: Chatto & Windus, 1928) p. VII. The conception of civilized living in this work is so limited and highbrow that it caused Virginia Woolf to remark:"He has great fun in the opening chapters but in the end it turns out that civilization is a lunch party at No. 50 Gordon Square". Quoted in Quentin Bell, <u>Bloomsbury</u> (London: Weidenfeld and Nicolson, 1968) pp. 88-9.
- (37) 'E.M. Forster (1879-1970), <u>New York Review of</u>

INTRODUCTION

　　　　Books, 23 July 1970, p.4.
(38) A Bibliography of E.M. Forster (1965; rpt. London: Hart Davis, 1968).
(39) See Chris Cook, P.47.
(40) Havighurst, p.175.
(41) See Bentley, p.180, Havighurst, p.276 and Hyams pp. 109-19.
(42) Goldsworthy Lowes Dickinson, p.146.
(43) Hyams, p.125.
(44) Hyams, pp.165-7.
(45) 'Introduction' in Hyams, p. XIII.
(46) Furbank II, pp. 53 & 63.
(47) Dangerous Estate - The Anatomy of Newspapers. (London: Longmans, Green & Co., 1957) pp. 189-91.
(48) Asa Briggs, History of Broadcasting in the United Kingdom: The Golden Age of Wireless (London: Oxford Univ. Press., 1965), vol. II, pp. 280-90.
(49) "... to get a review or article from him, during my twenty five years on The Listener, was the highest prize any literary editor could hope to win ..." J.R. Ackerley, E.M. Forster; A Portrait (London: Ian McKelvie, 1970) p.4.
(50) Independent Review, November 1903, vol. 1, pp. 311-13 (p.313). Rpt. AH, (p.189).
(51) 'The Personality of E.M. Forster', Encounter (London), November 1970, vol. 35, No.5, pp. 61-68 (p.61).
(52) The Cave and the Mountain, p. 348.

CHAPTER ONE

FORSTER'S VIEW OF THE NATURE OF MAN AND HUMAN EXISTENCE.

It has been remarked that while a few men create philosophical systems, everyone follows out a philosophy either consciously or unconsciously. Even when it is not formulated theoretically, a world view can usually be inferred from a writer's opinion on different subjects. Forster himself notices in his obituary note on Roger Fry - "...the belief which underlies all his aesthetics and all his activity; the belief that man is, or rather can be, rational, and that the mind can and should guide the passions towards civilization." (1) Forster's own criticism possesses a similar overarching personal vision. This is expressed as a sort of 'theory' in 'What I Believe' (1938), but for a comprehensive grasp of Forster's philosophy it is necessary to trace the general consistency of certain ideas and values within the whole body of his criticism. While at an obvious level Forster's essays discuss specific texts, authors or topics, at an underlying level they may be seen to explore, strengthen and disseminate a personal view of life.

Forster expounds no holistic Philosophy because he thought himself incapable of abstract speculation, (2) and because, seeing life as complex rather than logical, he feels that every conceptual framework denies to a certain extent the multiplicity and amplitude of life. His liberal temperament is obvious from his scepticism towards all theory, all systems, all Faiths and Causes. Yet the concern of his own work to advance specific values underlines his desire to recommend a sensible middle-course between anarchic subjectivity and the rigid 'objective' truth of any astringent and logically ordered Belief. One may observe in his work what he himself observed in Virgil's:

FORSTER'S VIEW OF THE NATURE OF MAN

> Spiritual things interest him keenly, and
> those who seek a spiritual guide have sometimes
> tried to find one in him. But here, as else-
> where, his movements are spasmodic. He does
> not adopt, or wish to adopt, a 'philosophy'.(3)

Not to propound a Philosophy is consistent with Forster's philosophy, but his consciousness of a world view or a broad framework of values unifies the otherwise scattered and patchy essays, book reviews, broadcasts and scribbled notes which constitute his criticism. The first general principle which it seems possible to isolate within this body of writing is a conception of the nature of man and human existence.

After the First War Forster took an interest in newly emerging scientific ideas. Cambridge scientists like Eddington and Jeans were explaining the physical universe to the ordinary person, and writers like Aldous Huxley and Gerald Heard were popularizing a knowledge of science. Forster's <u>Commonplace Book</u> is full of notes from books about the origin and nature of the universe. In 1928 he read Eddington's <u>Stars and Atoms</u> (1927) and a little later his <u>The Nature of the Physical World</u> (1928). In the thirties and forties he read Huxley, Heard and Wells and in the fifties and sixties made short notes from books by Bertrand Russell, Julian Huxley and Fred Hoyle. (4) The general effect of this reading seems to have been to confirm Forster's scepticism about the existence of any natural or cosmic order in the universe, and to make him concentrate upon a level of existence at which it is possible to perceive some sort of coherence and order. This level is indicated in a note made in the sixties -

> Origin of Earth - 4700 millions back. Fossils
> frequent: 600 millions only. 'Life' - i.e.
> living molecules - must have started between
> the above. These considerations - like those
> about space - steady me, and help me to concen-
> trate upon what's small and immediate. They
> compel me to adopt values. (5)

The tone of this note might suggest that Forster is adopting a new attitude, but the note is really the culminating expression of a view dating back to the First War, when, in that world of gigantic horror, Forster's mind was propped by "the slighter gestures of dissent" in the hedonistic and private worlds

23

created by J.K. Huysmans and T.S. Eliot. (6) It is this attitude which has come to be associated most distinctively with the work of Forster, an attitude of scepticism towards cosmic as well as social order, counterbalanced by a reliance upon the inner life of the individual. The two most basic features of Forster's mind are an openminded empiricism which makes him consider the evidence of science and history before reaching a conclusion, and a concentration upon human imagination to supply personal values in an infinite and disordered universe. While science and history give proof of outer chaos, imagination reveals the possibility of discovering or constructing smaller spheres of order. When he speaks of the 'small and immediate', Forster is really referring to the individual, whose capacity for personal relationships "...is something comparatively solid... starting from them I get a little order into the contemporary chaos." (7) This dialectic of inner and outer, of objective observation and subjective evaluation, is everywhere apparent in Forster's criticism. Forster is a binary thinker, and his world view is an attempt to synthesize the dual nature of reality, to harmonize the facts of the external universe with the inner forces of human nature.

This view is presented succinctly in 'What I Believe', but a fuller notion of it emerges by examining the essays written between the mid-twenties and mid-forties. The core of this period, the mid-thirties, contains most of Forster's significant essays, for it was over this period that economic depression and the rise of Fascism forced writers to adopt a position in relation to the universe, society and politics. Forster's essays of this period provide several insights into the precise angle from which he views the universe and man.

II

In Britain in the Nineteen Thirties, Noreen Branson and Margot Heinemann point out that in the pre-Hitler years, political interest centred on strains within the Empire rather than any threat from outside it. The Russian Revolution did symbolize a potential problem, but Russia in the twenties was too weak to be a source of worry. Moreover, the Beaverbrook-Rothermere press ensured that "...most middle- and working class people regarded Russia with dislike and contempt... because the Soviet system was thought of as a bloodstained tyranny."(8)

FORSTER'S VIEW OF THE NATURE OF MAN

But with the emergence of Stalin as absolute dictator before the end of the decade and because of Russia's apparent immunity to the economic slump, the challenge of communism to liberal democracy was reinforced in a very real way. Most of the younger generation writers - Auden, Spender, Day Lewis, MacNeice, Caudwell, Julian Bell and many others - came to accept that freedom and equality were only possible in a socialist society and were incompatible within liberal democracy.

Much more alarming was the threat from Fascism. Oswald Mosley formed his British Union of Fascists in 1932, Hitler came to power the following year, and Mussolini invaded Abyssinia in October 1935.

A third source of tyranny was discovered to exist even within democratic government. In October 1932 the police brutally disrupted a national hunger march organized by the National Unemployed Workers' Movement, and in 1934 the government introduced an Incitement to Disaffection Bill (popularly called the 'Sedition Bill'), which when enacted would give police wide powers of detention and prosecution. Pacifism was one of the areas which the government intended to suppress, and the bill was seen by the public as a serious infringement of civil liberty. (9) The National Council for Civil Liberties, with Forster as its first President, launched a campaign which forced the government to water down the provisions of the Sedition Bill. By the middle of the decade, therefore, it was apparent to liberals that British freedom was under threat from the sudden and universal growth of tyrannical tendencies in Europe, and as a reaction, within Britain itself.

This change of interest from Empire to internal politics is reflected in Forster's career as the movement from A Passage to India to the essays of the second, non-fictional phase of his life. There is, however, a fundamental continuity, for Forster's attention continues to be centred on the 'small and immediate', on the spheres of human personality and creative imagination which exist within the larger spheres of a chaotic universe and a disordered society. The definition of Forster's conception of the individual and human existence will therefore begin with what Forster has to say about man's fundamental physical and psychological condition within this broad socio-cosmic context.

A convenient starting point is the essay 'The Menace to Freedom' (1935) which was written just after Mussolini's invasion of Abyssinia. Forster argues here that tyranny is not a mystical force, nor

FORSTER'S VIEW OF THE NATURE OF MAN

does it simply emerge from an ideology, whether Marxist or Fascist. Rather, it is a symptom of something within human nature, for "...politics are based on human nature, and our freedom is really menaced today because a million years ago Man was born in chains." (10) Forster sees three permanent characteristics within human nature - fear, love and a desire for personal freedom. He thinks that in the course of evolution a superior development of man's mind has enabled him to dominate the universe, and that this has gradually freed man from fear and strengthened his capacity for love. Yet human history has not been a simple and straightforward progress towards love and freedom, because even after millions of years, fear remains man's strongest instinct -

> Man grew out of other forms of life; he has evolved among taboos; he has been a coward for centuries, afraid of the universe outside him and of the herd wherein he took refuge. So he cannot, even if he wishes it, be free today. In recent centuries - Greece saw the first attempt - he tried to become an individual, an entity which thinks for itself, says what it thinks, and acts according to its own considered standards - and there has been much applause for this attempt in art and literature, but it is abortive morally because of those primeval chains. (11)

This summarizes Forster's view of the history of human development and points towards his values. Forster sees human freedom emerging through the assertion of creative individuality and wants the process to continue. But he realizes that the attainment of a separate identity and the feeling of selfhood can be suppressed by a more primordial instinct - the fear which has perennially chained the individual to his herd. Forster does not say that man is inherently free or that man is born free. On the contrary, he sees that the first condition of life is man's existence within society. Freedom, however, is an acquired condition of existence which has become constitutively human. Man has evolved in a way which makes freedom a characteristic of 'human' (as distinct from 'bestial') existence. Given the fact that man is born into society, it is also necessary to accept that during the course of evolution, individuality has become a fact of existence - or as Forster puts it in 'What I Believe' -

FORSTER'S VIEW OF THE NATURE OF MAN

> ...as for individualism - there seems no way of getting off this, even if one wanted to ... (men) are obliged to be born separately and die separately, and, owing to these unavoidable termini, will always be running off the totalitarian rails. The memory of birth and the expectation of death always lurk within the human being, making him separate from his fellows and consequently capable of intercourse with them. (12)

In conflict with the necessity of existence within society, the desire for freedom - which is manifest as the individual's effort to unlink himself from the social chain and assert his separate identity - is seen by Forster as an effort of the human spirit. Evidence of its existence is the rise of the enquiring mind and the responsive heart. The individual spirit breaks free of the material chain when it thinks and feels by itself, when, even though ultimately conditioned, it becomes capable of influencing its own destiny and is aware of its own internal completeness. Such an effort is always resisted by the stratification of fear into its specific forms - obscurantism, dogma and ideology. The claims of group-loyalty, nationalism, patriotism, Fascism, communism and grundyism are only, in Forster's view, modern forms of the animal fear inherited at birth by every generation -

> Man... has disguised the fear of the herd as loyalty towards the group, and has persuaded himself that when he sacrifices himself to the state, he is accomplishing a deed far more satisfying than anything which can be accomplished alone. (13)

Forster believes that while social order has ensured, and is necessary for, material survival, man's greatest accomplishment - the development of his individuality - has been spiritual. This has been possible only with a general freedom from fear, when social order has not suppressed creative individualism.

Forster also refutes the Romantic notion associated with Rousseau that man is born free but enslaved by social institutions. From Forster's perspective the menace to freedom is internal and only therefore external, so that its solution must be moral before it can be social. He notes that in the eighteenth and nineteenth centuries it was possible for Rousseau and Voltaire to think of freedom as a natural state, a lost heritage that could be recovered. But possessing a better knowledge of history and psychology, and having suffered under tyranny and democracy alike, modern man cannot cherish any antique faith in a Golden Age. "Many people do not believe in freedom any more" he writes, "and the few who do, regard it as something that must be discovered, not recovered." (14) Forster is one of the few who continues to believe in freedom, though he feels that man can recover freedom from within himself, from his knowledge of the past, and through the gradual transformation of his ideal of freedom into a material reality. He does not believe that man will discover any new forces within himself, nor that scientific discovery and planning will by itself create an ordered and free world. He thinks that any philosophy, Marxist or Fascist, Hegelian or Wagnerian, which sees human progress as a scientific movement towards a glorious goal, misconceives the nature of man.

That is why, unlike J.D. Bernal, J.B.S. Haldane, H.G. Wells and other scientific sociologists (15) who were at this time propagating applied science as a method of developing and organizing society, Forster argues that far from creating a free world, every scientific methodology has reduced the individual into a mere functionary. (16) In 1920 he reviewed the first volume of Wells's The Outline of History and says that Wells is too ready to impose his faith in scientific evolution upon history - "To him evolution is progress... There is no collaring these optimists. They asked for science in 1914, they got it, and in 1920 they still ask for science ..." (17) Through the twenties and thirties, Wells continued advocating a world state in books like The Open Conspiracy (1928) and After Democracy (1932). In the latter he asked for "a Liberal Fascisti" and "enlightened Nazis" to plan a new international order. (18) In a 1929 broadcast he announced -

> In the scientific world I find just that disinterested devotion to great ends that I hope will spread at last through the entire range of human activity... We can all be citizens of the free state of science. (19)

It was this outlook that Orwell devastated in his 1941 essay 'Wells, Hitler and the World State', and Orwell's criticism is gently echoed in Forster's

FORSTER'S VIEW OF THE NATURE OF MAN

views. In 'The Menace to Freedom', for instance, Forster remarks ironically -

> The human make-up is certainly changing ...
> Perhaps under the inrush of scientific inventions, the change will proceed still quicker.
> Perhaps after the storms have swept by and the aeroplanes crashed into one another, and wireless jammed wireless, a new creature may appear on this globe, a creature who, we pretend is here already: the individual. (20)

Later, during the Second War, Forster again discredits Wells's utopian scientisms, saying that technology always outstrips the moral values that are needed to cope with it. In 'The New Disorder' (1941) he feels that "If science would only discover and never apply...mankind would be in a far safer position." (21) Forster feels that 'apathy, uninventiveness and inertia' in the scientific world might better facilitate a development of the love that exists within the human spirit, and thereby remedy the disjunction between the physical and psychic worlds.
    Forster is equally sceptical of the optimism of writers like Gerald Heard, Aldous Huxley and Christopher Isherwood who thought that mysticism could lead to psychological discoveries which would create a free and loving world. Through the thirties there were any number of people who went 'Eastern' out of Spenglerian despair with disharmony in European civilization.(22) Middleton Murry found inspiration in Gurdjieff and Ouspensky, C.E.M. Joad expounded the philosophy of Sarvapalli Radhakrishnan in Counter Attack from the East (1933), the sage J. Krishnamurthi gained an immense following. Aldous Huxley and Christopher Isherwood produced an edition of the Bhagvad Gita and Gerald Heard recommended a scientific use of 'yoga' and 'shakti' to revolutionize society in his Pain, Sex and Time (1939). The view implied by all these writers - that freedom would be discovered through a "revelation in the human make-up which will allow it (freedom) to emerge" (23) - seems too pseudo-scientific and far-fetched to Forster for he does not believe that the personality conceals undiscovered virtues which will miraculously transform human existence. "No millennium seems likely to descend... no change of heart will occur" he says in 'What I Believe', but he does not succumb to fatalism either, for "it is presumptuous to say that we cannot improve, and that

29

FORSTER'S VIEW OF THE NATURE OF MAN

Man, who has only been in power for a few thousand years, will never learn to make use of his power."(24) The real need, as he sees it in this essay as well as 'The Menace to Freedom', is a moral realignment. Seeing that fear gives rise to tyranny, he defines the inner power necessary to combat the menace to freedom -

> Man has another wish, besides the wish to be free, and that is the wish to love, and perhaps something may be born of the union of the two... it is a tendency that must be reckoned with, and it takes as many forms as fear. (25)

One of the sources of Forster's sentimental belief in love is the Bloomsbury creed of personal relations, and perhaps more specifically in this context, Lowes Dickinson's idealistic politics. In The Meaning of Good (1901), Lowes Dickinson says that in love "...we have something which gives us, if it be only for a moment, yet still in a real experience, an idea, at least, a suggestion, to say no more, of what we might mean by a perfect Good..." (26) Despite the fanaticism with which Germany was hated and patriotism lauded during the First War, Lowes Dickinson remained staunchly apolitical and wedded to the Platonic (or ahistorically 'human') ideals of love, reason and harmony. In his biography of Lowes Dickinson, Forster defends this commitment to humanist ideals in an atmosphere hostile to sanity and reason. His own attitude during the fervent politics of the thirties corresponds with that of Lowes Dickinson's two decades earlier, in that he continues to stress the importance of moral and human ideals and refuses to be swept away by the new faiths - Marxism, Scientific Socialism and Mysticism. His own, tentatively argued faith is in the combination and more effective use of inner love and freedom. In 1944, for instance, Forster reviewed the conflicting ideologies of Harold Laski's Faith, Reason and Civilization and F.A. Hayek's The Road to Serfdom. Laski argues that the Bolshevik revolution, like Christianity, emerged after a decay in civilization and ought to replace Christianity as the human ideal. Hayek, on the other hand, sees Marxism and Fascism as parallel ideologies, both opposed to liberal-democratic freedom. In such a conflict of interests between 'liberty' and 'equality' Forster does not see any hope of resolution, except possibly through the moral faculty. "I myself am a sentimentalist who believes in the importance of love" he says in his conclusion to the review, "(for) the desire to love and the desire to be loved are the twin anchor ropes which keep the human race human." (27) 'The Menace to Freedom' similarly implies that if fear leads to tyranny, love leads in the opposite direction towards creativity and relationship. Forster always emphasizes the dual and complex nature of man - dual because fear and love, good and evil, coexist, and complex because these impulses intermesh and can only be made to balance each other -

> If the two desires (love and freedom) could combine, the menace to freedom from within, the fundamental menace (of fear) might disappear, and the political evils now filling all the foreground of our lives would be deprived of the poison which nourishes them. (28)

'What I Believe' reiterates the same basic idea in different words -

> 'O thou who lovest me - set this love in order' ...I do not believe that it ever will be, but here, and not through a change of heart is our probable route. Not by becoming better but by ordering and distributing his native goodness, will man shut up Force into its box...(29)

While this reliance on 'love' and the inner moral goodness of the individual emerges through Forster's response to his general intellectual milieu and criticism of a variety of personalities and currents of opinion, it owes something special to the writing of Henry Fitzgerald (or 'Gerald') Heard. Heard was a curious mixture of historian, anthropologist, mystic and popularizer of science. His writing is like an amateur version of Arnold Toynbee's work, for it combines an analysis of the growth and decay of civilization with mystical and psycho-religious solutions to prevent the decline of the West. But unlike Toynbee, who discovered the solutions to Europe's seemingly imminent collapse in creative minorities such as the Christian saints and martyrs, Heard eclectically combines Wellsian faith in scientific planning with the mystical and subjectivist solutions of writers like Isherwood, Huxley and Joad. Wells's <u>The Open Conspiracy</u> had argued for "a great multitude and variety of overlapping groups...organized for collective political, social and educational as well as propagandist action..."(30)

and Heard's work similarly pins all hope of
saving civilization upon spiritually superior groups
who, having discovered hidden sources of strength,
will help humanity to evolve a perfectly adjusted
psyche. In 'The Significance of the New Pacifism',
an essay anthologised alongside those of other
thirties pacifists like Aldous Huxley and Canon
'Dick' Sheppard, Heard propagates "a psychological
communism which (will) make war and competition
irrelevant". (31) This belief is spelled out in
greater detail by all his other books, which argue
that human history has been a progressive development of individualism from the tribal state, that
this has led to possessiveness, materialism and
anarchy, and that the only solution to the resulting
chaos is a dissolution of individualism into spiritual feelings of harmony for the tribe. By the mid-
forties Forster had read most of Heard's work and
reviewed some of it as it appeared. In general,
Forster agrees with Heard's historical analyses but
disputes his mystical and anti-individualistic solutions. On 13th August 1931 Forster recommended
Heard's <u>The Social Substance of Religion</u> (1931) to
his radio listeners, paraphrasing the book's argument as follows -

> The immediate cause (of human unrest) he finds
> is the growth of individualism...The sub-men,
> from whom the human race has evolved, were un-
> selfconscious, they had a common consciousness
> such as one may observe in a herd of animals.
> Then the individual develops, and is torn by
> conflicting aims. He wants at times to be
> 'himself' and at other times to 'lose' himself
> in the group consciousness...Religion, accord-
> ing to Mr. Heard is not an individual affair. It
> is a spiritual refreshment which can only be
> obtained in and through others and the problem
> of our society is not political, not economic,
> but psychological...A religion of love is in-
> deed necessary... we must lose ourselves in the
> group... (32)

The tone of the broadcast is mildly sceptical.
Forster distances himself from Heard's argument without specifically disagreeing. Four years later
Forster reviewed Heard's <u>The Source of Civilization</u>
(1935) just before he wrote 'The Menace to Freedom'.
In this book Heard points to the historical instanc-
es of harmony between society and self achieved by
the ancient civilizations of China and the Indus

FORSTER'S VIEW OF THE NATURE OF MAN

Valley, and argues that man is not by nature a fighting animal. Forster agrees that such harmony has been achieved in history and also endorses Heard's view that the cause of evolution of 'man' from 'beast' was the energy expressed in love and sensitivity. According to Heard, "When the struggle to survive was called off... Life became most inventive and various and dared explore and experiment." (33) This argument is outlined with implicit approval in Forster's review -

> The prehistoric lizards specialized, covered themselves with armour and weapons, and are fossils. Man, if he imitate them, will share their fate. He may be saved because he has the unique power of contemplating himself, and thus realizing his affinity with his fellows. (34)

Heard also argues that moral values must keep pace with material and scientific development, because "It is on sustaining (a) balanced advance of inner and outer powers... (that) has depended the success of man's transition from animal to man...on the self-same balance depends whether civilization shall continue and man survive." (35) Forster's agreement with this is clear from the extent to which it is made a personal argument in 'The Menace to Freedom' and 'The New Disorder'. However, Forster also makes clear his disagreement with Heard's view that destructive forces are only sporadic interruptions which somehow erupt from a basically peaceful being. He himself sees man as much more fearful, and therefore violent, than Heard. Nor does he have much time for Heard's specific solutions for achieving a harmonized development of inner and outer existence. Heard's solutions are an absurd hotch-potch of group therapy, Freudian psychology and Hindu mysticism. They are based on the supposition that physical evolution has ceased, and that psychological evolution must begin and gradually create a perfectly adjusted human nature. This is outlined in tedious detail in his book <u>Pain, Sex and Time</u> (1939) where it is suggested that a scientifically organized development of consciousness will create a conflict-free social order. Man's suppressed sexual energy and capacity for pain must be canalized away from violence into an evolutionary drive for the creation of a sect of 'neo-Brahmins' - psychological supermen who will eradicate conflict by disseminating inner harmony. Forster's review of this book concludes - "Mr. Heard's analysis works. His remedy would fail." (36)

FORSTER'S VIEW OF THE NATURE OF MAN

A 1943 broadcast review of Heard's Man the Master(1942), a book in which more or less the old arguments are repeated, similarly concludes - "his analysis of our troubles is convincing...his remedies are not."(37) The only antidote to the fear which deprives man of his freedom, Forster insists, is a better use of man's innate capacity for love. Applied psychology, like scientific socialism, is unlikely to resolve social conflict. The only hope lies, in his view, in man's better realization of his already existent moral self.

III

While the reality of love as a counteraction to fear is only insufficiently emphasized by scientists and historians, Forster believes that a much more dangerous threat exists to the liberal notion of 'freedom'. This is the charge, partly from Marxism but mainly from Fascism, that the liberal notion of freedom is a mere illusion. Since freedom has only been achieved after the creation of social order, the Marxist and Fascist argument is that man's first duty is to society and the state. Forster's criticism disputes this view, and in the process of re-arguing a liberal notion of freedom, further clarifies his conception of the nature of the individual and human existence.

In a light hearted essay called 'The Game of Life' (1919) Forster indicates (albeit whimsically) his view of the freedom of the individual within the wider framework of life. The essay analyses the phrase 'game of life' by showing its connection with the outlook of the English public-school. The public-school curtails freedom because it conceives of life as a game played by previously laid out rules. It recognizes only the material and not the spiritual dimension of life. Man's duty, in the public school, is simply to contribute to a larger whole of which he is a part, never to a distinctly personal vision or to spiritual ideals that may be at odds with social order. Forster suggests that a game resembles life only when it allows the existence of free will. In this respect piquet represents the true proportions of the controllable and uncontrollable elements which make up life, for -

> This savage pastime admits the element of Free Will. It is possible to retard or accelerate Fate. Play, subtle and vigorous play, goes on all the time, though the player is being swept

FORSTER'S VIEW OF THE NATURE OF MAN

>   to disaster or victory by causes beyond his
>   control, and it is in the play, rather than the
>   result, that the real interest in the game
>   resides. (38)

In Forster's view life is complex, unfathomable, and in many ways, determined, yet the individual's freedom to make his own choices is one of the forces by which existence is, and ought to be, determined. It is most important that men "retain the power of wriggling, of fighting with their star or against it", for it is only by this process that man can create order and meaning in a universe in which he is not otherwise free.

This subject, freedom, is treated at a more serious level two decades later when Forster argues that the concept of individual freedom is disproved neither by showing the supreme importance of social order nor by demonstrating that men have never been equally free. He argues that freedom, like love and fear, exists as an impulse within human nature. The pressure, in the thirties, to define freedom in socially specific terms rather than as a 'bourgeois' ideal only hardens Forster's insistence that the ideal of freedom is a manifestation of something intrinsic to the human spirit. This ideal has usually a specific implication in his mind. 'The Menace to Freedom', for instance, equates freedom with the individual's ability to think of himself as a separate and unique entity, while more generally Forster's criticism defines freedom as the ability to think and create in isolation. One of the anti-Nazi broadcasts contains a representative statement:

>   I do not want to exaggerate the claims of
>   freedom...Freedom is only a favourable step -
>   or let us say, three little steps. When
>   writers (and artists generally) feel easy, when
>   they can express themselves openly, when their
>   public is allowed to receive their communica-
>   tions, there is a chance of the general level
>   of civilization rising.(39)

This is an ideal of freedom which looks back to Milton's <u>Areopagitica</u> and J.S. Mill's essay <u>On Liberty</u>, both of which specifically defend the freedom to express opinions without fear of censorship. (40) But in a 1939 review of <u>A Handbook of Freedom</u> (1939) compiled by the Marxist critics Jack Lindsay and Edgell Rickword, Forster also insists that an

FORSTER'S VIEW OF THE NATURE OF MAN

ideal such as freedom can escape definition and yet exist:

> Freedom? But freedom to do what? How pat the dreary question falls! How the lecturer mouths as he settles himself on his subsidized seat to discuss it. Freedom to injure others? Freedom to starve? Freedom to feed while others starve? ...Freedom, like God, melts when we ask her to give an account of herself. But she has the power of re-forming behind our backs or when we look away, so that suddenly, in the midst of our ratiocinations, we exclaim 'She exists! I know she exists! I must win her! All men must win her!'(41)

Insofar as Marxists attack possessive individualism, a notion which implies the slavery of others, Forster has no quarrel. But he savages the doctrinaire Marxists who do not accept freedom as a psychological reality, as an impulse intrinsic to human existence. From Forster's perspective, freedom is simply a deep-rooted urge for a utopian state in which every individual is equally free.

This theoretical defence of freedom was probably incited partly by Andre Gide's Back From the U.S.S.R. which Forster reviewed in 1937, partly by Christopher Caudwell's Studies in a Dying Culture (1938) which Forster reviewed in 1938, and to some extent also by Lenin's view that absolute freedom is a bourgeois illusion (which Forster encountered in an anthology of Marxist criticism) - than by anything in the Lindsay and Rickword anthology. (42) In the Introduction to their anthology, Rickword writes that "it is not to any right by birth, but to the strong arms and keen brains of our ancestors that we must attribute our liberation", (43) and with this Forster has no quarrel. But in 1937 Andre Gide returned from a disillusioning tour of Russia to write a book which exposed the denial of creative freedom in that country. He said he doubted "whether in any other country in the world, even Hitler's Germany, thought be less free, more bowed down, more fearful (terrorized), more vassalized."(44) Forster was impressed by Gide's honesty in confessing his disappointment with the position of artists in Russia, and in his review of the book hoped that free expression would come to be seen as an important facet of social life in Russia. (45) Very soon afterwards, Forster read an anthology of Marxist aesthetics, and while pleasantly surprised

FORSTER'S VIEW OF THE NATURE OF MAN

by Marx and Engels's enlightened attitude to art and creative freedom, was less impressed by Lenin's views on the same subjects. He thought - "Leninism less cultured than Marxism - i.e. less interested in the creation and enjoyment of works of art" (46) and felt that in the deservedly important drive for equality the equally important respect for the ideal of creative individualism was insufficiently stressed within the Leninist social framework. All this was perhaps no more than a misgiving about Russia. Forster recognized that it was a period of transition for that country and that there was no reason why communism would not in the future allow its artists greater freedom and "become civilized." But when Caudwell's book appeared in 1938, Forster was impelled to defend the liberal-idealist notion of freedom because the last essay of Caudwell's book is a direct attack on what Caudwell supposes to be Forster, Wells and Bertrand Russell's view of freedom.

Caudwell's criticism stems from his interpretation of the bourgeois conception of freedom, which, he says, is the illusion that man is born free but crippled by society:

> Implicit in the conception of thinkers like Russell and Forster, that all social relations are restraints on spontaneous liberty, is the assumption that the animal is the only completely free creature...This is of course an ancient fallacy. Rousseau is the famous exponent. Man is born free but is everywhere in chains. Always in the bourgeois mind is this legend of a golden age, of a perfectly good man corrupted by institutions.(47)

This overlooks Rousseau's real ideal of social harmony as an antidote to the barren individualism of Hobbes, but more important in this context, it falsifies Forster's Hellenic ideal of harmony between society and the individual. Forster does believe that after a point social order constricts individual freedom, but he never argues for the re-adoption of animal instinct or upholds primitive man as a loving and noble creature. On the contrary, 'The Menance to Freedom' shows man as originally a fearful creature for whom the all-consuming importance of social order prevents the development of separate individuality.

From his inference that liberals postulate a futile and fantastic primitivism, Caudwell further

FORSTER'S VIEW OF THE NATURE OF MAN

misunderstands Forster's view of the progress of civilization through an increase in personal freedom. He writes -

> The man alone, unconstrained, answerable only to his instincts, is Russell's and Forster's free man. Thus all man's painful progress from the beasts is held to be useless. All man's work and sweat and revolutions have been away from freedom... (they believe that) civilization should be abandoned and we should return to the woods. (48)

This, in fact, is the antithesis of Forster's outlook and is rather neatly illustrated by his praise for Lindsay and Rickword for producing an anthologised record of the sweat and revolutions which lie behind English democracy. Indeed Forster believes as firmly as Caudwell that progress is definable as the development of selfconscious man from unselfconscious beast. He never disputes that freedom must be made compatible with equality, but he does hold that freedom must first be acknowledged as a human impulse, because only then can man erect a social superstructure within which the need for equality does not grind individuals into a mass. Caudwell misrepresents Forster as much because he disregards Forster's emphasis on the spirit of individual freedom as because he debases a humanist argument into a sterile, atavistic anarchism. In addition, he obliterates a level of agreement between his own outlook and Forster's. Like Caudwell, Forster does not dispute the need for socialistic co-operation to obtain material freedom. The real difference - the value placed on co-operation as an end in itself by Caudwell and on co-operation as a means to creative individuality and spiritual liberation by Forster - is perhaps less antagonistic than Caudwell's mis-analysis and the zeitgeist of the thirties make it seem. Ronald Dworkin says in an essay that -

> Unfortunately, liberty and equality often conflict: sometimes the only effective means to promote equality require some limitation of liberty, and sometimes the consequences of promoting liberty are detrimental to equality. In these cases, good government consists in the best compromise between the competing ideals... The liberal becomes the man in the middle, which explains why liberalism is so often now

> considered wishy-washy, an untenable compromise between two more forthright positions. (49)

Especially in the thirties, even slight hesitations about socialism could lead to reductive accusations. This is evident from Caudwell's criticism, in which 'liberty' is a bourgeois rather than a human notion, and 'equality' the sole preserve of socialism. (50) While Forster is severely critical of Caudwell's faith in Marx, equating it with the Christian's faith in Christ, his review of Caudwell's book also indicates a certain basic agreement -

> So long as Caudwell attacks the bourgeois conception of liberty, he goes on gaily enough. It is, in the first place indefinable. In the second place, although some people are comparatively free they cannot if they are decent enjoy their freedom while their less fortunate brethren are suffering. Both these points are incontestible...(51)

The problem, as defined repeatedly by Forster, lies in the confusion of man's desire for freedom with a completely abstract and deliberately vague notion which may be held to justify anarchy or class interest. In 'Liberty in Englan'' (1935) he says, "I know very well how limited and how open to criticism, English freedom is. It is race bound and it's class bound...inspite of them I do believe in liberty..." (52) Forster implies that freedom is neither a Platonic Idea remote from human life, nor just the right social organization, but an aspect of the human spirit which makes man create those aesthetic, social and religious orders which define and extend the freedom within. The progress of English democracy demonstrated in the Lindsay & Rickword anthology gives Forster the feeling that -

> ...from the depths of the English people, as no doubt from the depths of other people, there arises this desire for pure liberty, coloured by circumstances and class, but striving upwards to the land beyond logic, to the Beloved Republic which feeds upon freedom and lives, to the Good Place which is every poet's dream. (53)

Like love, freedom is a component of the human spirit, an aspect of 'the unseen'. Its persistence within man raises it above the frame of a logic that can argue its material shortcomings.

This faith in liberty or individual freedom is not simply a refutation of dogmatic Marxists like Caudwell - it is in fact usually upheld as the antithesis of the Fascist 'weltanschauung'. The Kidd obituary, which again defends the idea of freedom, like the obituary notice on Fry, stands alongside other essays and broadcasts such as 'Jew Consciousness' and 'Racial Exercise' (1939) and the 'Three Anti-Nazi Broadcasts' (1940). All these contradict the Fascist definition of liberty. Mussolini's mentor, Giovanni Gentile, spelt out the Fascist conception of liberty in 1925 -

> Always the maximum of liberty coincides with the maximum force of the state...Every force is a moral force, for it is always an expression of will; and whatever be the argument used - preaching or blackjacking - its efficacy can be none other than its ability finally to receive the inner support of man and to persuade him to agree to it. (54)

This belief was the essence of the Italian Labour Charter promulgated by Mussolini in 1927, which began - "The Italian nation is an organism having ends, a life and means superior in power and duration to those of the single individual or groups of individuals comprising it." (55) In Hitler's writing and speeches too, 'freedom' is twisted to mean something which individuals do not possess in themselves, but which they discover by working for the collective good as defined by those in authority.

It is impossible to be exact about what and how much of Fascist theory Forster actually read. In the 1940 pamphlet Nordic Twilight he shows awareness of Mein Kampf, quotes the speeches of Hitler and other Nazi leaders, and footnotes What Hitler Did to Us by Eva Lips (56) as well as a book called Carlyle und der Nationalsozialismus (1937) by Theodor Deimel. Furthermore, in his 1944 essay on Samuel Butler's Erewhon he says that Carlyle's Of Heroes, Hero-Worship and the Heroic in History influenced him negatively, and his Commonplace Book contains a note (dated 1952) from Eric Bentley's The Cult of the Superman - a book which traces the ideal of hero-worship in the work of Nietzsche, Wagner, Carlyle, D.H. Lawrence and Stefan George.(57) The important point is, however, that no one during this period could have been unaware of the main Fascist ideas.

FORSTER'S VIEW OF THE NATURE OF MAN

Despite the undoubted moral and intellectual superiority of Marxism over Fascism, from the liberal-democratic viewpoint both ideologies are ultimately unacceptable because they fail to acknowledge that each individual is spiritually distinct and must have the freedom to develop his own individuality. Both are dogmatic, both obliterate the distinction between areas of private judgment and public control, and both induce a frame of mind similar to religious fanaticism. This seems to be Forster's view. He is sympathetic to the Russian effort to eliminate possessiveness and create social equality. He says - "I am not a Communist, though perhaps I might be one if I was a younger and braver man, for in Communism I can see hope. It does many things which I think evil, but I know that it intends good." (58) Forster was also very impressed by John Strachey's The Coming Struggle for Power (1932), an influential book of the period which presents the Marxist argument that the capitalist-imperialist search for foreign markets is the cause of international war. (59) Nevertheless, Forster retains liberal convictions because his sympathy for communism is counterweighted by his recognition that one of the evils of the communist state is that it denies personal freedom.

By placing 'freedom' alongside the constitutively human instinct of 'love', Forster first acknowledges freedom as an impulse of the human spirit and only then defines it more concretely as the inalienable right of man to think, respond and create without interference. His conception of freedom is very close to that of J.S. Mill's who had written:

> If it were felt that the free development of individuality is one of the leading essentials of well being, that it is not only a co-ordinate element with all that is designated by the terms civilization, instruction, education, culture, but is in itself a necessary part and condition of all those things, there would be no danger that liberty should be undervalued, and the adjustment of the boundaries between it and social control would present no extraordinary difficulty...the evil is that individual spontaneity is hardly recognized by the common modes of thinking as having any intrinsic worth... (60)

Forster's realignment of inner forces, in line with Mill's belief, suggests that the drive for freedom

would not lead to anarchy or to disbelief in the
necessity of social equality. Whereas fear forces
man to forsake his separate identity, love or goodwill would restrain any impulse for 'absolute freedom', and might lead towards an order in which
liberty and equality do not conflict. This seems at
once a tame, simplisitic, idealistic and far-fetched
hope. As a method of social change it had been
proved invalid and ineffective. In his 'War and
Peace: Letter to E.M. Forster', Julian Bell rightly
pointed out that love and goodwill were inadequate
political weapons, particularly in the crisis-ridden
context of the thirties. (61) But in retrospect,
Forster's quiet defence of seemingly outmoded
liberal beliefs seems courageous, sensible, and far
from absurd. In the context of Spenglerian fatalism, the desperate fantasies of Heard, the parochial
Christian faith of Toynbee, the idealistic and un-
worldly pacifism of the Peace Pledge Unionists, the
Stalinist purges in Russia and the insane barbarism
of German and Italian Fascism, there is something
reassuringly human in Forster's essays of this
period. In a time of violent upheaval and radical
social change, humanism of this sort is undoubtedly
anomalous and limited in the hope it offers for
social improvement, but its virtue is that it recognizes the complexity and variety of human life and
exposes the limitation of doctrines which do not.
Though inadequate as a social theory, it is at
least progressive, both in the ordinary sense of
recognizing the urgent need for greater economic
justice, and in an importantly different sense - in
stressing that man's uniquely 'human' self must not
be destroyed in the process of creating a just
social order. (62)

IV

Alongside 'love' and 'freedom', there are in
Forster's criticism other examples of virtues which
constitute the human spirit. Forster's definition
of 'spirit' (or 'the unseen', as he calls it) can
vary, and is usually given a precise meaning within
its context. He approaches a definition in his essay
on his ancestor Henry Thornton. He says here, that
the human spirit is revealed not in ascetic medita-
tion and pious acts, but in "a touch of mysticism,
a sense of the unseen, and a capacity for martyrdom
... (in) poetry, mystery, passion, ecstasy, music."
(63) 'Spirit' in Forster's sense is synonymous with
intense experience, a collective term for the

FORSTER'S VIEW OF THE NATURE OF MAN

impulses which lead to creativity and self-fulfilment. Forster's fiction points to the Greek ideal of harmony of body and soul. Spiritual fulfilment is shown as that intense response to the arts (Helen Schlegel's response to Beethoven's Fifth Symphony), to human beings (Mrs. Moore's intuitive warmth for Aziz) or to nature (Rickie Elliot's feeling for the countryside) which indicates that man is more than merely carnal. As Austin Warren says, Forster is "a 'naturalist' with wings and humanistic manners (who believes)...that everything ideal has a natural basis and that nothing in nature is incapable of an ideal fulfilment." (64) This belief underlies the humanist values propagated in Forster's essays.

While emphasizing the importance of the spiritual dimension, Forster never denies the importance of the body. He feels that a denial of the body is a denial of human life - "I am against asceticism myself...since bodies are the instruments through which we register and enjoy the world" he says in 'What I Believe'. Forster read Kenneth Clark's The Nude in 1955, and transcribed one of Clark's comments on the Greeks into his Commonplace Book - "Nothing which related to the whole man could be isolated or evaded: and this serious awareness of how much was implied in physical beauty saved them from the twin evils of sensuality and aestheticism." (65) In 1931 Forster reviewed H.S. Ede's A Life of Gaudier-Brzeska (1930) (66), and though his review does not say much that is revealing, he noted privately - "'Christians and Pantheists may insist that the soul is separate from the body, but this is not true. There is a live body, that is all.' Gaudier-Brzeska gets there in one." (67) Unlike the pantheist who believes in the separate existence of spirit, the humanist believes that body and spirit are interfused within the human frame. This humanist tenet makes Forster as critical of beliefs which deny the material life because of their obsession with the spiritual after-life, as of materialist doctrines which fail to recognize the reality of the human spirit.

This viewpoint is to be found most explicitly when Forster examines the psychological effect of property upon the individual in 'My Wood' (1926). This essay criticizes property as a cause of the possessive individualism which inhibits human relationship and spiritual fulfilment. Like 'Notes on the English Character' (1926), 'My Wood' shows that caution, stolidity and lack of imagination are the attributes of land-owners. The acquisitive instinct prevents, for instance, a toleration of the distinctive individuality and right to freedom of other beings. When a bird flies out of Forster's wood, he realizes he feels deprived and finds himself reluctant to accept the view that the bird belonged not to him, but to itself. Furthermore, the essay shows that the need to defend property leads to aggressiveness, this grows into megalomania, and ultimately there develops a territorial-imperative which may be "the nucleus of universal dominion." Hobbes recognized long before Forster that the reason for man's restless quest for power "is not always that a man hopes for a more intensive delight... but because he cannot assure the power and means to live well, which he hath present, without the acquisition of more." (68) Forster's argument is similar. The apparently modest need for self-preservation enlarges into a quest for power and security for their own sake and to the exclusion of others, rather than for a more intense fulfilment for every individual -

> Creation, property, enjoyment form a sinister trinity in the human mind. Creation and enjoyment are both very good, yet they are often unattainable without a material basis, and at such moments property pushes itself in as a substitute, saying 'Accept me instead - I'm good enough for all three.' (69)

But dislike of materialism does not swing Forster towards asceticism. He disagrees with Tolstoy and the Christian gospels when they argue that property is in itself sinful - "they approach the difficult ground of asceticism here, where I cannot follow them", he says.

This remark echoes Forster's disagreement with the argument of Tolstoy's What, Then, Must We do, a book he reviewed a few months before writing 'My Wood'. Tolstoy argues that social equality can only come through a complete renunciation of all possessions. Describing his experience of poverty, he says he grew to realize the hypocrisy of charity and the need for a radical solution - "I came to feel that in money itself, in the very possession of it, there is something evil and immoral, and that money itself, and the fact that I possess it, is one of the chief causes of evil ..." (70) While admiring Tolstoy's sincerity and commitment, Forster says in his review that even if renunciation did create equality, it would also produce "a curtailed, denuded, castrated individual who would have aroused the contempt of the Ancient Greeks." (71) In 'My Wood', which is really a reply to Tolstoy's Christian Socialism, Forster feels that rather than forsake enjoyment of the material world, a better use of the spiritual self is necessary -

> Our life on earth is, and ought to be, material and carnal. But we have not yet learned to manage our materialism and carnality properly; they are still entangled with the desire for ownership, where (in the words of Dante) 'Possession is one with loss'. (72)

Although Forster is as critical of possessiveness and greed as Tolstoy, a sense of proportion, in his view, is located between the unattractive 'freedom' which comes with possessions and the equally inadequate 'equality' entailed by asceticism. Forster tries to keep both excesses of materialism and spiritualism at bay because in both extremes, he believes, man forsakes his visionary powers and thereby abandons his distinctively human individuality.

Eleven years after 'My Wood', Forster visited the Soviet Pavilion at the Paris Exhibition of 1937. His thoughts on it show some development from the Lockean attitude - the defence of property alongside the stress on moral and rational development - of the 1926 essay:

> One of the evils of money is that it tempts us to look at it rather than at the things that it buys. They are dimmed because of the metal and the paper through which we receive them. That is the fundamental deceitfulness of riches which kept worrying Christ. That is the treachery of the purse, the wallet and the bank-balance, even from the capitalist point of view. They were invented as a convenience to the flesh, they have become a chain for the spirit. Surely they can be cut out, like some sorts of pain. Though deprived of them, the human mind might surely still keep its delicacy unimpaired, and the human body eat, drink and make love. And that is why every bourgeois ought to reverence the Soviet Pavilion. (73)

However, while this shows that Forster took a balanced view of Soviet Marxism and did not defend private property even half-heartedly as he had in 'My

Wood' ("It is forced on us by our economic system as the alternative to starvation"), his essays, like his novels, never satisfactorily grapple with economic issues. Like Howards End and A Passage to India, the essays focus narrowly on morality, values and the inner life within an economic system, rather than on the economic system itself: "...the effect of private ownership upon the community as a whole is another question ... Lets keep to psychology..." Forster says in 'My Wood', and this is essentially true of his writing as a whole. As a liberal, Forster feels that only by the adoption of true values will social problems be solved non-repressively. He sees that given property, self-interest asserts itself to the detriment of love, freedom and social harmony, but he also sees that merely the external imposition of a new socio-economic order will only curtail love, freedom and a truly human existence. The first step towards maintaining a distinctively human life, therefore, has to be the development of better attitudes, self-awareness and human values - or in other words, a more effective use of moral order.

V

Forster's sceptical view of scientific planning, mystic socialism, Christian socialism, dogmatic Marxism, as well as his opposition to Fascism - collectively define his view of human nature and of what constitutes a fundamentally human existence. He conceives of the individual as an interfunctioning unity of material and spiritual impulses because he is aware of both good and evil - fear and greed as well as love and freedom - within the human make-up. As fear, an aspect of the animal condition of existence, remains a part of man's inner being and vitiates the love and desire for personal freedom which make up his truly 'human' aspect, social conditions are, in Forster's view, similarly mixed and imperfect. Forster segregates love and freedom from fear and points to their ultimate importance if material conditions are to be improved. He believes that self-expression, creative freedom and social harmony are material extensions of the inner ordering of love and freedom, and that love and freedom are impulses which have become quintessentially necessary for civilized, human existence. In fact, ever since the 'human' phase of history, when the individual emerged from the herd, love and freedom have, in his view, become the defining characteristics of human life. Though born in chains because he cannot wholly cease to fear the universe, man has also become an individual who desires freedom for himself and fulfilment of his love for others. By greater consciousness and effective utilisation of his inner potential, man may be able to create the kind of social order in which his humanity is preserved and universally extended.

According to one political theorist, "any doctrine of human rights must be in some sense a doctrine of natural rights ... in the sense that they must be deduced from the nature (i.e. the needs and capacities) of men as such, whether of men as they now are or of men as they are thought capable of becoming." (74) Broadly speaking, the definition of human nature which emerges from Forster's essays implicitly follows this dictum. It proceeds from the factual to the desirable, from man as he is to what he can make himself. If Forster is idealistic about individuality, love and creativity, it is because he sees that only by these means has man created little spheres of order within circumambient confusion and flux. In the next chapter I will try to show that Forster's ideas about social order, like his ideas about the nature of man and human existence, are a further step in the basic thrust of his criticism - the argument that true 'order' only exists at the microcosmic level of creative individuality, especially as this is manifested in art.

NOTES

(1) 'Roger Fry', London Mercury, October 1934, vol. 30, pp. 495-6 (p. 496). Rpt. as 'Roger Fry: An Obituary Note', AH (p.51).
(2) "He was not, however, a Moore-ite. In fact he always believed himself incapable of abstract thought." Furbank I, p.77.
(3) Introduction to Virgil's Aenid, trans. Michael Oakley (1907; rpt. (revised) London: Dent, 1957) pp. V-XII (p.XI).
(4) CB, pp.50-1, 61, 241, 272 & 274.
(5) CB, p.290. The title of the note is 'Notes from Melvin Calvin'. Calvin was a scientist who investigated the origin of living systems in the universe. Another CB note of the same period runs: "Astronomy via Hoyle can help my outlook. Earth 4000 million years old and coagulated out of cold bodies ... Life, or rather the chemical preludes to it could have started before coagulation. This and other ill-apprehended scraps have an effect on my

mind and counsel that nothing matters for humans except the immediate ..." (CB, p. 274).
(6) 'T.S. Eliot and His Difficulties', Life and Letters, June 1929, Vol. 2, pp. 417-25 (pp.417-18). Rpt. as 'T.S. Eliot', AH (p.102).
(7) 'Credo', London Mercury, September 1938, vol. 38, pp. 397-404 (pp. 397-8). Rpt. as 'What I Believe', TCD (pp.65-6).
(8) Noreen Branson and Margot Heinemann, Britain in the Nineteen Thirties (1971; rpt. St. Albans: Panther Books, 1973) p. 323.
(9) Robert Graves and Alan Hodge point out that "People feared that this act would introduce Russian Ogpu or German Gestapo methods into Britain." The Long Week-End - A Social History of Great Britain 1918-1939 (London: Faber, 1940) p. 313.
(10) 'The Menace to Freedom', Spectator, 22 November 1935, pp. 861-2 (p.861). Rpt. TCD (p.9).
(11) TCD (p.9).
(12) TCD (p.73).
(13) 'The Menace to Freedom', TCD (p.9).
(14) ibid. (p.10).
(15) See Branson and Heinemann, pp. 284-5.
(16) The same basic hostility to the scientific outlook is evident in Matthew Arnold's Literature and Science (1882), which is a polemic against T.H. Huxley. The same argument is broadly restated in I.A. Richards's Science and Poetry (1926), and given its most savage expression by F.R. Leavis's Two Cultures? The Significance of C.P. Snow (1962). The tradition of liberal-humanist hostility to science is defined in Lionel Trilling's 'The Snow-Leavis Controversy' in Beyond Culture: Essays on Literature and Learning (1955; rpt. London: Secker and Warburg, 1966) pp. 145-77.
(17) 'A Great History', Athenaeum, 9 July 1920, pp. 42-3 (p.42).
(18) After Democracy: Address and Papers on the Present World Situation (London: Watts and Co., 1932) p. 24.
(19) 'My Point of View' in Points of View: A Series of Broadcast Addresses (London: Allen and Unwin, 1930) pp. 49-69 (pp.68-9). Lowes Dickinson had also contributed to this volume and it was reviewed by Forster - 'A Broadcast Debate', Nation and Athenaeum, 10 May 1930, p. 191.
(20) TCD (p.10).
(21) 'The New Disorder', Horizon, December 1941, vol. 4, pp. 379-84 (p. 380) Rpt. as The New Disorder

(New York: 1949) p.8.
(22) See Graves and Hodge, pp. 201-8. Oswald Spengler's doom-ridden The Decline of the West which argued that civilizations blossom and decay like natural organisms, appeared over the early nineteen twenties.
(23) 'The Menace to Freedom', TCD (p.10).
(24) TCD (p.69).
(25) 'The Menace to Freedom', TCD (p.10).
(26) The Meaning of Good: A Dialogue (Glasgow: Maclehouse, 1901) p. 188. A detailed and brilliant analysis of Forster's debt to the moral idealism of Bloomsbury and Cambridge exists in The Cave and the Mountain, pp. 72-98 and passim.
(27) 'A Clash of Authority', The Listener, 22 June 1944, pp. 685-6, (p.686).
(28) TCD (p.11).
(29) ibid. (p.72).
(30) The Open Conspiracy: Blueprints for a World Revolution (London: Gollancz, 1928) pp.127-8.
(31) The New Pacifism (London: Allenson & Co., 1936) pp. 13-22 (p.17).
(32) 'Books', King's College Manuscripts, vol. 22, pp. 14-15.
(33) The Source of Civilization (London: Jonathan Cape, 1935) p.57.
(34) 'Notes on the Way', Time and Tide, 23 November 1935, pp. 1703-4 (p. 1704).
(35) The Source of Civilization, p. 126.
(36) 'The Trigger', The Listener, 14 September 1939, p. 542 (p.542). Rpt. as 'Gerald Heard', TCD (p.27).
(37) 'Some Books', King's College Manuscripts, 3 February 1943, vol. 22, pp.214-5 (p.214).
(38) ibid. (p.72).
(39) 'Two Cultures: The Quick and The Dead', The Listener, 26 September 1940, pp. 446-7 (p.447). Rpt. as 'Three Anti-Nazi Broadcasts, 1: Culture and Freedom', TCD (p.33).
(40) Forster's 1944 broadcast 'A Tercentenary of Freedom' on Milton's Areopagitica argues similarly and specifically for freedom from censorship. See The Listener 7 December 1944, pp. 633-4. Rpt. as 'The Tercentenary of the "Areopagitica"', TCD, pp. 50-3.
(41) 'Freedom For What', The Listener, 1 June 1939, p. 1177 (p. 1177).
(42) Stephen Spender's Forward From Liberalism is another book of the period which mentions Forster by name and questions the liberal

concept of freedom. Like most Marxists of this time, Spender asks the question "Freedom - but freedom for what?" Forward From Liberalism (London: Gollancz, 1937) p. 171. See also pp. 83-4.
(43) A Handbook of Freedom (London: Lawrence & Wishart, 1939) p. VII.
(44) Back From the U.S.S.R. trans. Dorothy Bussy (London: Secker & Warburg, 1937) pp. 62-3.
(45) 'A Smack for Russia?' The Listener, 12 May 1937, p. 943.(p.943).
(46) CB, p. 118. The anthology which Forster read was Les Grands Textes du Marxisme Sur Litterature et l'Art, ed. Jean Freville (Paris: 1936).
(47) Studies in a Dying Culture (London: Bodley Head, 1938) p. 211.
(48) Ibid.
(49) 'Liberalism' in Private and Public Morality, ed. Stuart Hampshire (Cambridge: Cambridge Univ. Press, 1978) pp. 113-43 (p. 123).
(50) Forster was not spared by the Conservative Right either. In a shallow and ill-tempered survey of thirties Marxism, Harry Kemp and Laura Riding write - "Mr. Forster admits to feeling the pressure of communism, but pleads that he is too old for active service. His is the gentle character that likes a clean house but shrinks from doing the dirty work himself. He is, in fact, a nice, harmless person with all the right views, but rather lazy - and therefore extremely modest." The Left Heresy in Literature and Life (London: Methuen, 1939) p. 194.
(51) 'The Long Run', New Statesman and Nation, 10 December 1938, p. 971-2 (p.971).
(52) London Mercury, August 1935, vol. 32, pp. 327-31 (pp. 327-8). Rpt. in AH (pp. 76-7).
(53) 'Freedom For What', p.1177.
(54) Che Cosa e il fascismo trans. in H.W.Schnieder, The Making of the Fascist State (1928).
(55) 'The Labour Charter' (of 21 April 1927) in Benito Mussolini, Fascism - Doctrine and Institutions (1935; rpt. New York: Howard Fertig, 1968) p. 133. An early section of this book called 'Fundamental Ideas' expounds the Fascist ideology.
(56) Eva Lips was the wife of a liberal anthropologist who was hounded out of his job and his country by the Nazis. She wrote a moving account of the plight of decent, ordinary

people in Nazi Germany in her What Hitler did to Us (London: Michael Joseph, 1938).
(57) Carlyle, of course, is not a Fascist. Nor, strictly speaking, are Nietzsche (who is criticized in 'What I Believe') and Stefan George (discussed in 'Humanist and Authoritarian', The Listener, 26 August 1943, pp. 242-3. Rpt. as 'Gide and George' in TCD). But the ideas about heroism and leadership in the work of these writers point in the direction of totalitarianism. Forster notes that "Carlyle (if we ignore his belief that thought is stronger than artillery parks) certainly had something of the Nazi about him; he protests against Individualism and yet exalts the Hero; he despises Liberty..." Nordic Twilight (London: Macmillan War Pamphlets, No.3, 1940) p.29.
(58) 'Liberty in England', AH (p.77).
(59) Forster reviewed this book alongside Heard's The Source of Civilization. See Time and Tide, op.cit. (p.1703).
(60) On Liberty (1859), Intro. Gertrude Himmelfarb (Harmondsworth: Penguin Books, 1974) p.120.
(61) Julian Bell: Essays, Poems and Letters, ed. Quentin Bell (London: Hogarth Press, 1938) pp. 335-90.
(62) Samuel Hynes has pointed out that before the end of the thirties decade, Forster's argument that liberal values were limited but nonetheless important for human life, gained him the admiration of the major thirties writers who had lost faith in Marxism. The Auden Generation - Literature and Politics in England in the 1930s (London: Bodley Head, 1976) pp.301-3.
(63) 'Henry Thornton (1760-1815)', New Statesman and Nation, 1 April 1939, pp.491-2 (p.492).Rpt. TCD (p.188).
(64) 'E.M. Forster' in Rage for Order (Chicago Univ. Press, 1948) pp. 119-141 (p.129).
(65) CB, p. 208.
(66) 'An Artist's Life', Spectator, 25 April 1931, p. 669.
(67) CB, p.240. This is dated c. 1959. Forster may have been looking over his review copy, or perhaps got the quotation from some other source.
(68) Leviathan, ed. C.B. Macpherson (Harmondsworth: Penguin Books, 1979) p. 161.
(69) 'My Wood, or the Effects of Property upon Character', New Leader, 15 October 1926, p.3.

FORSTER'S VIEW OF THE NATURE OF MAN

     (p.3). Rpt. AH (p.36).
(70) What, Then, Must We Do, trans. Aylmer Maude (Oxford: Oxford Univ. Press, 1925) p.110.
(71) 'Poverty's Challenge: The Terrible Tolstoy', New Leader, 4 September 1925, pp. 11-12 (p.11).
(72) 'My Wood', AH (p.36).
(73) 'The Last Parade', New Writing, Autumn 1937, No.4, pp. 1-5 (p.4). Rpt. TCD, pp. 3-8 (p.6).
(74) C.B. Macpherson, 'Natural Rights in Hobbes and Locke' in Political Theory and the Rights of Man, ed. D.D. Raphael (London: Macmillan, 1967) pp. 1-15 (p.14).

CHAPTER TWO

FORSTER'S VIEW OF SOCIAL ORDER

The initial focus in discussing Forster's criticism has been on all that he considers indefeasibly human. This may be summarized as the view that man responds to life in three basic ways - he fears, he loves, and he desires to exist as a free individual.
Forster also connects these basic human impulses to certain social manifestations. Fear is connected to materialism, tyranny, dogma and 'Belief', while love and freedom are linked to personal relations, creativity in private life, and an attitude of critical responsibility in public affairs. The famous exposition of this view in 'What I Believe', is prefigured in a letter to Lowes Dickinson dated 5 May 1917:

> Most men are unhappy and restless without Faith, and to cover up the path that led them to it, give out that Faith is only fully attained by the elect... Hence 'God' in the past and the 'Nation' now... Only by believing in a Germany have we become patriotic, just as we remained religious only so long as we believed in a Devil. A menace (is) essential to Faith.
> Man in his public capacity (is) a contemptible failure. Even when there was food and clothing to go round he could not distribute them... Privately most men attain to love and unselfishness and insight and <u>a priori</u> one would expect them to display these qualities in their social life... But some psychological hitch takes place... Gulf between private and public has in the last three years grown dizzying, and thanks to scientific organization more and more of man's energy is diverted to the public side.
> The obverse of love is not hatred but fear.

FORSTER'S VIEW OF SOCIAL ORDER

> Hatred is only one of the forms fear takes, cowardice being another and efficiency a third. (1)

The essays written two decades later make public this hostility to Faith and to the 'social' self. Forster considers adherence to any received system of beliefs a failure of the imagination, a reaction against the spirit of freedom and a submission to fear - in short faith is seen as an abrogation of individuality and of the essentially 'human' self. Faith is "a sort of mental starch which ought to be applied as sparingly as possible." (2) It is a consequence of the residual fear which remains within the human make-up and inhibits creativity - "... worry tempts him (i.e. man) to simplify since through simplification he may find peace. Nagging and stinging night and day, it is the undying worm, the worst of our foes. The only satisfactory release, I think, is to be found in the direction of complexity." (3) "Belief", he says in a review which criticizes Kipling's public-school outlook, "frustrates our desire to synthesize. That desire has raised us out of the brutes; it is only by digesting, comparing, generalizing, deducing, that we have come to realize we are men." (4)

Against the blind acceptance of a belief, Forster propagates an attitude in which the function of the imagination is central. By imagination man creates smaller, personal spheres of order. This is identified as a human activity, as the social antithesis of belief. Like love and freedom, which balance fear within the personality, the imaginative life of creativity and personal relationships is upheld as a foil to every dogmatic and totalitarian ideology. Forster disputes the view that social order is an independent whole and that the first duty of the individual is to contribute to his society. He sees social order essentially as the loose framework within which the smaller spheres of personality and imagination are allowed to flourish.

This is most coherently argued in 'What I Believe', which shows that the point at which it seems logical to perceive - and beyond which it becomes difficult to impose - order in life, is the individual. Although Freudian psychology suggests that man is not the composite whole he assumes he is, Forster sees evidence of order at the level of individuality and personal life. The reason is not just that "men are obliged to be born separately and die separately", but also that there is consistency

FORSTER'S VIEW OF SOCIAL ORDER

within the human personality - "...though A is not unchangeably A, or B unchangeably B, there can still be love and loyalty between the two. For the purpose of living one has to assume that the personality is solid." (5) Similarly, the first principle of order within society must be the spirit of love and loyalty which unites individuals meaningfully. Opposing the creation of order through Belief, Forster argues for a loose framework of diversely creative individuals - "The people I admire most are those who are sensitive and want to create something or discover something... They found religions, great or small, or they produce literature and art, or they do disinterested scientific research, or they may be what is called 'ordinary people', who are creative in their private lives." (6) Confronted with Fascism, the belief in order as something personal rather than social grows into a militant counterbalance. Hating the idea of causes, yet faced in the thirties with the necessity of formulating one, Forster defiantly proposes creativity and relationship against the totalitarianism within which fear is disguised as loyalty to the state, and allegiance owed not to those who mean something personally but to a larger order which can have little personal significance. "I hate the idea of causes" he says, "and if I had to choose between betraying my country and betraying my friend I hope I should have the guts to betray my country." (7)

The social premise of this liberal creed is that no order can be meaningful beyond the point at which love between individuals ceases. As love does exist between particular individuals but is impossible between all the individuals that make up society, there is no reasonable basis for elevating social order or the state over personal values. This is spelt out in a statement of central importance which disputes the historian's idea of order and argues the artist's notion of the same concept:

> Order is something evolved from within, not something imposed from without, it is an internal stability, a vital harmony, and in the social and political category, it has never existed, except for the convenience of historians. Viewed realistically, the past is merely a series of messes... (8)

This notion of order has been a fundamental postulate of liberalism since J.S. Mill. In his book _Liberalism_, for instance, L.T. Hobhouse says that

FORSTER'S VIEW OF SOCIAL ORDER

"Personality is not built up from without but grows from within, and the function of the outer order is not to create it, but to provide for it the most suitable conditions of growth." (9) Social order is necessary only insofar as it nurtures individuality and the inner order of the mind. The supremacy of ahistorical and transcendent personal values over social order is similarly the keynote of J.S. Mill's attitude. This is paraphrased by Hobhouse - "Compulsion may be necessary for the purpose of external order, but it adds nothing to the inward life which is the true being of man... Under self-guidance (in contrast) individuals will diverge very widely, and some of their eccentricities will be futile, others wasteful... But upon the whole it is good that they should differ. Individuality is an element of well-being." (10) A similar notion of order is also to be found in Kemp and Riding's The Left Heresy in Literature and Life. The authors had written to Forster to ascertain his political views and criticized his sympathy for communism in their book, so it is likely that Forster read their definition of order as something aesthetic and not political -

> ...the poet's interest of order is an all-inclusive one, not merely an interest of social order; the order which it is his responsibility to define cannot be stated in political terms. It must be an order for the entire scope of life... it must be impelled from within, begin in the mind. The politician has no aim of providing a complete picture of existence ... his subject is that of social equilibrium... order in its temporal, physical aspects. (11)

Forster's definition of order is thus a re-statement of these liberal views that social order is not important in itself, but only necessary as a rough arrangement which fosters inner order.

II

At this same time, as most men do not exist in a harmony of friendship and creativity, but rather in an impersonal and unequal world, Forster is a realist who knows it is necessary to accept order on a larger scale than individuality and personal life. In 'Love, the Beloved Republic which feeds upon Freedom and lives' (12) the categories of relationship and creativity might be enough, but Forster knows this to be a utopian dream and acknowledges

FORSTER'S VIEW OF SOCIAL ORDER

that personal order must be made compatible with social order. In his essay on Edward Carpenter, for instance, this combination of idealism and realism is evident. Carpenter's idea of democracy is an extension into the world of practical affairs of his mystical belief in love. Whitman, the <u>Bhagavad Gita</u>, Blake and Shelley lie behind his utopian vision of democracy and, according to Hynes, Carpenter "blamed the failure of love and the failure of society on the same two imprisoning institutions - Christianity and Commercialism - and he believed that man, freed from these two, might fulfil his potentials. The democracy of his most ambitious work, <u>Towards Democracy</u>, is not simply a political term: it is rather a synonym of Love..." (13) In his heart Forster sympathizes with this idealism - "He believed in Liberty, Fraternity and Equality - words now confined to platforms and perorations" - but rationally Forster also recognizes the shortcomings of such political idealism - "He saw the New Jerusalem from afar, from the ignoble slough of his century, and there is no doubt that it does look more beautiful from a distance. When the armies of the downtrodden enter its gate... the New Jerusalem becomes a more ordinary city, where the party leaders book the best rooms." (14) Realistically, the best hope of achieving a harmony of idealism and realism in the political sphere, he believes, is within the framework of a tolerant democracy.

Tolerant democracy is not an ideal, for it is not an expression of love and freedom. It is simply the least meaningless order within which individuals can coexist, and it allows most opportunity to develop all that grows out of love and freedom - relationship, sensitivity, disinterested enquiry and art. In his essay called 'Tolerance' this concept is identified as a specifically social virtue, an inferior manifestation of man's spirit which comes into operation when love ceases, a principle by which variety is made possible. It is the necessary substitute of love in public life, the <u>sine qua non</u> of democratic existence. By it the atomism of private creativity is reconciled with a larger, non-autocratic social order. Forster's political realism is obvious when he disputes the religious argument that love must be the basis of social order. His own view is that -

> Love is a great force in private life; it is indeed the greatest of all things: but love in public affairs simply does not work. It has

57

> been tried again and again: by the Christian civilizations of the Middle Ages, and also by the French Revolution... it has always failed ...The fact is we can only love what we know personally. And we cannot know much. In public affairs ... something much less dramatic and emotional is needed, namely tolerance...(15)

Forster's belief in tolerance is restrained and wholly pragmatic. He realizes that tolerance can degenerate into apathy and fecklessness, and his definition of the concept tries to exclude it meaning either of these. "Putting up with people does not mean giving in to them. This complicates the problem. But the rebuilding of civilization is bound to be complicated" (16) he says. Tolerant democracy, however, is the necessary social framework for rebuilding civilization because it allows love, freedom, creativity and diversity, and is a viable alternative to fear, force, belief and totalitarianism. The first category comprises all that is civilized and human, the second all that is primitive and anti-human.

Forster's dialectic is argued at other levels. Fear against love and freedom and tyranny against democracy lead to hero-worship against creative individualism. Hero-worship is a testimony of the primitive fear which finds relief in blind subservience. Leaders become god-substitutes for the "timid and the bored" who feel exalted and strengthened by images of strength and violence. Like the Holy Trinity of Christianity, the trinity of heroes often erected by the state performs the same dehumanizing fiction. From Forster's perspective the hero - whether Hitler or Christ - fails because he thwarts creativity and reduces man into a believing rather than thinking and responsive being. (17)

But the hero-figure is not the solitary villain who enforces social order at the expense of private creativity. Forster sees that the individual is subjugated even within democracy, when a government arrogates too much power to itself and crushes individuality with an omniscient bureaucracy. His term for this in 'Liberty in England' is 'Fabio-Fascism'. The growth of bureaucracy had alarmed liberals like J.S.Mill (18) but it caused particular concern in the thirties when the machinery of state became more bloated than ever before. Lord Hewart, who was Lord Chief Justice, wrote <u>The New Despotism</u> (1929) criticizing the power of ministerially instituted non-statutory bodies: "...there is in existence a persistent and well-contrived system, intended to produce and in practice producing, a despotic power which at one and the same time places government departments above the Sovereignty of Parliament and beyond the jurisdiction of the Courts" he said. (19) C.K. Allen in <u>Bureaucracy Triumphant</u> (1931) pointed out that "While the total population of Great Britain has, within a century, quadrupled itself, the class of officials has multiplied itself by more than twelve." (20) Sir Ernest Benn's <u>Modern Government as a Busybody on Other Men's Matters</u> (1936) argued similarly against governmental control and restriction of personal freedom. One of Forster's broadcasts is an attack upon the English fabio-Fascist bureaucracy which arbitrarily and high-handedly imposes social order. Forster says that by curtailing creative freedom and diverse development, bureaucracy tries to institute social order as the ultimate goal of individual life. Men are easier to manage when, like sheep, they obey rules unthinkingly:

> I don't deny that many restrictions are inevitable, but how they increase! ...Organization must lead to standardization, that's the trouble... if you want people alike you must give up the nineteenth century fad of liberty and like prison. (21)

When government regulates personal life, expression and movement it oversteps its proper limits. Shakespeare's Richard II, says Forster, could comfort himself by imagining his prison a world but the modern-day individual, ironically, finds the real world being transformed into a prison. "...the spirit of prison is the spirit of modern civilization. Everything that is spontaneous and personal gets stopped." (22) Democracy is perverted if it tries to create equality by smothering the spirit which renders each person an individual. In keeping with the Millite liberal tradition, Forster argues for a democratic social order within which progress towards greater economic equality does not preclude diversity of spiritual development.

Laski remarks that liberalism has always made "an antithesis ... between liberty and equality. It has seen in the first the emphasis upon individual action for which it is always zealous ... in the second the outcome of authoritarian intervention of which the result, in its view, is a cramping of individual personality." (23) In trying to reconcile this antithesis Forster says that equality must be sought in the economic sphere, liberty and individuality in the spiritual and aesthetic spheres. This argument is put forward in 'The Challenge of Our Time' (1946) where Forster expresses the belief that laissez-faire capitalism must give way to some form of centralized economic planning, but that planning must leave room for freedom of expression. Historians have pointed out that after the Second War the national mood was in many ways the very opposite to the mood of 1918. In the earlier period there had been a desire to get back to 'the good old days' whereas later the pre-war world of the thirties "seemed so insecure and blameworthy that there was little nostalgia for the past... Uppermost in their (men's) minds was the desire for fuller social justice..." (24) The concept of the Welfare State crystallized by the 1942 Beveridge Report began to be translated into a reality by the Labour Government of Attlee. Forster's essay shows that he shares this mood for a just social order. In fact his acceptance of economic regulation is evidence of a progress from his scepticism in the twenties about any kind of planning. The desirability of social planning is likely to have been driven home by at least two factors. First, no one could have failed to appreciate that the Allied victory in the Second War could not have been achieved without state planning. Second, Forster's experience of Indian poverty in 1945 probably helped him recognize the supreme necessity of a just economic order. "I do not know what political solution is correct. But I do know that people ought not to be so poor ..." he says. (25) However, the primary emphasis of 'The Challenge of Our Time' continues to be upon the necessity for a social order which recognizes the importance of creative freedom. Forster is wary, not of social justice but of the rigid and potentially tyrannical social order which is often thrust upon people in the name of equality. This is why Laski's argument that liberalism declined because it "refused to confront squarely the fact that this changed world demanded, especially in the economic realm, massive social controls if the freedom it deemed the supreme good was to have any meaning in the lives of the multitudes" (26) - is only partially true when applied to Forster. Forster agrees with Laski that the original liberal stress on uncontrolled free enterprise is outdated but also argues a step further and tries to salvage the liberal belief in spiritual freedom for the individual from being lost along with the belief in laissez-faire when he says - "We must have planning and ration books and controls or millions of people will have nowhere to live and nothing to eat. On the other hand the doctrine of laissez-faire is the only one that seems to work in the world of spirit; if you plan and control men's minds you stunt them ..." (27) Forster accepts the need for a planned economy but what he really 'believes' in and values is the continuation of a human tradition through intelligence and creative work. His faith is in an intellectual minority which is represented in 'What I Believe' as an aristocracy of the spirit.

This is another strand which links Forster to liberal social tradition as expounded in J.S.Mill's On Liberty and Arnold's Culture and Anarchy. Mill's philosophy coalesces the Romantic focus on the creative, human faculties with the Benthamist emphasis upon man's material, acquisitive nature. Mill moderates the Utilitarian view of ideal society, in which satisfaction of the individual's material needs is optimized, by stressing the importance of spiritual and ethical values for a truly 'human' society. This, in his view, involves the generalized development of faculties which are uniquely human. Reading Wordsworth gave Mill the impression that the materialism of industrial society destroys man's spirituality, and thereby his quintessential humanity. Reversing the crisis of materialism required, at the cultural level, the development of a secular intelligentsia which would foster emotional, intellectual and spiritual development more widely in society. In his essay 'Civilization', Mill speaks about the necessity of "some organized co-operation among the leading intellects of the age, whereby works of first rate merit, of whatever class, and of whatever tendency in point of opinion, might come forth ..." (28) and in his essay On Liberty he writes that "...there are but few persons, in comparison with the whole of mankind, whose experiments, if adopted by others, would be likely to be any improvement on established practice. But these few are the salt of the earth; without them, human life would become a stagnant pool." (29) The assumption underpinning these suggestions is that the creative consciousness transcends society inasmuch as it is capable of producing works which are of universal and human relevance, as opposed to the material development of society which has become debased and anti-human. Mill also assumes that human capacities exist in an unrealized state within every individual. These capacities are diminished by fear, greed and materialism, but actualized and developed by spiritual pursuits - by all that is denoted by the word 'culture' the arts and disinterested intellectual activity.

Similar assumptions underlie Arnold's treatise, in which culture is heralded as the new transcendent substitute of religion and clergy replaced by a cultured minority. Arnold's position is encapsulated in this remark - "Religion says: The Kingdom of God is within you; and culture, in like manner, places human perfection in an internal condition, in the growth and predominance of our humanity proper, as distinguished from our animality." (30) Later in the essay Arnold defines an aristocracy which contributes towards the development of a humane social order -

> Natures with this (cultural) bent emerge in all classes, - among the Barbarians, among the Philistines, among the Populace. And this bent always tends to take them out of their class, and to make their distinguishing characteristic not their Barbarianism or their Philistinism, but their humanity. They have in general a rough time of it in their lives; but they are sown more abundantly than one might think, they appear where and when one least expects it, they set up a fire which enfilades, so to speak, the class with which they are ranked... (31)

Forster's contemporary L.T. Hobhouse similarly stresses that only those forms of social order are valuable which allow the free development of spiritual order - "There is no true opposition between liberty as such and control as such, for every liberty rests on a corresponding act of control. The true opposition is between the control that cramps the personal life and the spiritual order, and the control that is aimed at securing the external and material conditions of their free and unimpeded development." (32) Hobhouse's effort, like that of the Oxford Idealist philosopher T.H. Green, was to reconstruct liberal social philosophy so that the traditional value placed upon creative individualism could be preserved and harmonized with a more just and better planned economic order. He tried to avoid both laissez-faire liberalism and economically deterministic Marxism, and posited an ideal of 'liberal socialism' within which there was a better balanced stress upon spiritual freedom and diversity on the one hand and general socio-economic welfare on the other. Forster is no systematic social thinker and his stress is more upon moral values and legislation for the spirit than upon socio-economic regulation, but his outlook is broadly compatible with this tradition of social philosophy. He is unconvinced by the socialist view that a desirable morality will evolve out of a planned economy, but he says he is "both convinced that a planned change must take place if the world is not to disintegrate, and hopeful that in the new economy there may be a sphere both for human relationships and the despised activity known as art." (33) However, despite the better balanced stress upon an egalitarian social order as well as free individuality, the crucial difference between liberal and socialist philosophy is that in the former the weight of emphasis always falls upon personal freedom. This is very obviously true of all of Forster's essays. As an artist himself, Forster draws attention to the importance of creativity and free expression within society, and emphasizes that social order is meaningless unless it provides opportunities for human self-development. He believes in the artist and the sensitive individual because they try to fulfil the creative urges within them and thereby contribute meaningfully to society. He argues for a diverse, loosely-knit and creative society and points out that any social order born out of tyrannical imposition thwarts the very reason for which social order is valuable. Like Mill, Arnold and Hobhouse, Forster lays a dual emphasis upon social improvement and personal freedom, and like them points out that spiritual values are crucial to the concept of social improvement. While acknowledging the need for economists, sociologists and politicians - those who plan and maintain the material development of society - Forster's faith is in artists, philosophers and men of ideas - those who create the spiritual order by which social order is best enriched. These "represent the true human tradition, the one permanent victory of our queer race over cruelty and chaos. Thousands of them perish in obscurity, a few are great names." (34)

Much of Forster's criticism is about the people who comprise this aristocracy. By defining their values, he puts forward his own. In one of his broadcasts he says that his great concern is "the problem of value, the problem of maintaining and extending aristocracy in the midst of democracy."(35) This broadcast is a variation on the basic theme of 'What I Believe' and 'The Challenge of Our

Time'. It stresses that social order cannot be meaningful if its concerns are purely economic or material, for the individuals that make up society are dehumanized as much by unwareness of human values as by hunger. A society which ignores pioneers, artists, and people of exceptional ability who do not work to rule is taking man backwards to the bestial state, for these are the types "...who have helped the human race out of the darkness in the past. And if they vanish now, if they dissolve into the modern world's universal grey, what is to happen to the human race in the future. Into what final darkness will it disappear? (36)

III

The essay which stitches together all the various strands discussed so far - Forster's view of human nature, his belief in inner harmony, moral values, tolerance, variety, eclecticism, synthesis of social order with creative individualism, and an enlightened aristocracy which contributes to the formation of a democratic society by extending awareness of the values necessary for human life - is the essay 'The Ivory Tower' (1938). This is a companion piece of 'What I Believe' and remains perhaps the most important uncollected essay within the body of Forster's criticism. If 'What I Believe' is an answer to Fascism, 'The Ivory Tower' is Forster's most clearly thought and persuasive polemical retort to the Marxism of the thirties.

Over the thirties it was increasingly believed, as the battle lines between liberalism and Marxism sharpened, that the writers of the twenties had taken refuge in ivory towers to experiment with words that had no relation to life. Julian Symons identifies a cross-section of the intelligentsia of this period which he calls 'the Pragmatists', and says that it was from this predominantly left-wing section of society that there came exhortations "about moving out of the ivory tower of the imagination into the market place." (37) Most of the young writers of the time similarly argued for a more direct alliance between artists and the masses. Poets, like philosophers, seemed to them to have said a great deal about the world but done very little to change it. John Strachey's <u>The Coming Struggle for Power</u>, Caudwell's <u>Studies in a Dying Culture</u>, Julian Bell's 'Open Letter' to Forster, Spender's <u>Forward from Liberalism</u> and <u>The Destructive Element</u> were some of the thirties works which suggested that artists had been guilty of escaping from social responsibility into private havens of the imagination. The more liberal minded writers, usually of an older generation, disagreed with this argument. In his essay 'Poetry and Politics' (1937) Robert Graves concludes that "The goodness of poets and poetry is unquestionable, but it is not a goodness to be piously exemplified in a partisanship of humanitarian causes. It is practically demonstrable only in poems written as poems... The poet is concerned with that truth which is not a historical product but which is always there of itself because it is reality: he is concerned with final truth only." (38) Forster's essay similarly argues that not only every poet, but every human being, requires an 'ivory tower', and that the phrase implies no anti-social escape from life. (39)

Forster says that detachment from society is a human need, for - "Man is an animal, but a queer one. He possesses the herd instinct, so that he readily forms tribes, gangs, nations. But unlike other gregarious animals, he has the instinct for solitude as well... He wants to be alone even when he is feeling fit. That is one of the differences between a man and a chicken." (40) This echoes his earlier paraphrase of Heard's The Social Substance of Religion and his own essay 'The Menace to Freedom', where the instinct for solitude is seen as the first step towards personal freedom and creative living. The phrase 'ivory tower' is defined as a symbol of this human impulse and is dissociated from the 'aestheticism' and 'escapism' with which it had become synonymous within Marxist terminology. Forster carefully distinguishes between an ivory tower which implies creative retreat and that which implies a subterfuge from the problems of real life. Retreat, he says, is a necessary condition of creativity and valuable because it contributes to civilization. Subterfuge, on the other hand, is indefensible because it is born of fear, and "... Most of the misery of mankind, both in its political and social relations, arises from fear. It has done more harm even than greed. It breeds not only cowards, but bullies, and between them they drag down civilization." (41)

Thus, in Forster's view, complete isolation from the real world, like blind commitment to a cause, represents a failure to be truly human, and he defends the ivory tower only as a symbol of man's human need to express his separate identity and thereby contribute to his society. If social order is to remain recognizably human it must comprehend not only political, economic and industrial development, but also "these symbols of personal retreat, Ivory Towers". 'Ivory Tower' or 'escapism' in this sense - "...is not new, not a bourgeois weakness or an economic by-product, but is to be deduced from the queer nature of man, who gathers into groups like his cousins the monkeys ... but who also wants to build up a private life of his own. Both these tendencies contribute towards civilization." (42) Forster's view here again contradicts the simplistic and narrow Marxism of Caudwell, whereas it seems quite compatible with the more sophisticated Marxist position of Marcuse. Criticizing the devaluation of the notion of 'subjectivity' in orthodox Marxist aesthetics Marcuse says:

> ...even in bourgeois society, insistence on the truth and right of inwardness is not really a bourgeois value. With the affirmation of the inwardness of subjectivity, the individual steps out of the network of exchange relationships and exchange values, withdraws from the reality of bourgeois society, and enters another dimension of existence. Indeed this escape from reality led to an experience which could (and did) become a powerful force in <u>invalidating</u> the actually prevailing bourgeois values, namely, by shifting the focus of the individual's realization from the domain of the performance principle and the profit motive to that of the inner resources of the human being: passion, imagination, conscience. (43)

This seems to me to be a more complex way of saying what is said very simply in 'The Ivory Tower'. Forster's essay uses examples as diverse as Marcus Aurelius, Machiavelli, Milton, Wordsworth and Marx to illustrate how the desire for personal solitude is a positive contribution to social life. Forster suggests that the greatness of these writers lay in producing from their ivory towers, work which contributed to the improvement of society. In their lives he detects a 'wobble' between private creativity and social concern, and the ideal social order in his view is that which permits and nurtures individuals who fuse their private life with a desire to contribute to public life. 'Order' in this Forsterian sense is ultimately personal. It is not something discerned at the social level, but in the lives of those individuals who exemplify the ideal that "...we are here on earth not to save ourselves and not to save the community, but to try to save both." (45) Forster's own career as a critic seems to be an attempt to live by his composite ideal.

Ronald Dworkin has defined the basic principle which underlies the liberal view of society. He writes that all non-liberal theories hold that "... the content of equal treatment cannot be independent of some theory about the good for man or the good of life, because treating a person as an equal means treating him the way the good or truly wise person would wish to be treated." The liberal theory, on the other hand, supposes that "... political decisions must be, so far as is possible, independent of any particular conception of the good life, or of what gives value to life. Since the citizens of a society differ in their conceptions, the government does not treat them as equals if it prefers one conception to another..." (46) The non-liberal emphasis is upon social equality and well defined social ideals towards which individual effort must be directed. In contrast, the liberal view of society is atomic because it stresses diversity and personal ideals rather than uniformity of social goals. As we have seen, Forster recognizes the necessity of uniformity and planned development in the economic sphere, but as a whole his views on society are very much within the liberal tradition. He believes less in creating a uniform and well-regulated social order than in continuing a very diverse and loosely knit human tradition. The essential concern of his criticism is to point towards his aristocracy of the spirit which upholds those uniquely human ideals without which life would not be identifiably human. In this sense, Raymond Williams's analysis of Bloomsbury within its larger socio-historical context contains an observation which applies to Forster's concept of society - "(Bloomsbury was) against ignorance, poverty, sexual and racial discrimination, militarism and imperialism. But it was against all these things in a specific movement of liberal thought. What it appealed to, against all these evils, was not any alternative idea of a whole society. Instead, it appealed to the supreme value of the civilized individual, whose pluralization, as more and more civilized individuals, was itself the only acceptable social direction.' (46)

Forster's conception of human life is not narrowly limited, and the aristocracy propagated by much of his criticism is an eclectic mixture of

FORSTER'S VIEW OF SOCIAL ORDER

artists (from Shakespeare to Roger Fry), historians (Voltaire, Gibbon), scientists (James Simpson), theologians (Clement and Origen), thinkers (Plotinus, Lowes Dickinson) and even a god (Krishna). Forster holds them up to view as examples of diverse ways of fulfilment, as the creators of those ideals from which meaningful social action can ensue. At the same time he is always aware that his heroes are complex beings, mixtures of good and evil in whom the good predominates rather than symbols of perfection. Like Lytton Strachey, Forster is often deliberately irreverent about his heroes. He is all too aware of their fallibility as human beings, of the petty and the ridiculous in their character. This renders his heroes human rather than mythical or heroic. One has only to glance at his essays on Voltaire to recognize the truth of this. Against totalitarian forms of social order which set up supermen for obedience and against religious anthropomorphism which invests a supernatural being with all virtue and demands worship, Forster's social outlook is anthropocentric. He transfers attention to a variety of individuals and admires those traits which are positive and valuable within them. This, rather than any well defined and holistic social ideology, is the 'order' in which Forster believes. In this view salvation lies only in remembering, assimilating, cherishing and personally expanding the values of an aristocracy which has been sporadically thrown up over the whole stretch of human history. 'What I Believe' expresses this belief succinctly - "The saviour of the future - if he ever comes - will not preach a new Gospel. He will merely utilize my aristocracy, he will make effective the goodwill and good temper which are already existing." (47) This is the essence of Forster's social faith. Often set down with almost religious fervour it is only, according to Stone, "a humanist's term for what is holy in a secular world." (48)

NOTES

(1) 'Letters to G. Lowes Dickinson', King's College Manuscripts. Quoted in Furbank II, pp.45-6.
(2) 'What I Believe', TCD (p.65).
(3) 'The 1939 State', New Statesman and Nation, 10 June 1939, pp. 888-9. (p.889). Rpt. as 'Post Munich', TCD (p.24).
(4) 'That Job's Done', The Listener, 10 March 1937, Supplement No. 33, pp.III-IV (p.III).

FORSTER'S VIEW OF SOCIAL ORDER

(5) TCD (pp. 65-6).
(6) ibid. (p.67).
(7) ibid. (p.66).
(8) The New Disorder, p.7.
(9) Liberalism, intro. Alan P. Grimes (1911; rpt. New York: Oxford Univ. Press, 1964) p.76.
(10) ibid., p.60.
(11) The Left Heresy in Literature and Life, p.87
(12) Forster found this phrase in Swinburne's 'Hertha', a very Shelleyan poem in which the soul of man is seen to achieve its highest fulfilment - Love and Freedom - through an expression of individuality, and after rejecting the fetters of religious belief. Stone (pp. 61-2) sees a connection between Forster's admiration of 'Hertha' and the political idealism of McTaggart.
(13) The Edwardian Turn of Mind (London: Oxford Univ. Press, 1968) pp. 150-1.
(14) 'Edward Carpenter: A Centenary Note', Tribune, 22 September 1944, pp. 12-13. Rpt. as 'Edward Carpenter', TCD (p.206).
(15) 'The Unsung Virtue of Tolerance', The Listener, 31 July 1941, pp. 160-1 (p.160). Rpt. as 'Tolerance', TCD (p.44).
(16) ibid. (p.46).
(17) 'What I Believe', TCD (p.70). Forster's rejection of Christ, as the next chapter will show, is almost as uncompromising as his rejection of Hitler.
(18) Chapter Five of On Liberty contains an attack on bureaucracy.
(19) The New Despotism (London: Benn, 1929) p.14.
(20) Bureaucracy Triumphant (London: Oxford Univ. Press, 1931) p.103.
(21) 'Seven Days Hard', The Listener, 14 March 1934, p. 452.(p.452).
(22) ibid. (p.452).
(23) The Rise of European Liberalism, p.17.
(24) England in the Twentieth Century (1965; rpt. Harmondsworth: Penguin Books, 1978) p. 218.
(25) 'India After Twenty Five Years', The Listener, 31 January 1946, pp. 133-4 (p.134). Rpt. as 'India Again', TCD (p.316).
(26) The Decline of Liberalism: Hobhouse Memorial Lecture, 1940 (London: Oxford Univ. Press, 1940) p.21.
(27) 'The Challenge of Our Time', TCD (p.55).
(28) 'Civilization' (1836) in Mill's Essays on Literature and Society, ed. J.B. Schneewind (New York: Collier Books, 1965) pp. 148-82

(pp. 171-2).
(29) *On Liberty*, p. 129.
(30) *Culture and Anarchy: An Essay in Social and Political Criticism* (1869), intro. J. Dover Wilson (London: Macmillan, 1938) p.11.
(31) ibid., p.93.
(32) *Liberalism*, p.78.
(33) 'The Challenge of Our Time', TCD (p.57).
(34) 'What I Believe', TCD (p.70).
(35) 'The Fifth Anniversary of the Third Programme', *The Listener*, 4 October, 1951, pp. 539-41. (p.540). A note in the CB is of interest in this context - "I have always wanted to share my advantages with others. But I am asked to give up my advantages so that others may have things I don't want; to build a world I should find uninhabitable. It is a severe demand. The generous minded of the past century - Shelley and the liberals - have not appreciated its irony. They have assumed that, once the chains had fallen, art, scenery, passionate personal love, would become popular. One is placed in the equivocal position of the aristocrat who believes in the real goods, for they are real - and is tempted to defend them against democracy." CB, c. 1947, p.185.
(36) 'Fifth Anniversary of the Third Programme' (pp. 540-1).
(37) *The Thirties: A Dream Revolved* (London: The Cresset Press, 1960) p.38.
(38) *The Common Asphodel: Collected Essays on Poetry 1922-1949* (London: Hamish Hamilton, 1949) pp. 273-84 (pp. 283-4). Virginia Woolf's essay 'The Leaning Tower' (1940) is another example of the liberal backlash against the Marxism of the younger generation. See Collected Essays (London: Hogarth Press, 1966), vol. IV, pp.162-181.
(39) The presupposition upon which this is based is again traceable to J.S. Mill's view that "In proportion to the development of his individuality, each person becomes more valuable to himself, and is, therefore, capable of becoming more valuable to others." *On Liberty*, p.127.
(40) 'The Ivory Tower', *London Mercury*, December 1938, Vol. 39, pp. 119-30 (p.119).
(41) ibid. (p.126).
(42) ibid. (p.122).
(43) Herbert Marcuse, *The Aesthetic Dimension* (London: Macmillan Papermac, 1979) pp. 4-5.
(44) 'The Ivory Tower' (p.130).

(45) Ronald Dworkin, 'Liberalism', p.127.
(46) 'The Bloomsbury Fraction', <u>Problems in Materialism and Culture</u> (London: Verso, 1980) pp. 148-69 (p.165).
(47) TCD (pp. 71-2).
(48) <u>The Cave and the Mountain</u>, p.7.

CHAPTER THREE

FORSTER'S VIEW OF RELIGION

Like his approach to social and political order, Forster's criticism of religion is entwined with his view of man and deep concern with human values. Intense conviction about the reality of a human spirit allied with an equally ardent agnosticism makes his attitude to religion ambiguous, as implied in these two remarks - "My temple stands not upon Mount Moriah but in that Elysian field where even the immoral are admitted. My motto is: 'Lord I disbelieve - help thou my unbelief.'" (1) - and, "I like, or anyhow tolerate, most religions so long as they are weak, and I find in their rites an acknowledgement of our smallness which is salutary. But I dread them all, without exception, as soon as they become powerful..." (2) Insofar as religions inspire personal fulfilment and social harmony they have a value in human life, but because they usually advocate faith and otherworldliness above self-development and earthly enjoyment, Forster mistrusts them. Religious belief leaves him cold, ultimately, because in contrast to the order which grows out of personal creativity, he sees all religions as external impositions which seek to control and subdue individuality.

This ambivalent sceptical mysticism is also evident from Forster's diametrically opposite views of religious mysticism and religious belief. In The New Disorder Forster accepts the possibility of divine order - "...the mystic harmony, which according to all religions, is available for those who can contemplate it. We must admit its possibility, on the evidence of the adepts..." (3) This is consistent with humanism because the mystic's belief in the separate reality of a spiritual order evolves from a direct and intense personal experience. As one humanist philosopher puts it, "the rapt experience of religious worshippers and mystics ... are akin to those deeply felt aesthetic experiences a Humanist can know in looking upon the magnificence and beauty of the external world." (4) When it implies intense experience of this kind, religious mysticism denotes a deeply personal connection between the material and the spiritual dimensions of life, a connection which Forster accepts because he feels that - "Religion is more than an ethical code with a divine sanction. It is also a means through which man may get into direct connexion with the divine... In Germany the reformation was due to the <u>passionate conviction</u> of Luther." (my emphasis). (5) Forster connects deep feeling with the life of the spirit and believes that man's connection with the divine comes from an intensified sense of life. He sees this not as indication of an afterlife, but as a fruition of the life within. Man realizes spirit not through worship but by fulness of response, and the mystic, like the artist, is the individual who is spiritually alert and whose passionate nature leads him to create work which enriches man's awareness of the possibilities of human life.

In contrast, the ordinary religious believer's faith tends to impinge upon the notion of an external, heavenly order. This is groundless because -

> The Stars, the Army of Unalterable Law, with which George Meredith discomfited Lucifer and comforted the Victorians, prove to be a flying rout of suns and galaxies... No longer can we find a suitable contrast to chaos in the night sky. The heavens and the earth have become terribly alike during the last twenty years. (6)

Religion is therefore rejected when it is merely a belief in the existence of order 'somewhere up there' but highly regarded when it derives from intense personal experience such as that of mystics. The former connotation of the word implies mere preoccupation with metaphysics and eschatology, whereas the latter suggests a deeply felt response to earthly life. Forster's personal view is probably best summarized in a quotation he wrote down in his <u>Commonplace Book</u>:

> Flying induces a mood of religious scepticism. One realizes the fallacy of supposing that God can be 'up above' and can 'look down' on us. For the view of the observer up above is

necessarily one of indifference. One sees a
man bicycling, one sees a little farm with its
stream and bridge, and they have nothing human
about them. One does not wish to help the man
on his road or to drop a blessing on the little
house. To feel well or ill disposed towards
them one must see them horizontally, on the
human level. Man can only be man to those who
walk on the earth beside him. (7)

A final characteristic of Forster's criticism
of religion is its tendency to become an analysis of
central figureheads. The importance Forster attaches to individuality makes him analyse religious
ideas as aspects of the specific personalities from
whom they stem, so that this branch of his criticism
is quite largely a series of character-sketches.
Forster evaluates each religion according to the
human appeal of its idol and does not discriminate
seriously enough between a religion as a whole and
the specific personality which he sees as its symbol.
In particular, Forster's rejection of Christianity
and approval of Hinduism are very closely connected
to his dislike of Christ and admiration of Krishna.
This is a serious methodological limitation of
Forster's atomic liberalism, though in all fairness
it has to be remembered that Forster did not write
everything with equal moral earnestness; nor would
he have expected all his writing on religion
to be scrutinized with the apparatus of criticism.

II

Forster's criticism outlines a specific attitude to three religions - Christianity, Hinduism and
Islam. His view of Christianity may be outlined
first, because the reasons for its rejection point
towards Forster's more tolerant attitudes to Hinduism and Islam.

Between September 1955 and April 1956 Forster
engaged in a correspondence with the B.B.C., having
been annoyed by the preferential treatment the
corporation gave to Christian broadcasts. "Day after
day", he writes in one letter, "the various Christian bodies are free to broadcast their teachings
without being attended by a critic. And it is obviously right that they should have such freedom. But
why is the freedom not occasionally extended to the
non-Christian? Why should not he too be allowed to
speak unattended?" (8) Forster also suggests a
series called 'The Non-Christian Point of View' to

which he would be one contributor, but as the series never materialized he perhaps decided to present his point of view in an address to the Cambridge Humanists in 1959.

Forster's disavowal of Christianity within the Cambridge ethos dominated by the influence of G.E. Moore is the subject of this address. He says that he had to abandon his faith once he began to think for himself - "...my Christianity quietly and quickly disappeared... partly because of the general spirit of questioning that is associated with the name of G.E. Moore."(9) Christianity seemed specially unpalatable because of the personality of Christ. Unlike Renan and Wilde who debunk Christ's claim to divinity and yet eulogise him as a man, Forster infers an unappealing personality from the teachings of Christ. He does find something to praise - "the preference of Mary to Martha which so annoyed Rudyard Kipling, the marriage at Cana ... the reminder that adultery is an aspect of sex ... the blasting of the sterile fig tree" (10) - but these do not sufficiently redeem Christ for Forster. He finds on the whole a disproportionate otherworldliness, too much "preaching and threats, so much emphasis on followers, on an elite, so little intellectual power (as opposed to insight), such an absence of humour and fun" - that he cannot help disliking Christ. "I would on the whole rather not meet the speaker .... and since personal relations mean everything to me, this has helped me to cool off from Christianity." (11) Forster responds much more positively to the Virgin Mary because she appears more human. She appeals as a suffering human and is untarnished by Christ's grand illusion of saving man from sin - "The mother gave birth to the child, saw him grow up and saw him killed. Here is something immediately comprehensible to which we can accord heartfelt pity, and the fact that Mary seldom said or did anything notable on her own account only makes her the better medium between mankind and the incomprehensible." (12) It is typically Forsterian to elevate ordinary, unpretentious humanity towards the sublime, and contrariwise to cast doubt upon all who claim superhuman status. He is moved by the Virgin Mary, whereas Christ's belief in salvation, atonement, self-denial, the necessity of suffering, and worship add up to an ideal of human life wholly at odds with Forster's own ideal of 'self improvement' - "Improve! Such a dull word but it includes more sensitiveness, more realization of variety and more capacity for adventure. He who is enamoured of improvement will never want to rest in the Lord." (13)

This hostility to Christianity appears sporadically in Forster's criticism. In 1920 Forster reviewed books by Chesterton and Belloc and had devastating things to say about both. Chesterton's The New Jerusalem is a ponderous and digressive travelogue, ostensibly a historical account of Jerusalem, but one which mixes this up with the author's opinion on dozens of trivial and irrelevant issues. Forster thought the book biased, badly organized and a parody of historical research because for its author "All objects that intersect at right angles become proofs of the truth of Christianity." (14) Belloc's Europe and the Faith is a history of Europe written from a blatantly dogmatic and self-assured point of view. In his Introduction Belloc announces that "The Catholic brings to history ... self-knowledge ... others, not Catholic, look upon the story of Europe externally, as strangers ... he sees it all from its centre, in its essence, and together." (15) Forster's review demolishes Belloc's ultramontanism -

> In his introduction Mr. Belloc states his qualification for writing a book about Europe ... In a deep and mystic sense, he is one with his subject matter, and for this reason: because he is a member of the Roman Catholic Church. As a Catholic he has 'conscience', 'con-scientia', that intimate knowledge of Europe through identity that is denied to Protestants, Agnostics, Japanese and Jews ... Mr. Belloc has consented to read some documents, but intuition comes first, information afterwards. He reads rather to confirm the documents than to be confirmed by them, and he would have realized Europe quite as fully if he had read nothing, or if there was nothing to read. He is unable to make a mistake. Whatever he says is true, because he has the Faith. Others may argue or persuade, he announces, and however much he may stoop to the normal methods of scholarship we must never forget that he is mystically Europe at bottom. (16)

Two weeks later Forster reviewed four books by missionaries in the Orient. One of the books, S. Pollard's In Unknown China, appealed to him because the author seemed sincerely interested in developing personal relations with the Chinese and was not hell-bent on propagating his religion. But C.E.Tyndale-Biscoe's Character Building in Kashmir comes in for severe criticism because of the author's complacent assumption that all heathens dwell in darkness until enlightened by the word of Christ. (17)

The subject of Christianity next drew Forster's attention during the thirties crisis when religious belief of one sort or another was becoming popular. Arnold Toynbee published a talk in the Listener of 20 January 1937, titled 'Post-war Paganism versus Christianity', which drew an angry retort from Forster. Toynbee, says Forster, is merely another pleader for "blind belief in belief". He fails to see the contradiction in advocating religious worship as a substitute for dictator worship. The real problem, Forster argues, is the fact of worship and not the object of it - "... what our tormented planet most needs at the present moment is not more but less faith. People believe much too ardently, and consequently desire to kill those who differ from them." (18) Another observation which eloquently condenses Forster's view of the irrelevance of Christ and Christian belief in the modern world occurs in an otherwise insignificant book review, when Forster quotes a paragraph in a letter written by the minor novelist Ouida. The paragraph is quoted as an example of brilliant prose, but Forster could hardly have been less struck by the convictions it expresses -

> If you do not believe in the divinity of Christ, what remains? What of course was always there, a poor man of fine instincts sore troubled by the suffering and the injustice which trouble Tolstoy today. He drew the poor after him, naturally, by his assurances that the future would compensate them for their painful labour. But I have never been able to understand how theories so crude, so illogical, so uneducated and unsupported, could ever attract or satisfy intellectual minds. One must believe something, I am told. Why? Why should one need a belief? (19)

Later in life Forster seems to have become even more vehemently anti-Christian. His Commonplace Book is replete with sardonic notations on Christian belief. He seems to have been afraid that in a moment of weakness he might recant his disbelief, and so takes a nearly obsessive care to record his agnosticism. (20)

FORSTER'S VIEW OF RELIGION

A less angry and therefore more palatable note of agnostic humanism informs Forster's account of the Christian phase of the spiritual history of Alexandria. The historical section of _Alexandria_ is not just a simple factual narration of events. Forster's own predilections and prejudices emerge reasonably clearly within his record of the significant historical figures and issues connected with the development of religious philosophy in Alexandria. For anyone interested in his values, his narrative may be seen as a personal response to the course of the city's spiritual progress.

Forster's narrative begins with the migration of Jews from Jerusalem to Alexandria in about the third century B.C. Coming into contact with Alexandrian Hellenism, the Jew of the Dispersion became "more and more conscious of the churlishness and inaccessibility of his national God." (21) Forster's dislike of Jehovah, apparent from this remark, is expressed in an even more forthright manner in a book review of 1920 titled 'Jehovah, Buddha and the Greeks'. The review contrasts two books - G.N. Banerjee's _Hellenism in Ancient India_ and Norman Bentwich's _Hellenism_. Both these books discuss the influence upon the eastern world of the Hellenism which followed in the wake of Alexander the Great. Forster likes Banerjee's book for it shows that Buddhism greeted Hellenism with flexibility, synthesizing it with its own traditions to create a new and vigorous aesthetics in the Gandhara school of art. Conversely, Bentwich's book, which defends the hostility of Judaism to Hellenic ideas, comes in for sharp criticism from Forster. (22) In _Alexandria_ Forster points out that a narrow and dogmatic belief in Jehovah had survived unscathed within Palestine, but once the Jews were free to receive the influence of another culture they became tolerant and liberal and managed to absorb themselves into Alexandria. The subsequent fecundity of religious thought in the city was partly a product of this intermingling and hybridization of cultures.

The Alexandrian Jews sought ways of rendering Jehovah more human and accessible. The earliest evidence of their effort is 'The Wisdom of Solomon' - in Forster's view an admirable text which shows that the Jews conceived of Sophia or Wisdom as the link between man and the divine. This marks the initial step in the movement from dogmatic conservatism towards a tolerant and eclectic humanism, for it indicates belief in man's capacity to realize God within this world. Wisdom is here like "a messenger who bridges the gulf and makes us friends of God."(23) Subsequently, says Forster, the fundamental religious question which Alexandria tried to answer was how the human and the divine could be connected and brought closer together. Since this is also one of the fundamental questions posed by Forster's own writing, his attitude to the various answers offered by Alexandrian thinkers has an obvious value in indicating how he looks at this religious problem.

The idea of an intermediary between man and God is signified in the writing of Philo (a contemporary of Christ) by 'logos' or 'word'. Forster admires this notion as an allegory which "made the Hebrew Jehovah intelligible and acceptable to the Alexandrian Jews." (24) Philo spelt out this notion with some reserve since it did not exist in the Old Testament, but beneath the surface timidity of his writing Forster perceives a real sublimity. Philo, he feels, has the imagination to break free of scriptural restraint, and thereby anticipate Plotinus' emphasis upon mystic vision (rather than worship) as the path to the divine.

Three centuries later Plotinus offered an answer to the Alexandrian question. Although in the neo-Platonic tradition which Plotinus followed, the physical world is an imperfect copy of an ideal one and therefore negligible, the Plotinian <u>Enneads</u> contain one of the most compelling descriptions of the beauty of the universe. They reveal a cosmology which is broadly consistent with a humanist worldview - one within which response to natural beauty replaces admiration of supernatural glory. While the orthodox believer reveres the unseen beauty of God, a humanist considers earthly beauty the only firm evidence of spirit. Plotinus's philosophy bridges the gulf that usually exists between a religious and a humanist outlook, because Plotinus values the physical universe not as a mere reflection, but as a part of an all-encompassing spirit. Thus Forster ignores the fact that Plotinus places great emphasis upon an ascetic quest for mystic vision, and selectively concentrates upon Plotinus's monistic cosmology and his affirmation of human endeavour. For Forster the attraction of Plotinus's system is its view that "Not only do all things flow from God, they also strive to return to him; in other words the whole Universe has an inclination towards good. We are all parts of God, even the stones, though we cannot realize it; and man's goal is to become actually, as he is potentially,

divine." (25) Forster also notes the affinity of
the Plotinian view with that of Hinduism, its stress
on behaviour and training before one acquires a
vision of the divine, as well as the idea that "the
vision of oneself and the vision of God are really
the same, because each individual is God if only he
knew it. And here is the great difference between
Plotinus and Christianity. The Christian promise is
that a man shall see God; the neo-Platonic, like
the Indian - that he shall be God." (26)

   Forster then discusses some of the early church
fathers of Alexandria. Christianity absorbed
Philo's idea of the logos and borrowed other notions
from neo-Platonism, but was distinct in insisting
that Christ was the only intermediary between man
and God. Once this was established, controversy
arose as to the precise nature of Christ. Forster
comments sketchily upon these developments, and his
sympathies once again are with the thinkers who do
not narrow religion into a rigid order and emphasize
worship, but who are concerned with making
salvation more easily accessible. The first
important church father is Clement, whose outlook
was tolerant and eclectic. He did not denounce
either Hellenism or Judaism, saying instead that
they were preparations for Christ. "Learned and
enlightened, he set Christianity upon a path she did
not long consent to follow. He raised her from
intellectual obscurity, he lent her for a little,
Hellenic persuasion, and the graciousness of God
seems in his pages not incompatible with the Grace
of God." (27) Forster's account of Clement shows
that he tends to overlook the importance attached
to asceticism in Alexandrian philosophy when the
latter is also informed by a humane and enlightened
spirit. In actual fact, according to one historian,
"Clement greatly stressed the importance of asceticism in the progress of spiritual advancement: the
true Gnostic (seeker after knowledge) seeks to be
like God, and since passionlessness is a divine
characteristic the ideal life involves freedom from
desire." (28) Forster looks only at another aspect
of Clement's writing, that which is summed up here
by Maisie Ward - "Clement's longing for the life to
come never seems to take its rise from distaste for
the life that now is... This world is a pilgrimage
but a happy one; the halting places are only inns,
but an inn can furnish good cheer to mind and body."
(29) After Clement, his pupil Origen continued this
enlightened tradition. Like Plotinus, Origen was
ascetically inclined and even castrated himself to

be free of desire, but he did continue the humane thrust of early Alexandrian theology. He maintained that man and God have been linked since the beginning of things, that evil is only transitory, that Christ is a mediating influence through all time, and that Christianity is simply the heir of the past. Origen appeals to Forster for the same reasons as Plotinus and Clement - his teaching is undogmatic. The church still has reservations about Clement and Origen, especially the latter. Among Origen's 'dangerous' ideas was one which, according to Burkill, "envisaged a time when the precosmic paradise would be regained... and when all men and all demons - including the Devil himself - would be redeemed." (30) It is no wonder that Origen appeals to Forster. His philosophy allows scope for variety and personal creativity, and does not seek to impose order by demanding strict religious conformity. Origen, in Forster's view, is the last of Christianity's tolerant spokesmen in Alexandria. After him the religion hardens doctrinally and is transformed from a benevolent philosophy into a 'faith' which proclaims itself the sole truth. The conception of God stratifies into the image of a stern father-figure, and Christianity becomes involved in futile academic disputes. Forster's account more or less finishes with the third century A.D. because of his lack of interest in sterile theological warfare. Forster says nothing, for instance, about the theological rivalry between Alexandria and Antioch in the fifth century, when Cyril of Alexandria and Nestorius of Antioch had a furious fight about whether Christ was a composite unity of the divine and the human or whether he was partly divine and partly human. (31) There is, however, one last figure who arouses Forster's interest. This is Arius, the church father who provoked controversy in the fourth century. Forster sees him as the last church father to try to elevate man towards God. Arius held that as Christ was the son of God, there must have been a time when he did not exist. In his creed Christ becomes more human than divine, and this resists the thrust of Christianity towards belief in a remote, adjudicating deity. "It is easy to see why Arianism became popular" says Forster. "By making Christ younger and lower than God it brought him nearer to us - indeed it tended to level him into a mere good man..." (32) It is interesting to contrast Forster's sympathy for Arius with Hilaire Belloc's orthodox view - "Arianism lacked vision. It was essentially a hesitation to accept the Incarnation, and therefore it would have bred sooner or later a denial of the Sacrament; and at length it would have relapsed, as Protestantism has, into nothingness." (33) The conclusion to this section of <u>Alexandria</u> sums up Forster's personal opinion of the strength and weakness of religious philosophy in Alexandria. The weakness, he says, was the effort to locate the link between man and God too precisely. This led away from genuinely spiritual concerns towards doctrinal absurdities. The strength, he feels, was that "she (Alexandria) did cling to the idea of love, and much philosophical absurdity, much theological aridity must be pardoned to those who maintain that the best thing on earth is likely to be the best in heaven." (34)

III

    Moving from Forster's interpretation of Christianity (and doctrines associated with its early development) to his idea of Hinduism, it is noticeable that Forster's tone loses its sarcasm and becomes mellow. This is because in contrast with Christ who symbolizes austerity, ascetic self-denial, hero-worship, a deliberate search for pain and martyrdom, and a generally barren outlook, the Krishna of Forster's imagination represents some of the more engaging human qualities such as vitality, sensitivity and gaiety. Krishna is the fun-loving god who combines seriousness with the playfulness which Forster finds missing in the cold and emotionally deficient figure of Christ. He prefers Krishna's earthiness to Christ's sternness because at a human level, Krishna the teacher-god cum worldly-lover seems more congenial than the heroic and forbidding personage of Christ. Krishna is seen as an embodiment of that universal spirit which is only known through a response to the beautiful things of the world.

    Forster was baffled by the enthusiasm and high spirits at the Dewas celebrations of Gokul Ashtami. In fact the chaos and confusion of the occasion made him feel that "There is no dignity, no taste, no form, and though I am dressed as a Hindu, I shall never become one." (35) However, when he moves beyond the trappings and suits of Hinduism to the actual figure of Krishna, Forster discovers insights which he thinks truly spiritual. In both <u>The Hill of Devi</u> and the address to the Cambridge <u>Humanists</u>, Forster contrasts Christ with Krishna. "The canonical gospels do not record that Christ laughed or played. Can a man be perfect if he never laughs or plays? Krishna's jokes may be vapid, but they bridge a gap." (36) - and - "It may seem absurd to turn from Christ to Krishna... Krishna is usually a trivial figure. But he does admit pleasure and fun and jokes and their connection with love. And in one of his aspects, that of the charioteer to Arjuna, he manages to produce the most famous of the Indian's utterances." (37)

This utterance, the Bhagavad Gita, is the subject of Forster's 1912 essay 'Hymn Before Action'. This essay is a brief exposition of the philosophy of life contained in Krishna's reply to Arjuna who, about to battle his kinsmen, questions the god about the meaning of his action and of human life in general. Krishna's first reason for action does not appeal greatly to Forster. Krishna argues that death is negligible because man's soul is indestructible, and therefore action need not be feared when its consequences are merely physical. This is unconvincing since it might equally be an argument for fatalism. However, Krishna offers a second reason which gives a more positive meaning to action by linking it to the progress of the soul. He says that though the material consequences of action are merely temporary, the impulses that give rise to action have an eternal importance because they determine the destiny of the soul. Even this reason for action is not entirely satisfactory because while action may have a bearing on the eternal soul, how does a man reconcile this fact with the exigencies of present existence - how does one harmonize the needs of the immortal spirit with those of the immediate, human self? This is considered in Krishna's third reason for action which Forster believes "deals with the problems of renunciation, and attempts to harmonize the needs of this life with eternal truth." (38) According to Krishna, only the saint may renounce action, while the ordinary man must renounce only the desire for material reward and seek to attain spiritual fulfilment from his action. Transcending the sterility of the inactive man and the action of the man motivated by greed, there is the man whose action is informed and fulfilled by visionary insight. This is implied when Krishna reveals himself in his full glory to Arjuna and when Arjuna, inspired by this vision, fights without self-doubt. In this way Krishna postulates a message which is truly humane. He locates the meaning of life neither in faith nor in asceticism nor in material success, but in a personal realization of the inner, spiritual value of one's action.

Besides this, one can infer other reasons why Krishna, and some features of Hinduism, should appeal to Forster. Krishna is a figure who embraces varied qualities. In the *Gita* he speaks of himself as the spirit which exists in all things, and it is possible for Forster to cull from this multi-faceted figure those virtues that appeal most to his own temperament. At one level, Forster is attracted by the sage who emphasises the need for inner vision to make action meaningful, but at another he commends the Krishna of folklore, the god who revels and frolics. One of the features which connects Forster with Bloomsbury is the value he attaches to irreverence, whimsy, and the folly praised by Erasmus. The chief characteristic of the Krishna of folklore is his love of fun, and this is precisely what charms Forster - "Even if he kills a dragon he dances on its teeth, which St. Michael would not do. He is gay to the point of silliness." (39) Krishna, like Forster, shuns greatness. Forster also notes the variety of human accomplishments elevated to divine status in the figure of Krishna - "warrior, counsellor, randy villager, divine principle, flautist, great king...the destroyer of dragons ..." and adds - "Hindu religion has the high distinction of being non-propagandist. But if it abandoned the distinction ... and competed with Christianity and Islam as the unique representative of Truth, it might well push Krishna forward as its champion." (40)

The non-propagandist character of Hinduism seems to Forster an aspect of its wider belief in tolerance and respect for the individual. The *Gita* emphasizes the overarching unity of the universe, but simultaneously acknowledges individual differences and says that the pathways to salvation are manifold. This acknowledgement of the value of diversity within unity, in Forster's view, is one of the most profoundly democratic conceptions of Hinduism - "... Hinduism emphasizes the fact that we are all different. But it also emphasizes the other side of the human paradox - that we are all the same ... these two contradictory beliefs do really correspond to two contradictory emotions that each of us can feel, namely, 'I am different from everybody else' and 'I am the same as everybody else'". (41) A variation of this very idea is the theme of 'The Ivory Tower', and indeed of Forster's criticism as a whole.

FORSTER'S VIEW OF RELIGION

Forster's admiration of this aspect of Hinduism was reinforced by a better understanding of Indian art and architecture. During the Second War, an exhibition of pictures on Indian art by the art historian Stella Kramrisch gave Forster a further insight into the Hindu way of thought. Kramrisch, he writes, showed him that

> ...the temple was the World Mountain on whose exterior is displayed life in all its forms, life human and superhuman and subhuman and animal, life tragic and cheerful, cruel and kind, seemly and obscene, all crowned at the mountain's summit by the sun. And in the interior of the mountain she revealed a tiny cavity, a central cell, where, in the heart of the world complexity, the individual could be alone with his god. Hinduism - unlike Buddhism, Islam and Christianity - is not a congregational religion: it by-passes the community and despite its entanglement with caste it by-passes class. Its main concern is the individual and his relation to reality... (42)

Such an outlook appears sound because it is based on true psychology. It suggests that Hinduism makes allowance for the different nature and needs of every individual, and expounds an ideal in which self-realization rather than the mere worship of something external is the important thing.

From his interpretation of Krishna and some aspects of Hinduism it is evident that Forster is attracted by those Hindu values which are consistent with his own aesthetic-humanist and liberal-democratic ideals. While he kept a distance from the confusion of Hindu rituals, he was able to perceive that the religion is admirable in some of its conceptions of human life - most specifically in its respect for the individual's need to be free to think or meditate in solitude. Hinduism, in other words, suggests the need to harmonize social order with the private ivory towers of every individual. Furthermore, Krishna appeals to Forster as a sage, a visionary and a rounded individual whose engaging humanity, manifest in his love of fun and occasional stupidity, propagates the value of life over abstraction, renunciation and otherworldliness. As a general symbol of the best in Hinduism, Krishna seems to become one of the numerous representatives of Forster's aristocracy. Forster's criticism interprets and extends the message of Krishna in much the same way as it does those of (for example) Voltaire and Lowes Dickinson. Strange though it may seem, Krishna too stands alongside Forster's other champions of aesthetic, democratic, and humane values

IV

While Forster admired Hindu ideals, at a more personal level it was the mosque rather than the temple which moved him. In its proselytizing and congregational aspects Islam is closer to Christianity than to Hinduism, and these are not features which appeal to Forster. Nor is the relative unimportance it attaches to 'love' an endearing aspect of its outlook. In his short note on Islam in <u>Alexandria</u>, Forster sees that the religion emphasises a powerful and not a loving god. However, Islam appeals because of its simplicity, its serenity and the sense of peace it conveys. Forster got this feeling from Islam after his bewilderment with the Dewas rituals, and it stayed with him. "I do like Islam", he writes, "though I have had to come through Hinduism to discover it. After all the mess and profusion and confusion of Gokul Ashtami, where nothing ever stopped or need have begun, it was like standing on a mountain." (43) In addition, whereas Hinduism seemed to stress man's relation with god, Islam suggested personal relationship and the brotherhood of man. Forster's friendship with Ross Masood and other Muslims, as well as his contact with 'orientals in spirit' like Wilfrid Blunt and T.E. Lawrence, probably had much to do with his own intuitive sympathy with Islam.

Like his interpretation of Hinduism and Christianity, Forster's interpretation of Islam is selective. It is a very personal view, achieved not from the Koran but mainly from evocations of spiritual feeling by Mosque architecture. Like temple architecture, which suggests something about the nature of the Hindu religious outlook, Forster's intimations of the spirit of Islam derive in part from some of the structural features of the mosque. Forster writes that whereas a cathedral seeks to locate god within its interior, a mosque is more truly exalted because its uncomplicated structure suggests the omniscience of God:

> (A mosque) embodies no crisis, leads up through no gradation of nave and choir, and employs no hierarchy of priests. Equality before God, so doubtfully proclaimed by Christianity - lies at

> the very root of Islam... The Christian has a
> vague idea that God is inside the church, pre-
> sumably near the east end. The Moslem, when
> his faith is pure, cherishes no such illusion,
> and attaches no sanctity to it beyond what is
> conferred by the presence of the devout.(44)

Mosques with an elaborate architecture do not appeal to Forster. He was happiest in Cairo's Amr mosque - "There was nothing particular to look at - only old stones - but peace and happiness seemed to flow out and fill me. Islam means peace. Whatever the creed may have done, the name means peace, and its buildings can give a sense of arrival, which is unattainable in any Christian church." (45) Despite its historical record as a fiercely militant and dogmatic faith, Forster is moved by the sublime simplicity of the central Islamic tenet that "there is no God but God and that even Mohammad is but the Prophet of God". This is the message which Forster found enshrined within the mosque.

V

Forster's view of Christianity, Hinduism and Islam establishes that he values only select aspects of these religions and does not believe that any one of them by itself deserves allegiance. Whereas isolated religious conceptions and ideals seem admirable, no single religion is acceptable to him as an ordered totality - when it asks to be accepted as a binding doctrine which dictates the rules by which every individual must live. In this sense, religion becomes an order which is imposed from the outside upon passive believers rather than something which contributes to personal creativity and self-development. This is why despite the attraction of a variety of religious principles, Forster does not believe in religion in the way that he does in art. In the end, Forster's attitude to religion as an order or system of beliefs can be inferred from an essay of 1934 and a radio broadcast of 1956.

The essay, titled 'Our Greatest Benefactor', was written as a part of a series in which well-known public figures were asked to choose and discuss humanity's greatest benefactor. Andre Maurois spoke on the collective benefaction of the people who had freed mankind from pain and fear, H.W. Nevinson chose the creative artist, Sir Charles Grant Robertson chose Shakespeare and Pasteur, Sir Eustace Percy said every age has its own benefactor, Arnold Wilson discussed Christ. Forster spoke about James Simpson, the discoverer of chloroform. He begins by considering the claims of prominent inventors but dismisses them because inventions "only become important to us after we have got used to them." He then collectively considers the claims of artists, moralists and religious leaders but dismisses them too because their spheres of influence are always limited. Christ's claim, as much as Beethoven's, he says, is questionable because the majority of human beings have never responded to him. The benefits of religion, in particular, have been overweighed by persecution and tyranny. Forster's choice falls upon James Simpson because Simpson "symbolizes the decrease of pain", and because he had to resist the obscurantism and religious dogma which held that "pain was divinely ordered, and chloroform a criticism of the Almighty." (46) Simpson, as Forster's greatest benefactor, is not only the discoverer of a drug but one of the enlightened humanists who helped free mankind from the oppression of religious belief.

The broadcast which condenses Forster's attitude to religion is really a summarization and assessment of Lowes Dickinson's humanism. Dickinson's view of religion is concisely expressed in a broadcast where he says -"Religion in my judgment is not a fixed body of doctrine revealed by Buddha or Jesus or Mahomet ... (it) is an attitude of the informed and passionate imagination towards the whole world. Such an attitude, if one is intelligent, honest and bent upon truth, is necessarily being continually modified by new truths." (47) This eclecticism is allegorically expressed in Dickinson's The Magic Flute where Jesus, Satan, Buddha and Voltaire's Candide confess to flaws in their philosophies. Forster's broadcast shows how Dickinson tried to demonstrate that no doctrine can contain the whole truth, and that the truth may be arrived at by culling the best from diverse doctrines. Dickinson's Jesus, for instance, admits that his gospel was both true and false. The Buddha similarly admits that he was true in advocating selflessness and love but false when he preached flight from life. Approached in this way, religion is not accepted as belief but is sceptically scrutinized. By this procedure it aids and enriches the development of an open minded and tolerant outlook. At the end of his broadcast, Forster sums up the humanism which Dickinson propagated as an alternative to religious belief, and this humanism is the composite ideal of which Forster is himself a most memorable symbol:

He challenges the materialism of our age. He also challenges the religiosity, the revivalism, the insistence on sin that are so often offered as correctives to materialism. In place of those false goods and gods he offers the human spirit which tries to follow reason, knows that reason sometimes fails, yet when it does fail does not scuttle to take refuge in authority. Add to this his belief that it is through poetry and through music that man comes closest to the Sacred Fire, and his claim to be remembered is confirmed. (48).

The belief that man's connection with the divine is established not through religious worship but via the arts is the next subject of enquiry.

NOTES

(1) 'What I Believe', TCD, p.65.
(2) 'A Letter', Twentieth Century, February 1955, vol.157, pp. 99-101 (p.100).
(3) The New Disorder, p.9.
(4) Corliss Lamont, Introduction to Humanism as a Philosophy (London: Watts & Co., 1952) p.XII.
(5) 'Notes on the English Character', Atlantic Monthly, Jan. 1926, vol. 137, pp.30-7 (p.34). Rpt. AH (pp. 20-1).
(6) The New Disorder, p.9.
(7) The quotation is from a travel book by Gerald Brenan called The Face of Spain (London: Turnstile Press, 1950) pp. 21-2. CB, c. 1951, p.202.
(8) Letter to Mr. Newby of the B.B.C. dated 11 October 1955, King's College Ms.
(9) 'A Presidential Address to the Cambridge Humanists', University Humanist Federation Bulletin, Spring 1963, No.11, pp. 2-8 (p.4).
(10) ibid. (p.6).
(11) ibid. (p.6).
(12) ibid. (p.7).
(13) ibid. (p.8).
(14) 'The Untidy Gentleman', Nation, 4 December 1920, pp. 344, 346 (p.344).
(15) Hilaire Belloc, Europe and the Faith (1920; rpt. London: Constable, 1924) pp. 5-6.
(16) 'A Cautionary Tale', Nation, 9 October 1920, pp. 47-8 (p.47).
(17) This review - 'Missionaries' in Athenaeum 22 October 1920, pp. 545-7 - has been discussed in G.K. Das, E.M. Forster's India (London: Macmillan, 1978) pp. 32-3.

(18) 'Church, Community and State' (a letter). Listener, 27 January 1937, p.177 (p.177).
(19) 'A Bedside Book', The Listener, 7 November 1940, p. 675 (p. 675).
(20) See CB pp. 128, 215, 269, 272, 279 & 284.
(21) Alexandria: A History and a Guide (1922; rpt. Alexandria: Whitehead Morris, 1938) p. 55.
(22) Athenaeum, 4 June 1920, pp. 730-1.
(23) Alexandria, p.55.
(24) ibid., p.56.
(25) ibid., p.59.
(26) ibid., p.60. The parallelism between this outlook and Hinduism, and the contrast between it and the Christian outlook which stresses innate sinfulness as well as clear cut categories, is one of the themes of A Passage to India. It has been expounded with scholarship in John Drew, 'A Passage via Alexandria?' in E.M. Forster: A Human Exploration, ed. G.K. Das and John Beer (London: Macmillan, 1979) pp. 89-101.
(27) Alexandria, p.65.
(28) T.A. Burkill, The Evolution of Christian Thought (Ithaca: Cornell University Press, 1971) p.66.
(29) Early Church Portrait Gallery (London: Sheed and Ward, 1959) pp. 37-8.
(30) The Evolution of Christian Thought, p.71.
(31) Forster later noted - "I have too imperfectly considered him (St. Cyril) in my Guide. He was one of the worst, and I should like some day to go deeper into him" CB, c. 1942, p.150.
(32) ibid., p. 67 'St. Athanasius' in Pharos and Pharillon is an imaginative reconstruction of the dispute between Arius and Athanasius - the church father who ultimately subdued Arianism.
(33) Europe and the Faith, p.152.
(34) ibid., p.69. There are some notes of marginal importance on the church fathers of the third and fourth centuries in CB, c. 1942, pp. 139-50.
(35) The Hill of Devi: Being Letters from Dewas State Senior (London: Edward Arnold, 1953) p. 107.
(36) ibid., p.119.
(37) Humanist Address, pp. 6-7.
(38) 'Hymn Before Action', AH (p. 366).
(39) 'The Blue Boy', Listener, 14 March 1957, p.444 (p.444).
(40) ibid. (p.444).
(41) 'The Mission of Hinduism', Daily News and Leader, 30 April 1915, p.7 (p.7.).
(42) 'The World Mountain', The Listener, 2 December

FORSTER'S VIEW OF RELIGION

        1954, p.977-8 (p.978).
(43) The Hill of Devi, p.127.
(44) 'The Mosque' Athenaeum, 19 March 1920, pp. 367-8 (p.367). Rpt. AH, pp. 292-5 (pp.293-5).
(45) 'The Last of Abinger', TCD (p.354).
(46) Spectator, 15 June 1934, p.914 (p.914).
(47) Points of View, p.31. A more detailed version of this view exists in Dickinson's 'Religion: A Criticism and a Forecast', Letters to John Chinaman and other essays, introduced by E.M Forster (London: Allen and Unwin, 1946) pp.106-58.
(48) 'A Great Humanist: E.M. Forster on Goldsworthy Lowes Dickinson', The Listener, 11 October 1956, pp. 545-7 (p.547).

CHAPTER FOUR

FORSTER'S AESTHETICS

Before one begins writing about Forster's aesthetics, it is salutary to remember one strong argument against suggesting that he possesses any well worked out 'theory' of art. Forster's opinion of aesthetic theories is expressed unequivocally - "...to the irreverent eyes of some of us they appear as travelling laboratories, beds of Procrustes whereon Milton is too long and Keats too short." (1) This however, is not so much an opposition to the existence of aesthetic theories, as to their application as standards of judgment in literary criticism - "...if we wheel up an aesthetic theory - the best obtainable , and there are some excellent ones - if we wheel it up and apply it with its measuring rods and pliers and forceps, its calipers and catheters, to a particular work of art, we are visited at once, if we are sensitive, by a sense of the grotesque."(2) But though he may be cautious of constructing and applying any theory of literature, Forster, like every other artist or critic, does possess a loosely consistent 'aesthetics'. This, in his case, consists of a body of opinions on a variety of aesthetic issues such as the etiology of art, the nature of a work of art, the relation between art (or culture) and society, the role of criticism, the nature of the difference between literary genres, the ways in which novels are structured, and the way in which the ideal novel might be structured.

The conclusion of <u>The New Disorder</u> lists the four kinds of order which human beings have created. The first, social and political order, is seen as 'relative disorder'. It is valued insofar as it promotes individual freedom and creative self-development, but its claim to supreme value in human life is disallowed. The second, astronomical order, is shown to have been disproved by science while the third, religious or divine order, is tentatively accepted but again believed to be of value in human life only when it aids the development of inner order or personal creativity. These categories of order have been discussed in the earlier chapters. The fourth category is aesthetic order or art, and it occurs at the top of Forster's value scheme. Here I will show that Forster's discussion of art and related issues assumes as well as enlarges the framework of personal beliefs earlier discussed. His aesthetics both follows from and is the most important segment of his view of life.

Forster's world-view may be captioned as 'mystical materialism' or as 'eclectic humanism'. His metaphysics, ethics, sociology and politics are a part and peculiar extension of the broad tradition of Millite liberalism which integratively implies commitment to inner vision, gradual social progress through enlightenment and economic reform, diversity, tolerance, and the moral values - achieved through inner cultivation - which define a distinctively human existence and make possible the progress of civilization. The greatest stress within this eclectic philosophy falls upon the need for widespread self-fulfilment through self-expression and response to the beautiful in art and nature. Art, in particular, is seen from a Romantic position as the most sublime medium of spiritual fulfilment. Like Plotinus's conception of a universal soul which is manifest in all earthly objects but which becomes more powerful as these transcend their connection with material existence, Forster seems to conceive of an unseen spirit which is latent in all creation but which is more fully realized by man as he evolves into a truly civilized human being. The most advanced stage in this evolutionary process entails the cognition, appreciation and development of aesthetic form. Art, in this conception, is the most sublime material expression and expansion of an immanent spirit. It is the outermost spiritual extension of the deepest levels of human personality, the most intense, ordered and disinterested response to what is beautiful in life. Art is also thought to be superior to the other kinds of order because, while drawing upon and reflecting the material world, aesthetic form is dictated by the inner spirit - by what Coleridge called the shaping spirit of Imagination. Whereas social, political and religious order depend upon what is necessary or useful in life, are consciously created and have specific purposes, art is the creation of order without conscious purpose.

FORSTER'S AESTHETICS

Unlike the other categories, art is ordered according to the dictates of an inner, transcendent ideal of beauty. It is the means by which spirit is actualized and by which man forges a connection between his human and divine selves. It is therefore, in Forster's view, the one perfect form between the confusion of life and the dogmas which fail to order it.

This reiteration of Romantic expressionist theory is the nucleus of Forster's aesthetics, and from it radiate ideas which amplify and supplement the core. The important essays in aesthetics were written over a scattered period, between 'Inspiration' (1911) and 'The Raison d'Etre of Criticism in the Arts' (1947). This period saw major developments in literary theory but Forster was not significantly influenced by these. His aesthetics can be explained with reference to the Romantics, Matthew Arnold, A.C. Bradley, Roger Fry and Charles Mauron - rather than Richards, Leavis and Empson.

Forster's view of the genesis of art in 'Inspiration' shows a naive belief in divine afflatus. Forster believes that the conscious mind counts for little in the business of creation, and argues that in the domain of aesthetics it is fallacious to attribute too much to the intellect at the expense of the soul, because - "The mind as it were, turns turtle ... and a hidden part of it comes to the top and controls the pen. It ... is the process termed by the ancients 'inspiration' and one wishes that the term were still in use for it is far nearer the truth than most accounts." (3) In later articles, however, the explanation is not so simplistic. Artists may "like it to be supposed that they have acquired experience in a prenatal dream" (4) but, says Forster, it is a complex combination of the subconscious life with conscious, worldly existence that lies behind a work of art. Every artist wobbles between normal and heightened consciousness when he creates, for his imagination both draws upon and transforms his real experiences. This is fully elaborated in 'The Raison d'Etre of Criticism' -

> He (the artist) lets down, as it were a bucket into the subconscious, and draws up something which is normally beyond his reach. He mixes this thing with his normal experiences, and out of the mixture he makes a work of art ... whether it is good or bad it will have been compounded in this unusual way ... (5)

FORSTER'S AESTHETICS

The most perfect demonstration of this process, in Forster's view, is the genesis of Coleridge's 'Kubla Khan'. He is greatly impressed by Livingston Lowes's The Road to Xanadu (1927), which reveals the extraordinary manner in which a substratum of ordinary details in Coleridge's mind was transformed by imagination into poetry. Forster was also aware of a paper by Lowes Dickinson titled 'The Emergence of a Latent Memory Under Hypnosis' (6) which concludes that an elaborate rearrangement of conscious experience occurs in the subconscious mind. This can be made to unfold under hypnosis, and may show astonishing signs of an inner inventive process. C.G. Jung's notion of 'cryptomnesia' or latent memory is also very similar, and in line with these psychological theories Forster suggests that the genesis of art involves the emergence of a latent memory in a condition akin to self-hypnosis.

There is also a similarity between Forster's view and some aspects of Romantic aesthetics. Forster's notion of an interaction between the conscious and subconscious mind is like Coleridge's notion of a 'counteraction' between the artist and what he observes. Coleridge believes that observation stimulates the conception of forms in the imagination, these grow and modify during an activity which involves the whole soul of the poet, and finally the activity resolves itself as the work of art. Writing may begin with a conscious design, but an interior power soon takes control and evolves something surprising or even contrary to the original intention. Wordsworth's theory (and its exemplification in Proust) of art as a combination of remembered feelings and associations stirred by the memory is also echoed by Forster - "The artist has the power of retaining and digesting experiences, which years later, he may bring forth in a different form; to the end of his life he is accompanied by a secret store." (7) There is an even closer parallel when Forster calls poetry an "emotional reconstruction of an actual or imagined past ... A poet hides things up or pares them away, not because he is refined, but because his method requires it. The living fact which he experienced was entangled with dead stuff which did not interest him: he has to isolate it before he can express it passionately..." (8)

'Sleep', 'dream' and 'discovery' are other words connected with creation in Romantic usage, and Forster uses them often. In 1931 he delivered six lectures on 'The Creator as Critic' in Cambridge, and in the first - which distinguishes creation from criticism - he says:

> I mean by creation an activity, part of which takes place in sleep. It has, or usually has, its wakeful alert side, but it's rooted in the region whence dreams also grow. The region has various scientific names and psychoanalysis tells us all about it: Jung, Freud ... Creation is an activity which selects and connects the images found in sleep. It is a universal activity. The great writer differs from the rest of us because he selects and connects properly. (9)

'Sleep', in Forster's sense, is just another term for 'inspiration' and implies that during creation the artist's everyday personality is asleep while a deeper consciousness awakens within. It indicates the ivory-tower withdrawal and detachment which characterizes the artist's submersion into his spiritual self. It also suggests that art is the result of an organic, almost physiological process, because "the artist looking back on it (his creation) will wonder how on earth he did it." (10)

In the same vein, creation is compared to a dream. Dreams, as in Jungian psychology, are connected with both a personal subconscious and an archetypal human subconscious. Whereas the memory is an attribute of the conscious self, dreams are seen as an aspect of subconsciousness and an impersonal self. "In mythology, as in experience, only a low barrier divides the present from all pasts", Forster says, and believes that dreams "preserve an emotional truth which no waking moment can command. Dreams remember the essential past, however wildly they distort its forms." Proust is Forster's example of the artist as dreamer, for "The taste of a cake, the unevenness of a tile, were sufficient to regain all childhood, all Venice, for Proust." (11) Proust's use of memory in A La Recherche du Temps Perdu is closely connected with Henri Bergson's conception of an involuntary memory. Bergson's Matter and Memory (1896) distinguishes between a voluntary memory which is under conscious control and an involuntary memory which throws up stored images from past experience of its own accord. Clive Bell's Proust (1928), a book which Forster reviewed alongside Scott Moncrieff's translation of Proust, mentions Bergson's importance for Proust, (12) and no doubt as someone who took a keen interest in Proust Forster was aware of Bergson's ideas - especially as Bergson had himself suggested the importance of involuntary memory for the novelist.

An even closer relation exists between Forster's thoughts on the genesis of art and an idea expounded by C.G. Jung. It was Jung who developed the idea of a connection between art and the artist's unconscious life which had been first suggested by Freud. Jung, however, felt that art was not so much a sublimation of repressed desires and energies as that it developed out of primordial images or archetypes latent within the human subconscious. Dreams and unusual states of mind were (one critic paraphrases him as saying) - "the hidden treasure upon which mankind ever and anon has drawn, and from which it has raised up its gods and demons, and all those potent and mighty thoughts without which man ceases to be man." (13) Dreams were also a method by which these archetypes were recovered and used as material in art. Jung's theory is hinted at in Livingston Lowes, who writes at one point that "... after making all allowance for those elements which are unique in Coleridge, as the incommunicable essence of every genius is, there remains a precious residuum which is peculiar to no individual, but which inheres in the nature of the imaginative faculty itself." (14) A few years later this theory was applied as a method of interpreting literature by Maud Bodkin's <u>Archetypal Patterns in Poetry</u> (1934). Forster's friend Charles Mauron speaks of art deriving from "a great reservoir" (15) and Bloomsbury, with its deep interest in psychoanalysis, was certainly aware of Jung's ideas. Fry, for instance, attributes the power of art to "all sorts of subconscious associations and feelings ... which have the power to stir up corresponding subconscious feelings in the spectator. It is this fact that the work of art acts as a transmitting medium between the artist's subconscious nature and our own that gives it its peculiar, and as we say 'magic' power over us." (16) Forster's remarks about the origin of art reveal an affiliation with this school of thought.

The connection with Jungian thought becomes even clearer when one understands Forster's concept of the work of art as a 'discovery'. 'Discovery' in Forster's criticism contrasts with the notion of art as 'self-expression'. Forster does not consider poetry merely the unique expression of a specific personality. He believes that the poet's self-absorption does not so much indicate an interest in himself as that it is a condition which makes him discover his kinship with all humanity. All art has a social, communal, and in its widest sense, human, base. It aspires to be 'anonymous' because it stems from a subconscious self which is not peculiar to the poet, but a common human inheritance buried within him. From Forster's perspective expressionism is not the same as self-expression. The quintessence of the artist's distinctive individuality from which his art emanates proves paradoxically to contain much that connects it to every other individual. Forster believes that art is the product not of what distinguishes, but of an archetypal undercurrent which unites, all men. Men are separate individuals insofar as they possess a surface selfhood, but they are also subconsciously similar in possessing a spirit which transcends the limits of selfhood. This is the premise upon which Aspects is based and it is adumbrated in the statement - "All through history writers while writing have felt more or less the same." (17) This belief is spelt out in 'Anonymity':

> ...each human mind has two personalities, one on the surface, one deeper down. The upper personality ... is conscious and alert, it does things like dining out, answering letters etc., and it differs vividly and amusingly from other personalities. The lower personality is a very queer affair. In many ways it is a perfect fool, but without it there is no literature, because unless a man dips a bucket down into it occasionally he cannot produce first-class work. There is something general about it ... It has something in common with all other deeper personalities, and the mystic will assert that the common quality is God ... as it is general to all men, so the works it inspires have something general about them, namely beauty. The Poet wrote the poem, no doubt, but he forgot himself while he wrote it ... (18)

Eliot's view of art as the extinction rather than the expression of personality accords with Forster's to the extent that both believe art expresses something deeper than just the artist's personality.(19) Only by forgetting his surface personality can the artist become a discoverer and prophet of the inner life."...earlier writers and readers knew that the words a man writes express him, but they did not make a cult of expression as we do today ... (they recognized that) a poem was not an expression but a discovery..." (20) Similarly, the artist in 'The Duty of Society to the Artist' who replies to the demand that his work be edifying and entertaining defines his work as a discovery - "I want to experiment. I want to extend human sensitiveness through paint ... (paintings are) the discoveries made by artists upon their walls..." (21)

What the artist discovers within his lower personality is a hidden source of love and sympathy, and out of these his art is born. Like creation in Plotinian philosophy, Forster sees art as a spilling over of love for life and of sympathy with living things: "When the novelist ceases to design his characters and begins to create them, 'love' ... becomes important in his mind ... the predominance of love in novels is partly because of this ..."(22) And like Blake, Forster believes that art is a manifestation of the human capacity to love, an appeal to the spirit which makes man human. To create art and respond to it is a natural expression of the fact of being human.

II

To move from the subconscious provenance and genesis of art to Forster's view of the artist - it follows that if art is an overflow from the matrix of a universal human spirit embedded in every man's subconscious, every man is potentially an artist and the artist is not inherently superior to the ordinary person. While emphasizing the value of the artist, Forster is at pains to avoid giving artists the nearly superhuman status which 'aestheticism' confers upon them. In one broadcast Forster approvingly quotes Paul Robeson's view that "'creative ability means more than the capacity of a few individuals to paint, to write, or to make music. Every man has something of the artist in him.'" (23) The artist is not genetically superior or part of a Chosen Race. However, while his emotional equipment is no different, the artist does make himself an exception by devoting unusual attention to his inner life. In the same broadcast which quotes Robeson, Forster also paraphrases Kenneth Clark's view that "The poet and the artist are exceptional precisely because they are not average men; because in sensibility, intelligence and power of invention they far exceed the average. It is exceptions of this type who have helped us into the light in the past ..." (24) Forster's paraphrase of Blake's opinion of the artist is probably the clearest version of his own -

> ...he (Blake) never supposed that creation is the prerogative of the small minority ... If this were so, humanity would be in a tragic plight. He believed that everyone can create ... The imagination ... waits within us, ready to redeem from inertia and chaos, and lead us through action to our eternal home, and the poet ... is only specially valuable when he reminds average men of the salvation they are neglecting. (25)

III

Forster's ideas about the etiology of art and the nature of the artist lead on to others about the nature of a work of art. Forster does not provide any precise definition of a work of art for the same reason that he does not define the human spirit. Like the human spirit which it embodies, art is identified not as an object but as an effect in the soul of the artist or the reader. This is, as M.H. Abrams has shown, a typically Romantic tendency. Coleridge, for example, discovers that to define poetry is nearly the same thing as to define a poet and describes the creative process more than the finished product. Wordsworth's 'Preface' and Shelley's 'Defence' are also mainly interested in the genesis and effect of art, and underscore Poe's remark that "When, indeed, men speak of Beauty, they mean, precisely, not a quality, as is supposed, but an effect ..." (26) Forster's aesthetics reveals a similar tendency, and his definition of a work of art does not get much beyond calling art an 'order'. While trying to define art he says first that the power of a poem is to be found in the creation by words of an 'atmosphere', then that it lies in "the order in which words are arranged - that is in style", and finally that the work of art is "a world, which, while it lasts, seems more real and solid than ... daily existence ..." (27) This order of words has in Forster's mind an identity not very different from that possessed by an individual. "Treat books as if they are human beings" he once said to university students - "Make friends and enemies among them ... it is as impossible to like all books as it would be to belong to all religions." (28) The analogy is relevant in other ways. The individual is an equilibrium of disparate psychological forces distinguished by possessing a unique individuality and inner completeness. Forster's definition of a work of art corresponds completely with this. Secondly, the individual, in Forster's view, reconciles his public life with his detached, private existence. He is both an independent entity and an aspect of his society, and his value must be recognized in both these respects. Forster suggests something similar when he discusses a work of art, arguing that artefacts are first things in themselves and only secondarily links within an artistic movement or objects with any social purpose and value. Like the individual, art does have social value - it makes people imaginative, sensitive, noble,etc., but it must first be recognized that art possesses a highly ordered identity, an impersonal and objective reality which transcends time and makes it valuable as an end in itself. Like the individual who contributes to society but exists in his own right, the work of art 'wobbles' between human life and existence within its own, circumscribed order. This is a conception which relates in an obviously direct way with the notion that art is at once something general, the expression of a human subconscious, and at the same time the particular product of the individual genius who taps the collective source.

The words which comprise a work of art thus perform a double function. They stand for themselves in possessing an identity and order of their own, and simultaneously bear a wider relation to the world by pointing to things outside themselves. In 'Anonymity' these functions are called 'atmosphere' and 'information'. In Plotinian cosmology a 'real' spiritual and an 'unreal' material phenomenon denote the two extremes between which lies the universe, partaking something of both extremes. Similarly, Forster's 'atmosphere' and 'information' are the two antinomies between which occur the various orders of words. Informative words function as signs and are purely functional and utilitarian. They give direction to material life and their value increases in proportion with their truth to life - to a reality outside them, a reality to which they merely refer. The word 'stop' "is an example of pure information. It creates no atmosphere ... If the tram comes the information is correct; if it doesn't come the information is incorrect." (29) But progressing upwards from this utilitarian base, words become the symbols of an atmosphere which is unique to them. They create a world other than the real one, a world which exists only within their own peculiar order.

The value of such words increases in proportion with their power to reveal an independent cosmos and with their capacity to point only to the order created by their own unique cohesion:

> ...at the end of pure information stands the tramway notice 'stop' ... at the extreme other end is lyric poetry. Lyric poetry is absolutely no use ... for it conveys no information of any kind ... when we are reading 'The Ancient Mariner', or remembering it intensely, common knowledge disappears and uncommon knowledge takes its place. We have entered a universe which only answers to its own laws, supports itself, internally coheres, and has a new standard of truth. Information is true if it is accurate. A poem is true if it hangs together ... Information is relative. A poem is absolute. (30)

In the final analysis, however, art, like 'spirit', is inexplicable and remains a structure with an unresolved centre, for - "It is also something else, and to define that other thing would be to explain the secret of the universe." (31) Revolving around this indefinable spiritual core, Forster's conception of a work of art is quasi-mystical, the humanist's equivalent of a theology. One of his highest compliments is to Stella Kramrisch, who he said could see that "aesthetics and metaphysics are identical. The outer (form) does not express the inner (spirit). The outer _is_ the inner." (32) Art, in other words, is "the surface crust of the internal harmony, it is the outward evidence of order" (33) - the only enduring evidence of man having set his love in order.

Leaving aside the spiritual centre, about which in any case very little can be said, it is otherwise apparent that Forster sees works of art as heterocosms, autonomous aesthetic worlds which require specifically aesthetic criteria to be understood. This is consistent with the Coleridgean aesthetic tradition. Coleridge says that poetic power "reveals itself in the balance or reconciliation of opposite or discordant qualities.. (of) a more than usual state of emotion with more than usual order.." (34) Taken along with his view of the poet as someone who duplicates the divine act of creation, this suggests that the object created is a uniquely organized and ordered universe - or to use Austin Warren's term - an 'equilibrism'. Warren himself puts this idea succinctly when he says - "The poet's passionate desire to perceive order for himself (not to accept it as a stereotype. 'given', handed down) makes his final creation a kind of world or cosmos." (35) A variation within this tradition inaugurated by A.C.Bradley's Oxford lecture 'Poetry for Poetry's Sake' and echoed in the aesthetics of Roger Fry is the probable starting point of Forster's ideas about art. There is no evidence to prove that Forster read Bradley's essay, but the essay is famous enough and its similarity with Forster's 'Art for Art's Sake' remarkable enough for it to seem extremely likely that Forster was aware of it. As regards Fry, Forster denied any aesthetic debt to him (36) and indeed there are fundamental differences between Fry's and Forster's views which will be discussed. Nevertheless, the concept of the autonomy of the aesthetic universe does link Forster to Fry.

Bradley's essay mediates between the extremes represented by 'aestheticism' (Wilde and Swinburne) and 'moralism' (Arnold and Tolstoy). It says that the experience of art is "an end in itself, is worth having on its own account, has an intrinsic value." (37) Poetry may possess other ends - cultural, religious, educative, etc.- but a consideration of these must not be allowed to diminish its specifically 'poetic' value. This is because "its nature is to be not a part, nor yet a copy, of the real world ... but to be a world by itself, independent, complete, autonomous." (38) Life has more mass, says Bradley, but poetry has a more perfect shape. Real life experiences have a fixed position in space and time, whereas the unity of a poem makes it transcendent and universal. Fry quotes Bradley and agrees that "the purpose of literature is the creation of structures which have for us the feeling of reality ... these structures are self-contained, self-sufficing, and not to be valued by their references to what lies outside." (39)

This is also what Forster means when he speaks of 'Art for Art's Sake' in the essay with that title. Art is unique ...

> ...not because it is clever or noble or beautiful or enlightened or original or sincere or idealistic or useful or educational - it may embody any of those qualities - but because it is the only material object in the universe which may possess internal harmony. All the others have been pressed into shape from the outside, and when their mould is removed, they

> collapse. The work of art stands up by itself,
> and nothing else does. It achieves something
> which has always been promised by society, but
> always delusively ... It is the one orderly
> product which our muddling race has
> produced. (40)

This argument hinges upon the definition of a work of art as a perfect and unique kind of construct, as something which, like the individual, must be acknowledged as important in its own right. Forster explains that the play <u>Macbeth</u> is educational (it documents something of early Scotland), and morally significant (it shows something of human nature), but more important than these, it is "a world of its own created by Shakespeare and existing in virtue of its own poetry. It is in this aspect 'Macbeth' for 'Macbeth's' sake..." (41) Art also contrasts with social order in being more permanent, for "The world created by words exists neither in space nor time: though it has semblances of both, it is eternal and indestructible ... Ancient Athens made a mess - but the Antigone stands up." (42) And whereas the legislator imposes social order upon individuals who desire personal freedom, the artist "legislates through creating .... he creates through his sensitiveness and his power to impose form." (43)

Like Bradley who first suggested that the offensive aspect of 'Art for Art's Sake' is the doctrine that art is the whole or supreme end of life - the doctrine more appropriately titled 'Life for Art's Sake' by Abrams (44) - Forster explains that his use of the phrase never implies "the silly idea that only art matters ... (for) Many things, besides art, matter ... Man lives, and ought to live, in a complex world, full of conflicting aims, and if we simplified them down into the aesthetic he would be sterilized." (45) Forster's effort is really to reinterpret the phrase into something acceptable, and he does this by showing that the notion of art for art's sake is genuinely valuable in human life. He shows that art is not created or enjoyed for merely moral, social and narrowly utilitarian purposes, but that it is a beautiful and ordered expression of the human spirit. To respond to it as such is to acknowledge that beauty and response to beauty are things valuable in themselves, to recognize that while something beautiful may have utility, it possesses a unique order of its own which separates it from the rest of the world.

FORSTER'S AESTHETICS

IV

But if Forster stresses the primacy of an 'aesthetic' response and defines art as something precious and detached from everyday existence, he also sees the close links between art and life, and recognizes that an aesthetic response is also ultimately a moral - or morally desirable - response. The nature of the moral connections between art and life is a topic which crops up at various times in Forster's criticism.

Until this point Forster's conception of aesthetic form has suggested affiliations with the aesthetics of Roger Fry and Clive Bell. However, Bell's book <u>Art</u> (1914) takes formalism to its logically absurd extreme by saying that the subject matter within works of art is of no relevance in arousing aesthetic delight. Bell argues that since the common quality in all artefacts is the perfect unity of form which distinguishes art from life, a truly aesthetic response is only to the formal aspect of art - "What quality is shared by all objects that provoke our aesthetic emotions? ... Only one answer seems possible - significant form. In each (artefact), lines and colours combined in a particular way, certain forms and relations of forms, stir our aesthetic emotions." (46) Similarly, Fry believes that "...in all cases our reaction to works of art is a reaction to relations and not to sensations or objects or persons or events." (47) Both Bell and Fry formulated their aesthetic theories with visual art in mind, but their hypothesis that the subject in art is entirely irrelevant is generally applicable. It was read as applicable to poetry by I.A. Richards who disputed it in <u>The Principles of Literary Criticism</u> (1924), and was applied on one occasion to the novel by Fry. (48) Forster's definition of aesthetic response on the other hand implies that a work of art depends for its effect upon both its formal beauty and the significance of its subject. A response to the work of art is neither merely to its complex form or structure, nor merely to its subject, but to a mixture of both. In an early unpublished fragment called 'Pornography and Sentimentality' (49) Forster writes - "From a work of art two pleasures - aesthetic. From colour, composition, etc., (and) sentimental, from subject matter. Sometimes we feel 'How perfect': at other times 'How much I should like to know that person, or walk in that view.' In my case the aesthetic pleasure is weak, the sentimental very strong. But every spectator feels both in varying proportions." (50) This is borne out by the later essay 'Not Looking at Pictures' (1939), where Forster confesses his difficulty in responding purely to the form of paintings without reference to their subject matter.

The absurdity of ruling out the importance of the subject is another aestheticist fallacy exposed in Bradley's 'Poetry for Poetry's Sake'. Bradley says that although poetic value resides ultimately in the poem rather than its subject, some subjects are inherently more poetic than others. A better poem could conceivably be written about the head of a pin than about the Fall of Man, but the Fall of Man "offers opportunities of poetic effects wider in range and more penetrating in appeal ... (and) has some aesthetic value before the poet touches it."(51) The excitement generated by a poem can therefore hardly be said to have no relation whatsoever with the objects, persons and events which constitute a part of the poetic totality. Forster implies agreement with Bradley when he comments upon a remark made by Virginia Woolf in her essay on Robinson Crusoe. According to Woolf a masterpiece is a book in which "the vision is clear and order has been achieved", and Robinson Crusoe qualifies as a masterpiece because it has a consistent perspective whereby "everything is seen precisely as it appears to Robinson Crusoe." (52) Crusoe is unimaginative, shrewd and middle-class, and consequently Defoe's novel contains nothing rapturous or sublime:

> There are no sunsets and no sunrises; there is no solitude and no soul. There is on the contrary, staring us full in the face, nothing but a large earthenware pot ... By believing fixedly in the solidity of the pot and its earthiness, he (Defoe) has subdued every other element to his design; he has roped the whole universe into harmony. And is there any reason, we ask as we shut the book, why the perspective that a plain earthenware pot exacts should not satisfy us as completely, once we grasp it, as a man himself in all his sublimity...(53)

Forster's comment indicates his opinion on Bloomsbury's indifference to the subject in art -

> Virginia says: 3 cardinal points of perspective, God, man, Nature, and Crusoe snubs us on each and forces us to contemplate 'a large

> earthenware pot' - i.e. Defoe has a sense of
> reality which she also calls 'common sense'.
> Passing onto the dreary Bloomsbury conclusion
> that the pot's perspective may be as satisfying
> as the universe if a writer believes in a pot
> with sufficient intensity. I say such a writ-
> er's a bore merely. (54)

This view is reinforced by Aspects, where (as I will show) novels are not evaluated by the Bloomsbury criterion of 'form' - a criterion concerned exclusively with how perfectly a novel is shaped. The idea of 'form' implied in Forster's criticism places a unified emphasis upon how well art is shaped and what significance it has in the emotional and spiritual life of human beings. If any definite influence does lie behind Forster's aesthetics it is as likely to have been that of Lowes Dickinson as of Fry. Lowes Dickinson contradicted the sterile formalism which separated art and life, form and content. He wrote - "There is a view of art ... which sets it altogether outside the general trend of national life and ideas; which asserts that it has no connection with ethics, religion, politics, or any general conceptions which regulate action and thought; that its end is in itself, and is simply beauty; and that in beauty there is no distinction of high and low ... so that for example a butterfly drawn by Mr. Whistler would rank as high, as the Pantheon." (55)

Another important essay in connection with this aspect of Forster's aesthetics is 'The Ivory Tower'. This essay has been discussed as a companion piece to 'What I Believe', but it also has a close thematic relation with the later 'Art for Art's Sake'. The attempt is again to give new meaning to a phrase which had fallen into disrepute because of its connection with aestheticism. Forster analyses the kind of 'escapism' implied when Marxists and bureaucrats use the phrase 'ivory tower', and contrasts it with his own, truer definition. In the first sense, 'ivory tower' is used to denigrate artists because it means "a retreat from life, a denial of life, a spiritual suicide" and its opposite is supposed to be the "expression" of life in all its aspects. Forster refutes this by arguing that in the case of the creative artist 'escape' and 'expression' are synonymous, because it is only by temporary retreat into an ivory tower of the imagination that the artist expresses himself. To be an expression of life in all its aspects, art is always implicitly an escape from life. Wordsworth created a poetic universe which contrasts with, and criticizes, industrialism, only because he first escaped into his ivory tower. This makes his poetry both an escape from, and an expression of, life. (56)

While 'The Ivory Tower' suggests that art is, willy nilly, an activity which contributes to moral awareness and a better society, Forster's belief in the moral function of art is stated even more explicitly when he analyses the nature of the aesthetic response. Once again a double process corresponding with the existence of art as simultaneously a separate entity as well as a part of life is shown to be involved in aesthetic response. In the first part of the process the reader responds directly to the ordered beauty of the work of art. Like the artist who forgets his personality and the world outside him when he creates, the reader forgets himself and reality and is absorbed into the autonomous dream world of art - "The poet wrote the poem, no doubt, but he forgot himself while he wrote it, and we forget him while we read. What is so wonderful about great literature is that it transforms the man who reads it towards the condition of the man who wrote it, and brings to birth in us also the creative impulse." (57) At the same time, if a work of art is necessarily a part of and comment upon human life, aesthetic response cannot be purely a sensation of ecstasy without relation to the moral being of the individual. A desire for the pleasure of "co-operation with the artist ... is the sole reason for our aesthetic pilgrimage" says Forster in 'The Raison d'Etre of Criticism', but elsewhere he also recognizes that aesthetic response involves more than a transient feeling of exultation. In his unpublished lecture notes on Arnold and Tolstoy he identifies a sort of morally benevolent seepage which is the second part of aesthetic response. It also shows how Forster adopts a mid-position between aestheticism and moralism:

> M.A. (i.e. Arnold) and T. (i.e. Tolstoy) ... (were) creative writers (who weren't mere preachers) and who thought that books could criticize life and could make us better.'Better' is an unfashionable word today, so substitute 'different' for 'better', and look at M.A.'s and T's claim again. It then appears not unreasonable. Books do influence us. The aesthete says 'no - or if they do its quite irrelevant - books are or should be works of art, and

> if they send us back to life with new standards
> that is nothing to do with their purpose'. It
> mayn't be, but it is always hanging onto their
> purpose; if its an irrelevancy its a widespread
> one, as common as a tail on a bird ...

Forster's hypothetical debate with the aesthete continues until there is little doubt in his mind that Arnold and Tolstoy were making a point which is substantially true-

> 'Well' says the aesthete - receding a little -
> 'if they do influence our lives, its by making
> us more sensitive to impressions, not by altering our standards of conduct.' But sensations
> and conduct - don't they react on one another?
> Can you tamper with one and leave the other untouched? I don't myself see where the line's
> to be drawn, and therefore feel that the position of critics like A. or T. is stronger than
> at first appears. You can easily argue that
> books oughtn't to teach <u>this</u> or <u>that</u>, resignation or unselfishness etc., but <u>it's</u> very
> difficult to argue that they oughtn't to <u>teach</u>,
> because they have kept on doing it and filtering into our lives ever since writing
> began. (58)

The two-fold nature of aesthetic response thus involves both the pleasure obtained from entering the autonomous universe of art as well as the moral influence gained obliquely from the experience. Clearly therefore the work of art, like the individual, is both detached from social existence and a valuable part of it. Writing about Arnold's 1853 Preface, Trilling says something which is precisely applicable to Forster's idea of art -

> With our own modern feelings about literature,
> we might conclude that Arnold's Preface proceeds from the ivory tower; quite the contrary,
> it is a theory which recognizes the conditions
> of modern life and is directed towards them. It
> is not to the purpose to call it an 'aristocratic' theory because it seeks self-cultivation - though it is perhaps 'aristocratic' in
> contrast with the bourgeois demand that art be
> immediately 'useful' in settling problems. It
> implies that true art can settle no questions,
> give no directives; that it can do no more than
> cultivate what is best in the reader - his

moral poise ... (59)

This Arnoldian idea is echoed by Forster in times of crisis, whenever the value of art is questioned or under attack. 'The Ivory Tower' outlines Forster's answer in the late thirties, and there are other examples from the First War and from the Second. In 'The Functions of Literature in War Time' (1915) Forster says that it is necessary to continue reading literature because it has a useful influence upon people. Literature influences life in two ways, directly and indirectly. The direct influence is the overt moral or "code of behaviour" which a book may recommend. This is unimportant because readers often disagree with the writer's viewpoint and yet enjoy his book. The important influence is indirect. It arises not from moral passages, but as an overflow from the initial aesthetic response, and it helps man to be "noble, gentle and brave." (60) At the conclusion of <u>Othello</u> the impressions that last are not simply pity for Desdemona and hatred of Iago. "But much more a general sense that we have been in a world much greater than our own ... the world of spirit, that helps us to endure danger and ingratitude and answer a lie with truth; the world that we look for also in religion ..." (61) By removing a reader from an impure to a pure world, art affords a perspective which influences values and decisions in life. It does not suggest particular courses of action in specific situations, but it "does teach us that hatred and revenge are wrong, because they cloud the spirit." (62) Art achieves this because it is anonymous and detached, because it is not the exclusive property of only its creator or a nation. Once created, the work of art is a well wrought urn, a perfect form with its own life and the common property of all who respond to its beauty:

> As soon as a writer dies, he ceases to have an axe to grind. All that is temporary and selfish, all that is excitable in his work, becomes meaningless and forgotten, and the pure emotion survives. To his contemporaries he may have been a jingo or pacifist ... but to us he only shows forth the wonderful works of God ... The individual writer may believe that his race is chosen, but literature ... declares that beauty and truth and goodness exist apart from the tribe, apart even from the nation, and that their only earthly dwelling is the soul of

man. (63)

An essay of 1934 repeats this view - "The propping quality in books, music etc., is only a by product of another quality in them; their power to give pleasure ... where there was intense enjoyment, grave or gay, thence will proceed the help which every individual needs ..." (64) - as does another during the Second War where the classics remind Forster "that our troubles are not just the troubles of a day" for they "throw light... (on) the little moment in which we live and for which we want help." (65)

V

Forster's belief in the importance of art for human life is not a mere theory. The theory is given practical shape by his effort to pass on the cultural gospel. Indeed it is impossible to believe in art so passionately without wishing to infect others. "The appreciator of an aesthetic achievement becomes in his minor way an artist; he cannot rest without communicating what has been communicated to him" (66) says Forster, and his essays after the twenties are more in the nature of propaganda for art and artists than literary criticism. During a period in which the general emphasis of intellectuals and bureaucrats is upon social organization and material well being - usually with the deliberate or indirect effect of condemning art as irrelevant - Forster's criticism trips up those who try to create order without considering the claims of art, i.e. those who have misunderstood the meaning of order. He believes that economists, architects and planners are not the only people concerned with social reconstruction. The artist, with his vision of the future and his intuitive capacity to understand spiritual needs, is as fundamentally necessary in society as the scientific planner. He says in a broadcast that "...this impulse to create for the sake of creating, not because it is useful, is peculiar to the human race ... Hence my dismay when most of the distinguished economists and sociologists ... have not so much as mentioned it in their lists of desiderata and agenda. I submit to you that they are being unpractical." (67) The same broadcast also states that art "is an activity which distinguishes us from the animals and has raised us from their level, and if we stop practising it we shall not rise higher. I also believe that it is worth practising for its own sake, whether it is appreciated or not." (68) The two related emphases are that art, as it is a humanizing agency which helps man to shake off his primitive bestiality, is a means towards an end - and in the same breath that it is such a means only because it is an end in itself.

But a basic difference between Forster's attitude and that of sterner fanatics of the gospel of art is his refusal to be elitist in any way. To enjoy art is simply to enjoy life more, and incidentally to become a morally better person. Forster's belief in art does not give any hint that he feels intellectual or moral superiority over those who find fulfilment in other aspects of life. The complete lack of any snobbery, as well as the lucid and unpretentious tone of his essays, makes his beliefs about art appealing and acceptable. The liberal belief in culture is presented as a human need rather than as the ideology of a social class because Forster is aware of the difficulty of arguing for culture in a period of social crisis. The importance of culture was unquestioned, he writes, while the arts were associated with social prestige and aristocratic life. But with radical changes in the socio-economic base, culture is endangered because of its age-old association with the elite. In Forster's view culture must shed this elitist image because it was never meant, in the first place, to be the prerogative of any single social class. With the emergence of a new social structure made up of people "who are in some ways, more clear sighted and honest ... (but) indifferent to the aesthetic products of the past" (69) the urgent duty of those who care for the arts is to step out of their seclusion and actively demonstrate that the arts are universally accessible and meant for the enjoyment of every person - "If 'the classics' are advertised as something dolorous and astringent, no one will sample them. But if the cultured person, like the late Roger Fry, is obviously having a good time, those who come across him will be tempted to share it and to find out how." (70) The arguments of F.R. and Q.D. Leavis against pulp fiction and gimmicky entertainment (71) are repeated by Forster when he says "If you drop tradition and culture you lose your chance of connecting work and play and creating a life which is all of a piece ... Crooners, bestsellers, electrical organists, funny faces, dream girls, and mickey mice cannot do it - they throw the weight all to one side and increase the split." (72) Forster, however, is more sensitive than the

FORSTER'S AESTHETICS

Leavises to the fact that arguments against the new forms of entertainment can lead to an excess of hostility. While generally approving of <u>Fiction and the Reading Public,</u> he also remarks that Mrs. Leavis's attitude leads to priggishness. (73) His own taste in literature is more catholic and relaxed than that of the Leavises and his essays recommend a very wide variety of writers, both major and minor.

Advertising and 'marketing' everything he thought enjoyable was Forster's preoccupation as a critic, and the writers that he propagated will be discussed later. Simultaneously, Forster was also engaged in trying to alter social opinion with regard to the function of art in society. He argues that since the artist creates work which has value for human beings in general and not for any particular society, society must accept that the queer nature of art makes it impossible for the artist to work to rule or to make specific and tangible contributions. The theme of 'The Duty of Society to the Artist' is that the artist cannot conform to social demands because he is involved in "the development of human sensitiveness in directions away from the average citizen." (74) At one level the artist is like the average citizen - he must respect the laws and not give himself airs - but at another level he is irrational and extraordinary - he does not give society what it wants but asks it to accept what he gives. The artist recognizes the importance of social laws, and society for its part must tolerate the artist and recognize that his work is valuable even though it may not be immediately comprehensible.

Pointing out the duty of society to the artist also involved Forster in a crusade against censorship of the literary imagination. In 1927 he joined the International P.E.N. Club, an organization which worked for freedom of expression for authors. When Radclyffe Hall's lesbian novel <u>The Well of Loneliness</u> was pronounced obscene and <u>forcibly withdrawn</u> in 1928, Forster attacked the government for knuckling under to an archaic morality and said it was entirely arbitrary to ban the book on the grounds that it was 'spiritually corrupting'. Such grounds, he felt, were obscure enough to license the authorities to censor anything of which they disapproved, and he concluded that "If, in the supposed interests of morality and education, more elaborate restrictions are devised, we shall only be left in a worse condition than we are in at present: we shall have been rendered less, not more, spiritual." (75) In the aftermath of the Radclyffe Hall case, two pamphlets appeared. The first by Lord Brentford (the Home Secretary) was called Do We Need A Censor and argued for censorship. The second, D.H. Lawrence's Pornography and Obscenity, argued against it. This was Forster's opportunity to show up the idiocy of a bureaucratic conception of social order as against the visionary conception of the artist. Brentford, Forster declares, does not dare to define indecency because "from his point of view, to define filth is to advertise it" (76) and his reader is left to discover by inference that all sex is sinful except within marriage. In contrast, Lawrence can see that indecency lies not in sex, but in the effort to suppress it, and that censorship is a cause, not a consequence of sex being considered indecent. Forster's own solution is practical rather than passionate. He asks for tolerance, a recognition by the government that people are all different and must be free to express themselves and read what they wish.

Over the thirties and forties Forster was similarly involved in other skirmishes in his battle for art against social order. In 1931 the B.B.C. suppressed a radio play produced by Day Lewis called Krassin Saves Italia in which a Russian ice-breaker rescues General Nobile's polar expedition. Forster pointed out in an article the stupidity of suppressing a literary work merely because it showed a communist ship achieving something heroic. (77) In 1935 he addressed an International Congress of Writers in Paris with his 'Liberty in England', which argues for the liberty of free speech. His 1944 address to a P.E.N. conference on Milton's Areopagitica is a variation on the same theme. Forster's involvement with the N.C.C.L. was also mainly to work for creative freedom, and when in 1935 James Hanley's homosexual novel Boy was condemned as obscene, he campaigned with the N.C.C.L. for a change in the law. Another law, the law of libel, had forced Forster to withdraw his article 'A Flood in the Office' from Abinger Harvest, and during 1939 he served on a government committee to reform this law. (78)

Forster's aesthetics, which sees the artist as an outsider but also as a legislator in society, is thus a courageous and level-headed effort to harmonize ivory towers and industrial landscapes, to quietly 'connect' art and life while defining them as distinct from each other. Forster clings tenaciously to the simple idea that just as the individual is allowed a private life in society, the autonomous world of art must coexist with social order. This may not have been anything wonderfully new or brilliant, but it saved Forster equally from retreat and isolation in the world of art (like Clive Bell), as well as from desperate and misplaced self-identification with public causes (like the Auden group). By remaining true to himself and simultaneously helping to improve his society, Forster managed to fulfil as an individual what he always considered to be the true function of art.

VI

Forster's view of art can be traced all the way back to Kant's aesthetics, which forms one of the major sources of Romanticism. Kant says that the aesthetic realm is entirely separable from science, morality and utility. He defines aesthetic pleasure as 'disinterested satisfaction' and by this he does not mean (says René Wellek) "some kind of art for art's sake doctrine. 'Disinterested' to Kant means the lack of interference from desire, the directness of our access to the work of art, undisturbed, uninterfered with ... by immediate utilitarian ends. Kant in no way denies the enormous role of art in society ... He merely wants to distinguish (it) from morality, pleasure, truth and utility. If art is simply pleasure, communication, experience, or inferior reasoning, it ceases to be art and becomes a substitute for something else." (79) By the end of the nineteenth century aesthetic theory had based itself on the two assumptions implicit in Kant's view - first that art possesses an extra-societal and transcendent order of its own, and second that art exercises a moral and intellectual influence within society by preserving and developing the spiritual self and the 'human' faculties. When too much emphasis was put upon art as something transcendent and exalted it led towards 'decadence' and 'aestheticism'. Conversely, when all the emphasis fell upon the efficacy of art in human life or society it led towards 'moralism'. "In Mallarmé", Wellek writes, "poetry absorbs all reality and becomes the only reality; in Zola and Tolstoy and many others, art is identified with life and becomes superfluous and finally useless. Clearly the task of a new era would be a reassertion of the balance, a recognition of the independence and autonomy of art, but also of its meaningful relation to the reality of nature, man and society." (80) A patchy synthesis of both these assumptions may be discerned in late nineteenth century critical theory (81) and is given its most balanced expression by A.C. Bradley's 'Poetry for Poetry's Sake'. Following the example of Bradley, Forster picks up and interweaves the two strands of traditional aesthetic theory and presents a formalism tempered with moral concern. His belief in art for its own sake cannot be seen in isolation for it is tied up with his concern for human values and the future of civilization. In this respect Forster advocates neither aestheticism nor moralism, but an eclectic blend which extracts the best from both contraries. By mediating between the definition of art as something precious and uncontaminated by life,and the orthodox moral defense of art in the tradition of the Romantic poets, Arnold and Leavis, Forster helps to reassert a balanced view of the nature of art and its relation to life.

NOTES

(1) 'On Criticism in the Arts, Especially Music', Harper's Magazine, July 1947, vol. 195, pp.9-17 (p.10). Rpt. (revised) as 'The Raison d'Etre of Criticism', TCD (p.106).
(2) ibid. (p.113).
(3) 'Inspiration', Author, July 1912, vol. 22, pp. 281-2 (p.281). Forster's belief in inspiration was founded on personal experience. See Furbank I, p.92; also Furbank's introduction to Maurice (1971; rpt. Harmondsworth: Penguin Books, 1977) p.7.
(4) 'Writers at Bay', Spectator, 21 May 1932, p.724.
(5) 'Raison', TCD (p.111).
(6) See Proceedings of the Society for Psychical Research, August 1911, vol. 25, pp. 455-67. Forster mentions this paper in GLD, p.101. A fuller account of Lowes Dickinson's view of the subconscious origins of art occurs in his After 2000 Years: A Dialogue Between Plato and a Modern Young Man (London: Allen & Unwin, 1930) pp. 176-82.
(7) 'A Camera Man', Life and Letters, May 1929, vol. 2, no. 12, pp. 336-43 (p.342). Rpt. as 'Sinclair Lewis', AH, (p.149).
(8) 'Ancient and Modern', The Listener, 11 November 1936, pp. 921-2 (p.921).
(9) King's College Ms., titled 'Miscellaneous', p.64. These are lecture notes, not fully written lectures, and therefore the syntax is

often elliptical.
(10) 'Raison', TCD (p.111).
(11) 'Recollectionism', New Statesman and Nation, 13 March 1937, pp. 405-6 (p.405).
(12) Proust (London: Hogarth, 1928) p. 38. Forster's review is 'Our Curiosity and Despair', New York Herald Tribune, 21 April 1929, Section II, Books, pp 1,6. Bergson's notion of involuntary memory is discussed more thoroughly in relation with Forster's idea of 'rhythm' in the next chapter.
(13) Frieda Fordham, An Introduction to Jung's Psychology (1953; rpt. Harmondsworth: Penguin Books, 1974) p.27.
(14) John Livingston Lowes, The Road to Xanadu: A Study in the Ways of the Imagination (London: Constable & Co., 1927) p.32.
(15) The Nature of Beauty in Art and Literature (London: Hogarth, 1927) p. 58.
(16) 'Art History as an Academic Study', Last Lectures, ed. Kenneth Clark (Cambridge: Cambridge Univ. Press, 1939) pp. 1-21 (p.13).
(17) Aspects of the Novel and related writings, Abinger edition, ed. O. Stallybrass (London: Edward Arnold, 1974) p.13.
(18) 'Anonymity: An Enquiry', Calender of Modern Letters, November 1925, vol. 2, pp. 145-56 (pp. 151-2) Rpt. (revised) in TCD (pp. 82-3).
(19) Forster took down extracts from 'Tradition and the Individual Talent' while preparing his 'Creator as Critic' lectures. See CB, p.63.
(20) 'Anonymity', TCD (pp.82, 84).
(21) The Listener, 30 April 1942, pp. 565-6 (p.565). Rpt. TCD (p.96).
(22) Aspects, p.38.
(23) 'The Claims of Art', The Listener, 30 December 1943, pp. 742-3 (p. 743).
(24) ibid. (p.743). Clark's view is also quoted in The New Disorder, p.11.
(25) 'An Approach to Blake', Spectator, 2 April 1932 p.474 (p.474). One of J.B. Beer's remarks about Blake is helpful in this context: "The paradox is that for Blake the 'genius' that is in every man and is therefore eternal and universal also makes each man unique. When he thought about social and political questions it was the eternal man that was most present to him ... In the end, however, he returned to the individual artist as the one man who could express his 'genius' and so awaken the 'genius' of other men." Blake's Humanism (Manchester:

Manchester Univ. Press, 1968) p.15.
(26) 'The Philosophy of Composition' in The Complete Works of Edgar Allan Poe, Essays and Miscellanies, ed. J.A. Harrison (New York: AMS Press, 1965) vol.XIV, p.197. Quoted in The Mirror and the Lamp, p.137.
(27) 'Anonymity', TCD (pp.80-1).
(28) 'The Enjoyment of English Literature', a paper read at Government College, Lahore, on 3 March 1913, King's College Ms., vol. 15, pp. 118-29 (pp. 128-9).
(29) 'Anonymity', TCD (pp.77-8).
(30) ibid. (pp.78-9, 81).
(31) ibid. (p.81).
(32) 'The World Mountain', (p.978).
(33) 'Art for Art's Sake', Harper's Magazine, August 1949, vol. 199, pp. 31-4 (p.34). Rpt. (revised) in TCD (p.92).
(34) Biographia Literaria: Or Biographical Sketches of My Literary Life and Opinions (1817), ed. George Watson (London: Dent, 1975) p.174. Quoted in The Mirror and the Lamp, p.120.
(35) Rage for Order: Essays in Criticism (Chicago: Chicago Univ. Press, 1948) p.V. This branch of poetics has been discussed in 'The Poem as Heterocosm', The Mirror and the Lamp, pp. 272-5.
(36) Forster told William van O'Connor that J.K. Johnstone's The Bloomsbury Group (1954) was mistaken in tracing his views on aesthetics to Fry. See William Van O'Connor, 'A Visit With E.M. Forster', Western Review, Spring 1955 XIX, pp. 215-19.
(37) Oxford Lectures on Poetry (1909); rpt. London: Macmillan & Co., 1959) pp.3-34 (p.4).
(38) ibid. (p.5).
(39) 'Some Questions in Aesthetics', in Transformations: Critical and Speculative Essays on Art (London: Chatto and Windus, 1926) pp. 1-43 (p.8). In this context, G.E. Moore's view that personal affection and the appreciation of what is beautiful in art and nature are worth having 'purely for their own sakes', is of relevance. So is Lowes Dickinson's remark - "Art is a refuge from life, not a substitute for it; a little blessed island in the howling sea of fact." The Meaning of Good: A Dialogue, p.162. The origins of Forster's aesthetics have been discussed in The Cave and the Mountain, pp.101-6, and Donald Watt, 'G.E. Moore and the Bloomsbury Group', English Literature in Transition,

vol. 12, No.3, pp. 119-34.
(40) TCD (p.90).
(41) ibid. (p.88).
(42) ibid. (p.90).
(43) ibid. (p.92).
(44) See The Mirror and the Lamp, p.283. Another critic, Solomon Fishman, writes - "The phrase 'art for art's sake' is highly ambiguous; in the context of literary criticism it has acquired an almost totally pejorative connotation ... If it refers to aestheticism as a theory of the conduct of life, a mode of achieving perfection of the self by means of a balance of culture and feeling, it should be interpreted as meaning art for the sake of a highly specialized morality. In the narrower context of aesthetics, insofar as it specifies the ontology of art ... (it) implies that the work of art be apprehended and judged on its own terms rather than by extrinsic standards." The Interpretation of Art: Essays on the Art Criticism of John Ruskin, Walter Pater, Clive Bell, Roger Fry and Herbert Read (Berkeley: Univ. of California Press, 1963) p.47.
(45) 'Art for Art's Sake', TCD (p.87).
(46) Art (London: Chatto & Windus, 1914), p.8.
(47) 'Some Questions in Aesthetics', p.3, According to Howard Hannay, in Fry's aesthetics "the artistic values of colour and form are quite self-contained and without any reference to external interests. This is the dominant tendency in Roger Fry's thought and completely overshadows ... (another) tendency, which concerns the emotional significance of art." 'Roger Fry's Theory of Art', Roger Fry and other essays (London: Allen and Unwin, 1937) pp. 15-51 (pp.17-8).
(48) Chapters 2 and 10 of Richards's book refute the notion that aesthetic experience is entirely different from every other. Fry's idea of the novel is discussed in my next chapter.
(49) This has been dated c.1911-12 by Elizabeth Heine in her Introduction to Arctic Summer and other fiction (London: Edward Arnold 1980) p.XVI.
(50) 'Fragments' in Kings College Ms. A letter from Forster to Lowes Dickinson dated 12 May 1907 is also relevant in this context: "All I write is to me, sentimental. A book which doesn't leave people either happier or better than it found them, which doesn't add some permanent treasure

to its world, isn't worth doing ... This is my 'theory', and I maintain it's sentimental - at all events it isn't Flaubert's" <u>King's College Letters</u>.
(51) <u>Oxford Lectures on Poetry</u>, p.9. Maud Bodkin points out that Bradley's essay, at this point, anticipates Jung's view that great literature contains archetypal themes which are inherently and eternally significant for human beings. See <u>Archetypal Patterns in Poetry - Psychological Studies of Imagination</u> (London: Oxford Univ. Press, 1934) p.5.
(52) 'Robinson Crusoe', <u>The Common Reader</u>, 2nd series (London: Hogarth, 1932) pp. 51-8 (pp. 54, 56).
(53) ibid. (pp. 54, 58).
(54) CB, p. 25. Rpt. in Appendix 'A', <u>Aspects</u>, pp. 121-37 (p.128).
(55) <u>The Greek View of Life</u> (1896; rpt. London: Methuen, 1957) p.207.
(56) Harry Kemp and Laura Riding point out that the term 'Romantic' suffered a degeneration of meaning in the thirties by being associated with 'bourgeois', 'ivory tower' and 'socially irresponsible'. It was forgotten that "The romantic poet was the 'exile' from society ... in the special sense that the world created by his writing was the world of the future - the world in which his interests as a poet would be identical with his interests as a social being." <u>The Left Heresy</u>, p.54.
(57) 'Anonymity', TCD (p.83). A nearly identical statement occurs in 'The Raison d'Etre of Criticism' - "We are rapt into a region near to where the artist worked, and like him, when we return to earth we feel surprised." (TCD.p.113). This matches with Fry's idea of aesthetic response - "(There is) the consciousness of a peculiar relation of sympathy with the man who made this thing in order to arouse precisely the sensations we experience ... We feel he has expressed something which was latent in us all the time, but which we never realized, that he has revealed us to ourselves in revealing himself." See 'An Essay in Aesthetics' (1909), in <u>Vision and Design</u> (London: Chatto & Windus, 1920) pp. 11-35 (pp.29-30).
(58) 'Criticism of Life' in 'The Creator as Critic' series, <u>King's College Ms. - Miscellaneous</u>, pp. 62-113 (pp. 104-5).
(59) <u>Matthew Arnold</u>, (New York : Norton & Co., 1939)

pp. 152-3.
(60) Working Men's College Journal, March 1915, vol. 14, pp.57-61. Rpt. in E.M. Forster, Albergo Empedocle and other writings, ed. George Thomson (New York: Liveright, 1971), pp.176-83 (p.179).
(61) ibid. (p.179).
(62) ibid. (p.180). Arnold says that "culture hates hatred" in Culture and Anarchy (p.11). Lowes Dickinson says this about his A Modern Symposium - "the object of such a book as mine, as it was Plato's object long ago, is to raise the mind above the fighting attitude." The Autobiography of Goldsworthy Lowes Dickinson and other unpublished writings ed. Dennis Proctor (London: Duckworth, 1973) p.171.
(63) Thomson, (pp.181-2).
(64) 'Notes on the Way', Time and Tide, 9 June 1934, pp.723-4 (p.723). Rpt. as 'A Note on the Way', AH (pp.86-7).
(65) 'Reading as Usual', The Listener, 21 September 1939, pp. 586-7 (pp. 586-7).
(66) 'Does Culture Matter', TCD (p.104).
(67) 'The Claims of Art', The Listener, 30 December 1943, pp. 742-3 (p.743).
(68) ibid. (p.742).
(69) 'Does Culture Matter', TCD (pp. 102-3).
(70) ibid. (p.104).
(71) In Mass Civilization and Minority Culture (Cambridge: Minority Press, 1930) and Fiction and the Reading Public (op.cit.).
(72) 'Does Culture Matter', TCD (p.101).
(73) ibid. (p.100).
(74) TCD (p.97). This roughly repeats J.S. Mill's view that "Persons of genius are, ex vi termini, more individual than any other people - less capable, consequently, of fitting themselves, without hurtful compression, into any of the smaller number of moulds which society provides in order to save its members the trouble of forming their own characters." On Liberty, pp. 129-30.
(75) 'The Censorship of Books', Nineteenth Century and After, April 1929. Vol. 105, pp. 444-5 (p.444). This topic is also the subject of 'The New Censorship', Nation and Athenaeum, 1 September 1928, p.696. The Radclyffe Hall case is discussed in Furbank II, pp. 153-5 and in C.H. Rolph, Books in the Dock (London: Andre Deutsch, 1969) pp. 76-80.
(76) 'Mr. D.H. Lawrence and Lord Brentford', Nation

and Athenaeum, 11 January 1930, pp. 508-9 (p. 508).
(77) 'The Freedom of the B.B.C.', New Statesman and Nation, 4 April 1931, pp. 209-10.
(78) This aspect of Forster's career has been discussed in Furbank II, pp. 191, 211, and passim.
(79) 'Kant & Schiller' in A History of Modern Criticism (London: Cape, 1955), vol. I, pp. 227-55 (pp. 229-31). Stephen Korner, whose Kant offers an introductory account of Kant's philosophy, writes that Forster's essay 'Art For Art's Sake' can be read as a simplified version of Kant's aesthetics. See Kant (1955; rpt. Harmondsworth: Penguin Books, 1974) pp. 185-6.
(80) 'Stephane Mallarmé', in A History of Modern Criticism (1965; rpt. London: Cape, 1966), vol. IV, pp. 452-63 (p.463).
(81) An excellent account of the unification of decadent aestheticism and moral humanism in the work of Pater, Symons, Lionel Johnson, Henry James and Yeats exists in Brijraj Singh, The Development of a Critical Tradition: From Pater to Yeats (Delhi: Macmillan and Co., 1978).

CHAPTER FIVE

FORSTER'S VIEW OF THE NOVEL

Forster's perception of the tendency in words to veer from a purely material function towards forms that are autonomous and spiritual - from 'information' to 'atmosphere' - indicates that like the Romantics he grafts a neo-Platonic cosmology on to an aesthetic scheme. Forster believes that art becomes more and more sublimely spiritual as it moves from a direct to a remote or fantastic or non-representational rendering of reality, as it conveys a power that is unseen behind the facts that are seen. Art becomes increasingly profound, he suggests, when simple representation of outer life is replaced by the ability to reveal the inner energy of living things. He values art less as a reflection of life than as a medium which sees into the life of things - or, to borrow a metaphor made famous by Abrams - he prefers art which possesses the incandescence of a lamp above art which is a realistic mirror of life. He seems to agree with Gauguin's view which he paraphrases in one of his book reviews - "(Creation) leads away from the realistic imitation of nature: if the picture bears the impress of the supreme moment (of inspiration) all is well, and the distortion justified." (1) The most sublime aesthetic form in this kind of hierarchy is, naturally, music. In Romantic criticism by and large, says Abrams -

> In place of painting, music becomes the art frequently pointed to as having a profound affinity with poetry. For if a picture seems the nearest thing to a mirror image of the external world, music, of all the arts, is the most remote ... it does not duplicate aspects of sensible nature, nor can it be said, in any obvious sense, to refer to any state of affairs

123

> outside itself ... Music, wrote Wackenroder, 'shows us all the movements of our spirit disembodied.' (2)

After William James's <u>Principles of Psychology</u> (1890) which described consciousness as a stream of thought, Freud's demonstration that the unconscious is a continuum of free association unmodified by logical thought, the recognition by Mallarmé and the French Symbolist poets of the intricate synthesis of music, poetry and drama in Wagner's operas, and Bergson's assertion that the artist is the flag-bearer of superior intuition against inferior logic and reason, there came about a revival of interest in the Romantic belief that music is the most spiritual and therefore the most superior form of art. (3) Bergson himself considered music the most exalted art, and Virginia Woolf, Aldous Huxley, Proust and Forster recognized that fiction might achieve a new intensity by adopting some of the techniques of music. Forster himself feels that "music is the deepest of the arts and deep beneath the arts" (4) and he places the other genres on successive rungs below music. Lyric poetry, which is musical and of "absolutely no use ... it conveys no information of any kind" (5) comes a close second. Beneath the lyric there is poetic drama in which "uselessness still predominates", followed by the novel - this being more 'useful' than music and poetry inasmuch as it records information. With journalism and the social sciences the aesthetic element decreases until with timetables it disappears entirely.

This generic hierarchy, however, is only a broad indication of values and is not meant to be taken too literally. What Forster enjoys may be at variance with his aesthetic scheme. All music is not automatically better than all poetry, nor all lyric poetry better than all novels. In fact Forster slightly prefers the mixed art of fiction. <u>Moby Dick</u> is less 'useless' than most ballads, but is greater as a work of art than most ballads. Joyce and Virginia Woolf are more atmospheric than Jane Austen and Fielding, but Forster prefers Fielding and Austen. Nor does Forster's inter-generic definition of all art as one kind of order imply that he does not distinguish between genres. On the contrary, while Forster wants each genre to aspire beyond its generic limits towards the spiritual condition of music, he can also see that each genre has some qualities appropriate only to itself. He writes that -

FORSTER'S VIEW OF THE NOVEL

> The play - that's going to be acted, so certain conventions are imposed upon it ... The lyric poem - that is of the nature of a song, and it will tend to express one main emotion. The short story - that has the same medium as the novel, but it is short, and so it must calculate beforehand what effect it wants to produce, and produce it or fail. The novel, in my view, has not any rules ... (6)

<u>Aspects</u> shows that the novel does indeed adhere to a few basic rules, but that the novelist is freer to order his art in the way he wants than the dramatist, the poet or the short story writer. Forster believes that this freedom can enable the novelist to elevate the art of fiction from its traditional commitment to social representation towards something like the spiritual revelation achieved by music. He argues in <u>Aspects</u> that the novel, with its roots in 'information', can approximate towards the 'atmosphere' and spiritual intensity of music.

Forster's view of music is of particular relevance to his concept of the novel, and even the little that he wrote about music helps in an understanding of <u>Aspects</u>. In 'How I Listen to Music' (1939) Forster says he hears music in two ways. In the first instance the notes of music, like the words of a novel, appear to be referential for they remind him of things other than the music. Wagner's music, in particular, conjures up real life associations because his musical phrases are closely connected to the themes of his operas. This gives Wagner's music a non-musical meaning. Forster does not mind this because "Only a purist would condemn all visual parallels, all emotional labellings, all programmes." (7) But Forster also hears musical notes as autonomous and non-referential and prefers music when it does not remind him of the world outside it - "... music which is untrammelled and untainted by reference is obviously the best sort of music to listen to: we get nearer the centre of reality. Yet though it is untainted it is never abstract: it is not like mathematics, even when it uses them." (8) In 'The Raison d'Etre of Criticism' he says that music is the only art form which exists simultaneously at two levels - within time and outside time, developing like history and transcendent like art - "I can conceive myself hearing a piece as it goes by and also when it has finished. In the latter case I should hear it as an entity, as a piece of sound architecture, not as a sound sequence, not as something divisible into bars." (9) To hear music not only within time but also outside time is to hear it not so much with the ears as with the spirit, and leads one to ask why it is that music, more than painting or architecture or the plastic arts, has such an intensely spiritual appeal. Forster's criticism offers two answers to this. First that as the only art form which does not mirror reality, music is wholly 'useless', as well as more completely spiritual (or 'atmospheric') and autonomous than anything else in life. The second reason is connected to the first. Because music does not refer to anything outside itself, it appeals with greater directness than the other arts to the subconscious, spiritual self of man. This seems to Forster to be evident from the fact that the pleasure obtained from music does not involve rationality or understanding or conscious thought. Whereas the pleasure from painting or sculpture presupposes knowledge and understanding of the things in the real world of which these are idealised representations, music is apprehended entirely intuitively. This also happens, in Forster's view, because though the notes of music are connected sequentially, music minimizes temporal sequence. The regular pulsation of time and the logic of the rational mind are replaced in music by an irregular rhythm and an illogical order which only the human spirit can apprehend. There are three interesting notations which vaguely define Forster's meaning. In his notes for **Aspects** Forster says - "... this pretence of a time sense may be common to the whole of literature and may be implied when one word is written after another. Yet it is **NOT** implied in music, nor in words under their musical aspect: these have nothing to do with the time sequence of ordinary life." (10) He also transcribes this remark from Thomas Mann's **The Magic Mountain** into his **Commonplace Book** - "Music's peculiarly life enhancing method of measuring time imparts a spiritual awareness and value to its passage. Music quickens time, she quickens us to the finest enjoyment of time." (11) Music is heard in time - it cannot be otherwise - but Forster believes its peculiarity as an art form is that it seems to enable the listener to transcend existence in time. The third comment runs - "There's an insistence in music, expressed largely through rhythm; there's a sense that it is trying to push across at us something which is neither an aesthetic pattern nor a sermon. That's what I listen for specially." (12) The notion that musical rhythm is something spiritual which transcends an aesthetic pattern is important for an understanding of 'pattern' and 'rhythm' in Aspects. It is a notion that is not adequately defined by Forster himself, but is was by Charles Mauron. Mauron criticized Fry's use of the term 'relations' to define art because he felt that "it at once suggests the idea of a numerical connection where numerical connections are irrelevant ... who will calculate the relation between the different musical variations of a single theme? Even if it could be calculated, how shall we explain why this number and no other, has so remarkable an effect?" (13) In place of a specific pattern or definable relations between parts, Mauron said that aesthetic response is to "the unexplained harmony in a work of art" (which) hangs on correspondences felt in their entirety ... the work should convey an impression, even though vague, of a reality richer in unforeseen correspondences than the ordinary world." (14) This, as the later discussion will clarify, is reasonably close to Forster's notion of how 'rhythm' can enhance the beauty of a novel. The kind of order towards which Forster would like fiction to approximate is, however, best defined by Wagner. Wagner believed that music at its best possesses a structure which enables the sensitive listener to achieve a mystic glimpse of a deeper spiritual reality. His own effort was to achieve through opera that zenith which he felt had been attained within the symphonic form by Beethoven. In a Beethoven symphony, Wagner writes ...

> ... with a hitherto unknown persistence, the purely musical expression enchains the hearer in an inconceivably varied mesh of nuances; rouses his utmost being to a degree unreachable by any other art; and in all its changefulness reveals an ordering principle so free and bold that we can but deem it more forcible than any logic ... So that this symphony must positively appear to us as a revelation from another world ... (it) guides our feeling with such a sureness that the logic mongering reason is completely routed and disarmed thereby. (15)

Though seemingly illogical because of the immense complexity with which themes are developed and related to each other, music is ordered in a way which only the spirit can follow. Forster wants fiction to be roughly what Wagner saw in a Beethoven symphony. By minimizing the time-sense of everyday existence and the patterns and plots of the conscious mind, the novelist might approach the higher fusion which music alone can fully achieve. Forster suggests that by emulating the complex and illogical structure of music, fiction may be elevated from its roots in 'information' and social representation into something which appeals to man's highest, spiritual faculties.

As a theory of fiction this represents a reaction against the 'realism' of Zola, Balzac and Flaubert. In England 'realism' is associated with the novels of Wells, Bennett and Galsworthy. Forster's dissatisfaction with the realist school is part of a general current of feeling which was one reason that caused Lawrence to write poetic and unsystematic novels like those of Hardy, and led Virginia Woolf to criticize the preoccupation with social rather than inner life in Edwardian fiction. (16) While Virginia Woolf and Forster differ over the ideal structure of the novel, both they and Lawrence give a new emphasis to psychological and spiritual representation in fiction. 'Plot' of the conventional sort is disparaged by all three. "Tell Arnold Bennett that all rules of construction hold good only for novels which are copies of other novels" says Lawrence in one of his letters. (17) A less deliberate, less discernible unity achieved through imagery, poetic intensity in the writing and the author's personal vision of life are thought more desirable than the traditional fictional order achieved through neat plot construction.

In Forster's case, however, the stress that fiction should aspire towards a musical order is also a reaction against the reliance on dramatic techniques by Henry James and his propagandists - Ford Madox Ford, Joseph Warren Beach, and most importantly, Percy Lubbock. (18) James was an admirer of Flaubert and was influenced by the 'dramatic' method of telling the story in Madame Bovary. This was one of the reasons why he tried to make his own fiction more dramatic. Broadly speaking this entailed cleansing fiction of its external, intrusive narrator. James felt that if someone within the fictional universe could be made the central consciousness through which all events were mediated, the novel would become autonomous and self-contained. Simultaneously, such a dramatization of events through a central consciousness would serve as an ordering principle, for everything within the novel would be seen from a consistent point of view.

FORSTER'S VIEW OF THE NOVEL

However, while James used this principle to great success in his own fiction, he himself was not dogmatic about the way in which fiction could achieve a unity of form. In 'The Art of Fiction' (1884) he says that "The only obligation to which in advance we may hold a novel, without incurring the accusation of being arbitrary, is that it be interesting ... The ways in which it is at liberty to achieve this result strike me as innumerable, and such as can only suffer from being marked out or fenced in by prescription." (19) James's advocate Percy Lubbock, however, is concerned precisely with prescribing the sole method - the dramatic method developed by James - by which fiction can become a work of art. Wayne Booth correctly observes that Lubbock reduces "James's treatment of dozens of literary problems ... to the one thing needful: a novel should be made dramatic ... a scheme that James can be made to support, but in James's account it is surrounded with important qualifications which in Lubbock are already beginning to be slighted."(20) The fundamental problem which all novelists must solve if they wish to succeed, says Lubbock, is how to "make the mind and the eye objective, to make them facts in the story. When the point of view is definitely included in the book, when it can be recognized and verified there, then every side of the book is equally wrought and fashioned." (21) Lubbock's theoretical restrictions upon fiction are admirable enough when they try to free the novel from its discursive imperfections, its habit of speaking chattily to the reader, but they also rule out variety and individuality. James is used inflexibly as a model against which other novelists are measured. One of the novelists who does not measure up to the Jamesian standard is Tolstoy. Lubbock feels that <u>War and Peace</u> is too loose and undramatic, and therefore less perfect as a work of art than it would have been had Tolstoy presented his action from an unvarying point of view. (22)

Forster's general argument for a musical rather than a dramatic aesthetic of fiction and his specific use of <u>War and Peace</u> as the greatest example of a vast, discursive, undramatic and musically ordered novel are a refutation of Lubbock's idealization of James's fictional method. Always sceptical of theory, Forster disputes Lubbock's aprioristic idea of good method because he feels that the only true method of evaluating fiction is empirically, by one's enjoyment of it: "...for me the whole intricate question of method resolves itself not into formulae but into the power of the writer to bounce the reader into accepting what he says ... All that matters to the reader is whether the shifting of attitude and the secret life are convincing." (23) If anything, it is the shifting perspective that is more likely to bring about a suspension of disbelief, for "We are stupider at some times than others; we can enter into people's minds occasionally but not always ... this intermittance lends in the long run variety and colour to the experiences we receive." (24) Lubbock's view that the novel becomes art only when an unvarying perspective has been perfected seems to Forster to make vitality and intensity of life subsidiary to shape and architecture. This is virtually a separation of form from content, for a novel judged by such a criterion may be dead and yet perfect. "The novelist who betrays too much interest in his own method can never be more than interesting: he has given up the creation of character and summoned us to help analyse his own mind, and a heavy drop in the emotional thermometer results"(25) - is Forster's view. For him the form of the novel is perfect, regardless of the novelist's method, when the novel communicates a world which is felt to be 'alive' and 'real' by the reader.

Consequently, in <u>Aspects</u> the novel is continually being dissociated from drama and compared to music. Forster feels that dramatic rules limit the scope of what the novel can achieve. A play has to be performed before an audience and must therefore conform to the Aristotelian stricture about the supremacy of action or plot over character. Action is the dramatist's only means of revealing character, and since the inner life of characters cannot be communicated with the depth and detail possible in a novel, the dramatist cannot be "so deeply committed to the claims of human beings." (26) The play must have a beginning, middle and end, a logical structure within which character is defined, but also in a sense, confined. A play cannot give pleasure if the plot is abandoned for a time and attention focussed on the thought processes of a particular character. This ultimate necessity of an overriding plot makes the drama less desirable as an ideal for fiction than music. Only a symphony permits themes to appear, disappear and then reappear almost at random, creating a structure which is at once vast, loose, spiritual and ordered. In Forster's conception it is this kind of musical structure, rather than the drama, which offers the novelist the possibility of a complete commitment to the claims of his characters, and allows him to create in fiction a world which is unfettered by preconceived ideas of form.

With these general assumptions about music, Forster's separation in *Aspects* of the formal properties of the novel into a hierarchy which ascends from story (which is time bound and rooted in the basely material world) towards rhythm and prophecy (which are spiritual and transcend time) becomes clearer. While *Aspects* is valuable for its discussion of various novelists, it is even more significant for its theoretical argument about the possibilities of fiction and for its insights into the narrative techniques which transform simple stories into complex, aesthetically pleasing fictions. In fact Forster's chief concern is to determine and define those formal aspects within the novel which make it a transcendent work of art, and not with novels or novelists *per se*. The latter serve really to illustrate Forster's theory of how fiction can approximate towards the intensity of music. Like his criticism of society and religion, Forster's criticism of fiction in *Aspects* seems ultimately directed towards a search for a more perfect kind of order - the perfect order which can exist within the universe of a fictional work. My discussion of the substance of *Aspects* will show that Forster conceives of the novel as a work which should be capacious enough to encompass the multiplicity of life, expansive yet intricately ordered like a symphony with many themes, and like music, something which may be capable of giving intimations of the spiritual energy which exists in the universe.

II

In the Introduction to *Aspects* Forster says his analysis of the novel will be ahistorical because his concern is not with the facts and personalities connected with the novel, but with the nature of its form. Personality and fact are located in time, whereas the various aspects of the novel form, like certain aspects of human nature (with which they are closely connected by Forster) are unchanging. This method of analysis is similar to that adopted by Shelley in 'A Defense of Poetry', and the neo-Platonic premise of this procedure is explained by Abrams's remarks on Shelley's 'Defense' - "... according to this outlook, the poetry of every age... reapproximates the same unaltering pattern. In Shelley's essay therefore, all the greatest single poems lose their particular locations in time and place, lose even their identity, and are viewed as though they were fundamentally simultaneous and inter-convertible." (27) Forster's basic premise is, therefore, that the novel possesses certain transcendent formal properties. His task is to isolate, analyse and evaluate these properties.

Secondly, Forster says that novels will not be classified by their subjects or points of view, because "...the novel's success lies in its own sensitiveness, not in the success of its subject matter." (28) This opposition to novel criticism which discusses the subject rather than the form is an attack upon Clayton Hamilton's <u>Materials and Methods of Fiction</u> (1909). Both Forster and Virginia Woolf were scathing in their criticism of Hamilton's book. Woolf said it was a book which tried to show that "every work of art can be taken to pieces, and those pieces can be named and numbered, divided and subdivided, and given their order of precedence, like the internal organs of a frog." (29) Forster similarly ridiculed the effort to anatomize and define fiction with pseudo-scientific expertise. His own analysis, he stresses, is not with the intention of dissecting fiction and naming each part as it is disclosed by the scalpel. It is undertaken to determine the value of each of the various attributes of the novel form in transforming ordinary life subjects into art. For Hamilton 'plot' is simply a category under which various novels can be listed. To Forster 'plot' indicates that the novelist who uses it is more intelligent than one who tells a story but less sensitive than the novelist who uses pattern and rhythm. Hamilton's categories are scientific, while the categories of <u>Aspects</u> are evaluative and form a sort of neo-Platonic aesthetic ladder beginning in matter (story) and terminating in the realm of intense spiritual awareness (prophecy).

Story is the element in the novel which is purely informative, referential, non-atmospheric and time bound. A story moves monotonously forward like the regular pulsation of time to an 'and then', 'and then' beat - as opposed to 'rhythm' which pleases because it is irregular and unexpected. It is, therefore, a purely mechanical, sequential, unmusical and shapeless order of facts or events. It merely shows 'what happens next' in time without pausing to reflect upon the significance of what happens, and without ordering what happens into a trans-temporal structure like music. Story is all matter and no art, for it reflects the most quotidian aspect of life - the life in time - without conveying anything of the timelessness of "the life by values" - the intelligence or poignance or sublimity whichconstitute the more eternal elements of existence.

This complete disentanglement of the story from all the other aspects of fiction such as plot and character (which are deeply embedded in the story) seems extreme (30) but the extrication is credible and in fact necessary if one remembers that <u>Aspects</u> builds a scheme which is evaluative rather than scientific. 'Story' can be understood as separate from everything else within the novel if it is recognized that its appeal is merely to an unintelligent and brutish curiosity, and not to the rational or reflective or emotional self. It is the caveman's art and implies a shallow audience. This notion of a correspondence between social ascent from a barbaric to a civilized state on the one hand and on the other an aesthetic hierarchy which begins in story and concludes with impassioned utterance is another feature which links Forster with the liberalism of J.S.Mill. Mill's well known essay 'What Is Poetry' evaluates literature by an affective method, connecting childhood and primitive society with interest in the outer life of incident, and civilized living with a more developed aesthetic sensibility which responds to the inner life of feeling and thought. (31) This is precisely why Forster distinguishes story from its finer outgrowths.

Like Plotinus who values the realm of spirit more than material existence but who also recognizes that earthly life is a means towards a spiritual goal, Forster is both an idealist who attaches immense importance to the spiritual self and a realist who knows that material life offers the only possibility of apprehending spirit. This mixture of idealism and humanistic realism is manifest, in this context, in the fact that while Forster denigrates story as base and time-bound, he also accepts that story is a necessary step up his Platonic aesthetic ladder. He knows that the human condition is time bound and cannot be entirely transcended, and correspondingly, he feels that if the novel tries to do away with story, an essential element of form would be lost and "the novel that would express values becomes unintelligible and valueless." (32) The experiments of Gertrude Stein to create fiction with words which do not connect logically with each other seem to him to be laudable but doomed, because fiction only gains aesthetic and spiritual value when it uses but moves vertically away from this prerequisite towards the transcendent dimension of music.

The first vertical offshoot from story into the dimension of values occurs when the novelist transfers interest from mere incident to the life of the people he creates. People exist in time as well, but less so than stories because they possess an inner life and are autonomous, uniquely ordered beings. The novelist's interest in people rather than sequences of events indicates a progress from that which appeals to a semi-bestial herd of primitives to that which stimulates a more human and civilized interest - from a sort of pure materialism (story) towards a materialism tempered with something spiritual (the human personality). The storyteller is a historian of life, the delineator of character an artist who reveals something spiritual - "The historian deals with actions .... it is the function of the novelist to reveal the hidden life ... 'All human happiness and misery' says Aristotle 'take the form of action'. We know better. We believe that happiness and misery exist in the secret life, which each of us leads privately and to which (in his characters) the novelist has access." (33) Characters are more interesting in fiction than in history or real life because their spiritual lives have been disclosed. Forster ascribes the aesthetic value of character in fiction to the fact that while in life "perfect knowledge is an illusion ... in the novel we can know people perfectly ... fiction is truer than history because it goes beyond the evidence ... that is why novels, even when they are about wicked people, can solace us: they suggest a more comprehensible and thus a more manageable human race, they give us the illusion of perspicacity and of power." (34) If the success of characterization depends not upon the point of view from which character is seen but upon the ability to lay bare the soul of people, then a very close connection is being drawn between aesthetic value and the intensity and vitality with which human life is represented. Aesthetic value is not, in this case, determined so much by the shape of the novel or by the perfection of its system of internal relations, but by its capacity to reveal the ordinarily hidden spiritual dimension. Virginia Woolf correctly pointed out that this is, properly speaking, a 'humane' rather than an 'aesthetic' view of fiction since value is attached preeminently to vitality and intensity of life rather than to perfection of shape. (35) This, it will be seen, is underscored in Forster's notion of 'prophecy'.

The classification of the techniques of characterization into 'flat' and 'round' is a convenient method of separating the novelist who succeeds in penetrating beyond the surface life of his characters from the one who does not. 'Flat' corresponds with the outer life and the life in time, 'round' indicates the 'life by values' or spiritual existence. (36) Flat characters connect with story and primitive appeal. They are easily remembered because like the humorous 'types' of Elizabethan drama, they do not develop psychologically. In contrast, round characters are unpredictable because they are endowed with conflicting emotions and possess a unique identity. They have the semblance of being alive independent of their creator, they have depth and an inner existence. They are therefore preferable to flat characters. They appeal in other words to the more developed intelligence which recognizes the value of the inner life, and it seems clear that Forster's aesthetic of fiction corresponds in the stages of its development with those of human evolution from a flat mindlessness to an intelligent roundedness.

The second offshoot from story towards spiritual revelation is 'plot'. Plot is "the novel in its logical, intellectual aspect" and implies an intelligent audience alive to the causality of events.(37) The primitive business of listening and the more civilized act of sympathy for people is now complicated by the need for an enquiring mind which probes for causes and responds to a fabric of relationships. "A plot cannot be told to a gaping audience of cave-men or to a tyrannical sultan or to their modern descendant the movie public ... a plot demands intelligence and memory also." (38) The reader must observe each fictional event in two ways - "isolated, and related to the other facts that he has read on previous pages." (39) Memory locates each event in time, ranging back and forth to "rearrange and reconsider" each event and its cause, while intelligence perceives a network of cross-correspondences and significant relationships between events. Plot is an unfolding mystery, and to appreciate it requires "a suspension of the time sequence" for events are not merely perceived as a sequence, but in their totality as an interconnected system. Like interest in people, which implies concern with entities which are autonomous and have spiritual value, interest in plot indicates the capacity to appreciate something shapely and unique. The final impression of a good plot, says Forster,is of a complex and architectured whole, of "something aesthetically compact, something which might have been shown by the novelist straight away, only if he had shown it straight away it would never have become beautiful." (40)

However, the very fact that plot is something which the novelist can show straight away means that plot is a preconceived form into which people and events are fitted and inter-related, as in drama. Thus a tug of war between people and plot is inevitable. If the novelist concentrates too much attention upon revealing character, the action of his novel cannot proceed and the symmetry of his plot suffers. Conversely, if his major concern is symmetry of action, this will tend to deprive characters of their vitality. This is something of a recurrence in aesthetics of the social problem of accommodating the individual into a larger order while allowing him to be true to himself. In keeping with his preference for individualism above totalitarianism as the basis of social order, Forster's aesthetic of fiction strongly favours the novelist who can provide the feeling of intensely 'real' characters to the novelist who adroitly arranges events and people into clever constructions. The plot constructing novelist is seen by Forster as a sort of autocrat who compels his people to conform to a preconceived order. This is precisely Gide's point of view in his Les Faux Monnayeurs (1926), a novel which Forster admires because it fights free of the limitations of the traditional plot. It has been shown that "Of fundamental importance to his conception of form in the novel (Les Faux Monnayeurs) is Gide's rejection of any prior plan, any set mould into which the material has to be stuffed according to fixed patterns or rules ..." (41) Forster does not think Les Faux Monnayeurs a very successful novel, but he admires Gide's ideal of a less stringent plot and like Gide, feels that plot is undesirable when it is a mould into which living tissue appears to have been squeezed. The anarchy and illogic of life need no superimposition because Forster's premise is that to create life with sufficient intensity is itself to create aesthetic form. "... to pot with the plot! Break it up, boil it down... All that is prearranged is false" (42) he concludes, making clear his preference for novels organized by a poetic intensity of vision over those shaped by a theory of form.

'Pattern', which Forster leaves for his last chapter, ought logically to follow the discussion of plot because it is "an attempt to elevate the plot to Aristotelian symmetry". (43) Pattern represents the novel's movement in the direction of painting and architecture rather than music. It is at one level nothing more than the visual design of the plot, a more precise visual image of "the something aesthetically compact" which might have been shown straight away. Like the division between story and plot, the division between plot and pattern is mainly credible in affective terms - "story appeals to our curiosity ... plot to our intelligence, the pattern appeals to our aesthetic sense, it causes us to see the book as a whole." (44) But this is a crucial difference, for whereas plot is essentially the satisfactory solution to questions about the causality of events and their internal relations, pattern achieves something more vital - it suggests the idea of a whole which is greater than the sum of its parts. Pattern is Virginia Woolf's pot - an architectural symmetry which radiates an atmosphere. To put it differently, plot is an intelligible jumble which becomes an aesthetic pattern when its inner order becomes more distinct, or when its sequence of events also suggests a visual shape such as an hourglass or a chain. When this happens, there is in addition to intellectual satisfaction, the feeling that something beautiful has been created. But at the same time, pattern, like plot, must not be a mould into which living substance is poured. To succeed fully, it must be in the nature of a spiritual thread "woven out of their (the characters's) own substance" (45) - a form which radiates from within the content it encompasses.

However, Forster agrees with H.G. Wells that more often than not, pattern is achieved at the expense of vitality of characterization. Both writers had Henry James in mind when saying this. James constantly urged the need to give life in fiction a shaping form and prevent discursive looseness. In 'The Art of Fiction' he also compared fiction to painting, saying that "the analogy between the art of a painter and the art of the novelist is complete. Their inspiration is the same, their process (allowing for the different quality of the vehicle) is the same, their success is the same." (46) A very similar view appears in one of Fry's rare comments on the novel - "in the novel, which as a rule has pretensions to being a work of art, the structure may be so loose, the aesthetic effects may be produced by so vast an accumulation of items, that the temptation for the artist to turn aside from his purpose and interpolate criticisms of life, of manners or morals, is very strong. Comparatively few novelists have ever conceived of a novel as a single, perfectly organic, aesthetic whole." (47) Virginia Woolf, too, endorses the theory of fiction as painting. Both in the essay on <u>Robinson Crusoe</u>, and subsequently in 'The Narrow Bridge of Art' (1927) where she criticizes the "looseness and freedom" of <u>Tristram Shandy</u> and argues that the novelist should "bring to bear upon his tumultuous and contradictory emotions the generalizing and simplifying power of a strict and logical imagination" (48) - she suggests a theory influenced by Fry and Post-Impressionist art. This is the tendency, of which James is the focal point, attacked by Wells and Forster. In his essay 'The Contemporary Novel' (1911), Wells opposed James's theory of a controlling form in fiction when he said

> But the novel I hold to be a discursive thing: it is not a simple interest, but a woven tapestry of interests; one is drawn on first by this affection and curiosity, and then by that; it is something to return to, and I do not see that we can possibly set any limit to its extent ... I rejoice to see many signs today that the phase of narrowing and restriction is over, and there is every encouragement for a return towards a laxer, more spacious form of novel writing. (49)

In, <u>Boon</u>, James's pictorial theory of fiction is attacked even more violently - "James has never discovered that a novel isn't a picture ... That life isn't a studio ... He wants it (the novel) to have a unity, he demands homogeneity ... Why <u>should</u> a book have that? For a picture it's reasonable because you have to see it all at once. But there's no need to see a book all at once ..." (50) The fictional equivalent of a picture, in James's conception, was a play, and making a novel like a painting meant making it perfectly ordered and arranged like a play. Like Wells, Forster disagrees with this conception. His remark that "the novel is not capable of so much artistic development as the drama: its humanity or the grossness of the material hinder it" (51) - indicates his agreement with Wells on this specific issue.

FORSTER'S VIEW OF THE NOVEL

Forster's own view of pattern is ultimately ambivalent. He connects pattern with atmosphere and values its appeal to the aesthetic sensibility, but cannot sufficiently distance it from the idea of externally imposed order and a theoretical concern with form. "... the sensation from a pattern is not intense enough to justify the sacrifices that made it ..." (52) is his last word on the subject, as he moves on to discuss an aspect of the novel more vitally connected with the life within it, an aspect inaccessible to writers "who plan their books before hand ...". (53) This is a passage to the higher elements of fiction, "the vague and vast residue into which the subconscious enters. Poetry, religion, passion..." (54)

'Fantasy' can be seen as an alternative to plot and pattern. It is the novelist's way of saying 'to pot with the plot' and letting his fancy shape his novel entirely. The novelist abandons the logic of conscious life and presents a fictional universe which could not exist in reality. Truth to ordinary life, appeal to intelligence and realistic representation are discarded for a purely imaginative construction. Fantasists are divided into two categories, the comic and the satiric. Forster prefers comic fantasists because he feels fantasy is only suited to charm and gaiety. Fantasy re-orders the real world into a new imaginative synthesis, and is thus a movement away from the logic and divisions of social existence. In contrast, satire relates to specific social problems in the real world. A fantasy can only be appreciated if one ceases to ask logical questions, but satire is precisely an appeal to recognize the truth about reality. Satiric fantasy is thus a contradiction in terms, because the element of satire prevents any thorough immersion of the reader into the illogical world of fantasy. An example may make this clearer. Forster can be understood as saying that <u>Gulliver's Travels</u> is unsuccessful because the reader is continually being jerked back from the fantasy world to the real world by his recognition of events and characters that represent real events and characters. Swift's fantasy world does not,therefore, exist for its own sake and is incompletely autonomous. This assumption may help to explain why Forster does not enjoy satire and why he is so tepid about writers like Swift and Joyce. He feels that art and satire are somehow incompatible - "Indignation in literature never quite comes off either in Juvenal or Swift or Joyce; there is something in words that is alien to its simplicity."

(55) One method of assessing the aesthetic merit of a fantasy (on account of its remoteness from reality) is, in Forster's view, by seeing how completely criticism fails to understand it. Plot and pattern are explicable, but fantasy - and later 'prophecy' - are not easily understood because they appeal to the spirit rather than to the intellect. "A gulf between the critical and the creative states exists in all cases, but in the case of a fantastical creation it is so wide as to be grotesque", writes Forster in his essay on Ronald Firbank. (56) Another essay on Lewis Carroll similarly warns that analysis is futile when it tries to explain Alice in Wonderland because Carroll's "grace is unanalysable." (57)

An even better substitute of plot and pattern than fantasy is the use of 'rhythm' in fiction. The word 'rhythm', as it is used by Forster in Aspects, is synonymous with his notion of music. When fiction is rhythmically structured it approximates towards the sublime form of a symphony. Forster says that rhythm in fiction is noticed in two ways - as a separate, self-contained theme or a "little phrase (which) has a life of its own" (58) within the larger flow of the novel, and also as a larger indefinable entity which is recognized after the novel is over. In the first case rhythm denotes the sporadically recurring images, something like Wagner's operatic leitmotifs, which make the novel a loosely and musically (as opposed to rigorously and dramatically) cohesive structure. Little half-remembered phrases recur unexpectedly to give a reader the impression of a work that has "no external shape ... and yet ... hangs together because it is stitched internally." (59) The pleasure from a rhythmic structure is also greater than that from fiction with a controlling pattern because it is always unexpected. The beauty of rhythm is precisely "not to be there all the time like a pattern, but by its lovely waxing and waning to fill us with surprise and freshness and hope." (60) Forster noticed this technique in Proust's A La Recherche du Temps Perdu, where a little phrase from a sonata by the composer Vinteuil recurs at unexpected moments in the life of one of the protagonists (Swann) and gives him intimations of spiritual reality. Both in Aspects and in his two essays on Proust, Forster is full of praise for this use in fiction of the equivalent of the Wagnerian leitmotif system. (61) Proust himself has been shown to have derived the idea of this rhythmic technique from his teacher and distant relative Henri Bergson. Bergson distinguishes between two forms of memory - voluntary and involuntary. The first is an aspect of consciousness, a creature of reason and will. The second underlies its counterpart and Bergson says that "This spontaneous recollection, which is masked by the acquired recollection, may flash out at intervals." (62) Its ways are capricious, it is manifest as fugitive insights which reveal obscure recesses of the soul, and "the recollections which it brings us are akin to dreams." (63) Memory in Bergson's philosophy is connected with intuitive and spiritual - as opposed to intellectual and material - perception of life. Ordinarily we perceive the world logically, so that all the objects of our perception seem discrete and separable from each other. But in the process of remembering, the remembered objects and events blend and fuse into each other, thereby suggesting that reality is not something as logically divisible as we are used to thinking, but a condition of perpetual flux. The artist is capable of this intuitive recognition of life's Heraclitean changefulness, and Bergson remarks in one of his major works - "Now, if some bold novelist, tearing aside the cleverly woven curtain of our conventional ego, shows us under this appearance of logic a fundamental absurdity, under this juxtaposition of simple states an infinite permeation of a thousand different impressions which have already ceased to exist the instant they are named, we commend him for having known us better than we knew ourselves." (64) Although Proust refused to acknowledge his debt to Bergson, the phrase of the Vinteuil sonata which echoes and re-echoes - not as a static symbol but as an image which acquires new meaning in different contexts - is the practical exemplification in fiction of this theory of involuntary memory. Proust's own description of 'la petite phrase' is at one point a poetic expression of everything that Forster might have wished to say about the nature and effect of rhythm:

> But at a given moment, without being able to distinguish any clear outline, or to give a name to what was pleasing him, suddenly enraptured, he (Swann) had tried to collect, to treasure in his memory, the phrase or harmony - he knew not which - that had just been played, and had opened and expanded his soul, just as the fragrance of certain roses, wafted upon the moist air of evening, has the power of dilating our nostrils ... An impression of this order, vanishing in an instant, is, so to speak, an

> impression sine materia ... this indefinite perception would continue to smother in its molten liquidity the motifs which now and then emerge, barely discernible, to plunge again, and disappear and drown; recognized only by the particular kind of pleasure which they instil, impossible to describe, to recollect, to name ... (65)

Thus, in preferring rhythm to pattern Forster is defining an aesthetic in which fiction is, at its best, an expression of the deepest and most spiritual aspect of life rather than a product of the conscious, logical and intelligent self.

Rhythm of the second sort, Forster says, is something unheard and yet apprehended when the novel is over. It cannot be pinned down or defined as anything specific within a novel, for it is a sort of revelation of the novel as a spiritual unity. It is the highest kind of beauty that a novelist can achieve. But if such a rhythm is so elusive, what is the novelist supposed to do to achieve it? Forster's answer is that this highest kind of beauty to which the novel can aspire implies the creation of an ordered and autonomous universe. Within this, the constituent parts, while contributing to the larger unity and perfection of the whole, have a life of their own and seem to have obtained a sort of liberation and fulfilment for themselves:

> Music though it does not employ human beings, though it is governed by intricate laws, nevertheless does offer in its final expression a type of beauty which fiction might achieve in its own way. Expansion. That is the idea the novelist must cling to. Not completion. Not rounding off but opening out. When the symphony is over we feel that the notes and tunes composing it have been liberated, they have found in the rhythm of the whole their individual freedom. Cannot the novel be like that? (66)

The similarity between this conception and that of a society in which each individual obtains a private fulfilment but also contributes to his world, is very evident. Forster's conception of the best way in which fiction can be ordered seems to correspond with his view of the ideal social order. It may be inferred that from this point of view the greatest works of art can be understood as models which society has in its own way to emulate before it can be truly ordered. The notion is very vague and insufficiently specified, but the fundamental point seems to be that music is the most perfect kind of order because the tunes which make it up are significant and valuable in themselves, but also contribute to the unity of the world of which they are a part. Rhythm in this sense can be understood as Forster's word for perfect order, a term which denotes the ideal spiritual form towards which both the novel and human society, in their own ways, must approximate. Forster himself considered that this kind of spiritual unity had been achieved in War and Peace.

The relation between plot and pattern has a higher analogue, namely the relation between rhythm and 'prophecy'. Prophecy is not to be understood "in the narrow sense of foretelling the future." (67) Rather, when the novel throbs with a living rhythm, when this pulsation seems to expand the novel out of its material and temporal confines, it becomes prophetic. However, the use of rhythm is only one method of making a novel prophetic. Prophecy itself denotes the existence of spiritual intensity within a novel and may be achieved in more ways than one. The novelist is a prophet when his work, like music, becomes a sensible embodiment of the unseen. The difference between fantasy and prophecy is roughly Coleridge's distinction between fancy and imagination. Fantasy is a charming absorption in the disparate particulars of life, prophecy the discovery of their underlying oneness. The fantasist is the novelist as conjurer, employing an elaborate machinery to perform amusing tricks. The prophet, on the other hand, is the novelist as mystic, whose work reveals the underlying spiritual unity of all creation. As an expression of the unseen, prophecy can be demonstrated rather than defined. Forster can only hope that the reader's ear is attuned to music so that he can hear this "accent in the novelist's voice." (68) The prophetic novelist's theme is "the universe, or something universal, but he is not necessarily going to 'say' anything about the universe; he proposes to sing ...Prophecy - in our sense - is a tone of voice." (69) The prophet celebrates the inner life - his song results from "the raising of human love and hatred to such a power that their normal receptacles no longer contain them." (70) Prophecy, in other words, consists precisely of what Virginia Woolf had thought irrelevant in a masterpiece - the depiction of human life in all its sublimity. The novelist is prophetic when he shows a sensitivity to the invisible essence which suffuses and unites all living things, and Dostoevsky's Mitya ...

> ... only becomes real through what he implies, his mind is not in a frame at all. Taken by himself he seems distorted ... we cannot understand him until we see that he extends, and that the part of him on which Dostoevsky focussed did not lie on the wooden chest or even in dreamland, but in a region where it could be joined by the rest of humanity. Mitya is - all of us ... The extension, the melting, the unity through love and pity occur in a region which can only be implied ... (71)

A masterpiece, in Forster's sense, is clearly not a book with singleness of vision, but one which possesses the spiritual anonymity that makes it universally accessible.

III

Thus the basic thrust of Forster's view of the novel, traceable to his aesthetics and even further to his view of life, can be summarized as follows. The progress of civilization, defined from the liberal perspective as the movement of man from a socially bound to an individually free and autonomous position has an analogue in the world of art, where the social and temporal character of a work of art is redeemed by its spiritual and transcendent autonomy. Like the individual, art is inextricably tied to time, matter and society, but - reaching its high point in music - art assumes an atemporal, circumscribed individuality. This is shown to hold good for the novel. Despite the generic limitations which make it time-bound and a reflection of social life, the novel can develop into a form like music, a medium concerned more with the spiritual essence of things than with existence in time and society. By emulating music, the novel can actualize more of spiritual reality within a material frame. But - and this is vital - the novel cannot and does not become more spiritual by becoming non-representation Unlike music, it cannot cease to reflect human life. Like the individual, even when he is a mystic, it cannot sever its connection with life in time and society. Forster does not want the novel to become music, he merely wishes it to reproduce the effect of music - to give intimations of the unseen like music. He feels that this is achieved through an intense absorption in life, when novelists are sensitive to the spiritual rhythms that constitute the underlayers of man's inner life. When Pater said that 'all art constantly aspires towards the condition of music' he did not mean, says Wellek, "that all art should become music, or even like music ... Good poetry should aspire to such an identity, but with its own means, and the arts should and will remain separate, since 'each art has its peculiar beauty, untranslatable into the forms of any other.'" (72) This seems to be very close to Forster's view and it is not correct to infer from Forster's notion of rhythm and prophecy that he would like the novel to become like 'music itself', "a kind of bodiless transparency flying off like a butterfly into divine realms." (73) The ascent from 'story' to 'prophecy' is a movement from the material to the spiritual, but is not a movement from life to sterilized aesthetic purity. It signifies, rather, a deep concern with human values, because it argues for the creation of a fiction which moves from an unintelligent imitation of the outer life of action towards an intense illumination of the inner life of value.

This personal theory of fiction has both a historical significance and a permanent value. Its permanent value is that by breaking up the novel into its constituent elements it has provided some of the interpretative terms - such as flat and round characters, rhythm, pattern, prophecy - with which fiction can be analysed and discussed. It is historically important as a departure from the prevailing premises about fiction. In his effort to make the novel respectable, Henry James had emphasized the necessity of shapeliness and a controlling form if fiction was to be taken seriously as art. This view had been endorsed by Fry and Virginia Woolf who also felt that a novel must possess the unity of perspective which exists in pictorial art. H.G.Wells disputed this emphasis on pictorial unity and argued that fiction must be as discursive, varied and loose as life. Forster agrees with Wells that singleness of vision is often constrictive, but argues further that fiction can reconcile the claims of art and life if it possesses a musical rather than a pictorial unity. <u>Aspects</u> demonstrates the possibility of obtaining such a musical unity to create a fiction which is varied and expansive but also spiritual, transcendent and ordered. This was not something radically new. A.W. Schlegel, a century before, had thought that the novel "aims at all-inclusiveness, and thus can use all the other genres. It hints at those riddles of life which cannot be actually expressed and thus every detail within it becomes meaningful and symbolic." (74) But this view remained undeveloped and unexplored, and Forster was the first to examine in detail how there can be "more in the novel than time or people or logic or any of their derivatives, more even than fate ... something that cuts across them like a bar of light ..." (75) In setting out to show this, Forster falls alongside James, Wells and Virginia Woolf as one of the pioneering propagandists of fiction. Like them he believes that the novel can appeal to the highest levels of human imagination. In the process of arguing this he also implicitly delineates another area of order created out of chaos by sensitive men, an area of relevance and value in human life.

NOTES

(1) 'The Extreme Case', <u>Athenaeum</u>, 4 July 1919, pp.561-2 (p.561).
(2) <u>The Mirror and the Lamp</u>, p.50.
(3) There is a lucid account of the implications for fiction of the philosophies of Bergson and William James in Shiv Kumar, <u>Bergson and the Stream of Consciousness Novel</u> (London: Blackie, 1962) pp. 1-35.
(4) 'Raison', TCD (p.105).
(5) 'Anonymity', TCD (p.79).
(6) 'The Art of Fiction', a B.B.C. broadcast dated 24 November 1944, Rpt. as Appendix 'D' in <u>Aspects</u>, pp. 143-7 (p.144).
(7) 'How I Listen to Music, 1: By E.M. Forster', <u>The Listener</u>, 19 January 1939, p.173 (p.173). Rpt. as 'Not Listening to Music', TCD (p.123).
(8) ibid., TCD (p.124).
(9) ibid. (p.116).
(10) CB, p.24. Rpt. in Appendix 'A' in <u>Aspects</u>, p.126n. Forster's GLD concludes - "... a biography of him (Dickinson), if it succeeded, would resemble him; it would achieve the unattainable, express the inexpressible, turn the passing into the everlasting. Have I done that? ... No. And perhaps it can only be done through music." (p.201).
(11) CB, c.1926, p.41.
(12) 'Not Listening to Music', TCD (p.124).
(13) <u>Aesthetics and Psychology</u>, trans. Roger Fry and

Katherine John (London: Hogarth Press, 1935) p.89.
(14) ibid., p.89. Since Aspects was written before Mauron's book there is no question of an influence. There is merely a close correspondence of views.
(15) Wagner on Music and Drama, ed. A. Goldman & E. Sprinchorn, trans. H. Ashton Ellis (1964; rpt. London: Gollancz, 1977) p. 187.
(16) In her essays 'Modern Fiction' and 'Mr. Bennett and Mrs. Brown' in Collected Essays (London: Hogarth, 1966) vol. 1, pp.103-10 and vol. 2, pp. 319-37. See also Samuel Hynes, 'The Whole Contention Between Mr. Bennett and Mrs. Woolf', Edwardian Occasions, pp. 24-38.
(17) Letter to J.B. Pinker, dated 16 December 1915, in Letters, ed. Aldous Huxley (London: Heinemann, 1932) p. 295.
(18) Ford wrote Henry James: A Critical Study (1913), Beach wrote The Method of Henry James (1918) and Lubbock wrote The Craft of Fiction (1921).
(19) The Art of Fiction and other essays, ed. Morris Roberts (New York: Oxford Univ. Press, 1948) pp. 3-23 (p.8).
(20) The Rhetoric of Fiction (Chicago: Chicago Univ. Press, 1961) pp. 24-5. A full account of the history of the 'point of view' controversy exists in Norman Friedman, 'Point of View in Fiction - The Development of a Critical Concept' in The Theory of the Novel, ed. Philip Stevick (New York: Free Press, 1969) pp. 108-38.
(21) The Craft of Fiction (London: Cape, 1921) p.116.
(22) See The Craft of Fiction, pp. 26-58. James had earlier remarked that Tolstoy was the great master whose method was disconnected from his matter. See James's Preface to The Tragic Muse (1908) and a letter (1913) to Hugh Walpole, both qtd. in Theory of Fiction: Henry James, ed. James E. Miller (Lincoln: Univ. of Nebraska Press, 1972), p. 262 and p.267.
(23) Aspects, pp. 54, 59.
(24) ibid., p.56.
(25) ibid., p.56.
(26) ibid., p.116.
(27) The Mirror and the Lamp, p.128.
(28) Aspects, p.13.
(29) 'The Anatomy of Fiction', Athenaeum, 16 May 1919. Rpt. in Granite and Rainbow (London: Hogarth, 1958) pp. 53-6 (p.54). Forster's attack is 'The Fiction Factory', Daily News,

23 April 1919, p.6. Rpt. as Appendix 'B' in Aspects.
(30) Forster might just have been taking on Henry James who wrote - "I cannot see what is meant by talking as if there were a part of the novel which is the story and part of it which for mystical reasons is not ... he would be a clever man who should undertake to give a rule ... by which the story and the no story should be known apart." 'The Art of Fiction' (pp.17-8).
(31) "At what age is the passion for a story, for almost any kind of story, merely as a story, the most intense? - in childhood ... In what stage of the process of society, again, is storytelling most valued, and the storyteller in greatest request and honour? - in a rude state ... Passing now from childhood, and from the childhood of society ... the minds and hearts of greatest depth and elevation are commonly those which take the greatest delight in poetry ..." 'What Is Poetry' (1833), in Mill's Essays on Literature and Society, ed. J.B. Schneewind (New York: Collier Books, 1965) pp. 102-17 (pp.104-5).
(32) Aspects, p.29.
(33) ibid., p.31.
(34) ibid., p.44.
(35) 'Virginia Woolf, Review, Nation' in E.M. Forster: The Critical Heritage, ed. Philip Gardner (London: Routledge and Kegan Paul, 1973) pp. 332-6, (p.334).
(36) This distinction is the literary equivalent of the one drawn by Fry between 'plastic' and 'flat'. "(Modern architects do not) feel plastically, their minds do not move freely in three dimensions, they think and feel in the flat." Architectural Heresies of a Painter (London: Chatto and Windus, 1921) p.31.
(37) ibid., p.67. Forster's conception of plot is not as all encompassing as that of the neo-Aristotelians. Like James who says it is impossible to distinguish between the story and the no-story, the neo-Aristotelians bring everything in a novel within the scope of its plot. R.S. Crane's 'The Concept of Plot and the plot of Tom Jones' suggests that all novels possess one of three kinds of plot - plots of action, plots of character, and plots of thought. Norman Friedman expands this into fourteen kinds of plot. See Critics and Criticism: Ancient

(37 cont.) and Modern, ed. R.S. Crane (Chicago: Univ. of Chicago Press, 1952) pp.616-47 and Norman Friedman, 'Forms of the Plot' in The Theory of the Novel, ed. Philip Stevick, pp. 145-66.
(38) Aspects, p.60.
(39) ibid., pp.60-1.
(40) ibid., p.61.
(41) Carlos Lynes Jr., 'Andre Gide and the Problem of Form in the Novel', Forms of Modern Fiction: Essays collected in honour of J.W. Beach, ed. William van O'Connor (Minneapolis: Univ. of Minnesota Press, 1948) pp. 175-88 (p.182).
(42) ibid., p.71.
(43) ibid., p.64.
(44) ibid., p.103.
(45) ibid., p.104.
(46) 'The Art of Fiction', (p.5.).
(47) 'Some Questions in Esthetics', p.7.
(48) Granite and Rainbow (London: Hogarth, 1958) pp.11-23 (p.22).
(49) 'The Contemporary Novel' in Henry James and H.G. Wells: A Record of Their Friendship, Their Debate on the Art of Fiction, and Their Quarrel, ed. Leon Edel & G.N. Ray (London: Rupert Hart-Davis, 1958) pp. 131-56 (pp.136-7). The Wells-James controversy is discussed by Edel and Ray in their Introduction.
(50) Boon, The Mind of the Race, The Wild Asses of the Devil, & The Last Trump (London: Fisher & Unwin, 1915) pp. 101-2.
(51) Aspects, p.112.
(52) ibid., p.112.
(53) ibid., p.115.
(54) ibid., p.71.
(55) ibid., p.85.
(56) 'Butterflies and Beetles', Life and Letters, July 1929, vol. 3, pp.1-9 (p.2.). Rpt. (revised) as 'Ronald Firbank', AH (p.130).
(57) 'My Poultry Are Not Officers', The Listener, 26 October 1939, Supplement No.III.
(58) Aspects, p.115.
(59) ibid., p.113.
(60) ibid., p.115.
(61) Forster's two essays on Proust are 'Our Curiosity and Despair' in New York Herald Tribune, 21 April 1929, Section II, Books, pp. 1,6, rpt. in AH; and 'Our Second Greatest Novel?' in The Listener, 15 April 1943, pp. 454-5, rpt. in TCD. E.K. Brown has shown that A Passage to India is rhythmically structured. See Rhythm in the Novel (Toronto: Toronto Univ. Press, 1950),

pp. 87-115.
(62) Matter and Memory, trans. N.M. Paul & W.S. Palmer (1911; rpt. London: Allen & Unwin, 1962) p.101. Quoted in Shiv Kumar, Bergson and the Stream of Consciousness Novel, p.27.
(63) Matter and Memory, p.102. It is possible that Forster read Bergson whose work was being published in English translations just before APTI was begun. When describing the working of unconscious memory one of the things Bergson says is - " ... the immediate horizon to our perception appears to us to be necessarily surrounded by a wider circle, existing though unperceived, this circle implying yet another outside it and so on ad infinitum." A few sentences later Bergson says - "... when a memory reappears in consciousness it produces on us the effect of a ghost whose mysterious apparition must be explained by special causes." Bergson's first image is very similar to that of the overarching sky in APTI. With regard to the second connection between memories and ghosts, Mrs Moore connects dreams with ghosts and later her ghost haunts the memories of Adela, Aziz and Godbole. Cf. Matter and Memory, pp. 185-7 and APTI, pp. 3, 34, 88-9, 229, 249, 278 and 281.
(64) Time and Free Will: An Essay on the Immediate Data of Consciousness, trans. F.L. Pogson (1889; rpt. London: Swan Sonnenschein, 1910) p.133. Qtd. in Bergson and the Stream of Consciousness Novel, p.31.
(65) Swann's Way, trans. C.K. Scott Moncrieff (London: Chatto and Windus, 1922) pp.287-8. Another revealing description runs - "Swann was not mistaken in believing that the phrase of the sonata did, really, exist. Human as it was from this point of view, it belonged, nonetheless, to an order of supernatural creatures whom we have never seen, but whom, in spite of that, we recognize and acclaim with rapture when some explorer of the unseen contrives to coax one forth, to bring it down from the divine world to which he has access to shine for a brief moment in the firmament of ours." Swann in Love, trans. C.K. Scott Moncrieff (London: Chatto and Windus, 1922) pp. 184-5.
(66) Aspects, p.116.
(67) Aspects, p.86.
(68) ibid.
(69) ibid.

(70) ibid.
(71) ibid., p.92.
(72) 'Walter Pater', A History of Modern Criticism: The Later Nineteenth Century (op.cit.), vol. IV, pp.381-99 (pp.391-2).
(73) Stone, The Cave and the Mountain, p.121.
(74) 'August Wilhelm Schlegel', in Rene Wellek, A History of Modern Criticism: The Romantic Age (London: Cape, 1955), vol. II, pp. 36-73 (p.51).
(75) Aspects, p.74.

CHAPTER SIX

FORSTER ON CRITICISM AND AS A CRITIC

Forster suggests that man has an innate capacity to enjoy art if only he makes sufficient effort to respond to it. Consequently he attaches little importance to criticism. An unpublished fragment in his late hand institutes a suggestive comparison between the role of criticism in interpreting art and the role of theocracy in interpreting God:

> A parallel could be drawn between the priest, the minister of religion on the one hand, and the literary critic on the other. Both seek to intervene between the individual and that which he desires to understand ... As long as the intervention is tentative and gentle, it may bring help ... But the moment the intervention becomes authoritive (sic) it changes its character and changes for the worse. For the literary critic to be authoritive is absolutely unjustifiable; let him practise the modesty which befits his unimportance and allow the reader to get at the book. (1)

Forster's admiration of Hinduism as a religion which allows the individual to be alone with his god helps, at this point, to clarify his generally disapproving attitude to criticism, for he believes that in aesthetic - as in religious - response, there should be no interference between man and the spiritual form which has evoked the response. This idea is anticipated in Aspects where Forster believes that "The final test of a novel will be our affection for it, as it is the test of our friends and of anything else which we cannot define." (2) A third example from an unpublished talk of even earlier date outlines Forster's view most clearly:

FORSTER ON CRITICISM AND AS A CRITIC

> A book is mainly talk - the words of a man, perhaps of a man who has been dead for three hundred years and is trying to talk out of the immense darkness to you. He talks, you listen. There is no-one and nothing between you, and you must get on with each other as best as you can ... always remember that the writer you are reading was once a man... there are other things no doubt that help - knowledge of the conditions under which it (his book) was written ... the influence it has had on other writers ... criticisms that have been made about it. But these are subsidiary ... Listen to the voice of the speaker. (3)

To turn to critical interpretations of literature is to respond at second hand. There is no substitute, in Forster's opinion, for the immediacy of personal response - even if such an effort is fumbling and imperfect.

Forster's writing also reflects his concern at the diminishing production of literature and the proliferation of criticism on it. He stresses the fundamental difference in kind and value between creativity and criticism and points out that creativity and personal response are what really matter, for it is more important to read literature than books about it. Criticism can describe the external structure of a work of art, but cannot penetrate into its ultimately mysterious core. It can break down the complex order achieved by artefacts but it cannot duplicate their essence. This is because of the fundamental dissimilarity between art and criticism as modes of communication. The creative and critical faculties "constantly occur in the same men - and they often fade into each other. But they are essentially different." (4) The difference between the two can be roughly explained as the difference between atmosphere and information, art and science, emotion and reason, the subconscious and the conscious self. In 'The Raison de'Etre of Criticism' Forster says that "The critical state has many merits and employs some of the highest and subtlest faculties of man. But it is grotesquely remote from the state responsible for the works it affects to expound. It does not let down buckets into the subconscious ... while not excluding imagination and sympathy, it keeps them and all the faculties under control, and only employs them when they promise to be helpful." (5) The assumption underpinning this view of criticism can be traced to Forster's view of

art. Insofar as an artist's conscious self and his
real life experiences are involved, the work of art
reflects the specific social and cultural environ-
ment within which the artist lived and wrote. But
since the artist is also believed to derive his material unconsciously from the great reservoir of
human feelings, the work of art is quintessentially
an autonomous entity which appeals to deep rooted
human emotions and thereby transcends its socio-
cultural conditions. The two sources of art, inner
and outer, enmesh within every work of art, but what
renders an entity 'art' rather than social document
is its ability to 'bounce' readers and engender in
them the deep feelings which went into its making.
This is obviously something which only art, by definition, can do, and explains why criticism is
"grotesquely remote" from what it expounds. Criticism is futile precisely because it can only expound
and explain experience but not generate it. In
Bell's view "art is not something to come at by dint
of study; let us try to think of it as something to
be enjoyed as one enjoys being in love. The first
thing to be done is to free the aesthetic emotions
from the tyranny of erudition." (6) Mauron says the
same thing - "Aesthetic order is meant to be felt
rather than analysed ... if it is to become a source
of pleasure (it) must remain hidden in a sort of
twilight where we may have the joys of discovering
it." (7) The view that criticism is inappropriate
because it breaks up and analyses something which
can only be truly grasped as a synthesis and a unity
is common in the 'heterocosm' theory of art, and is
also a traditional reason for the hostility of artists towards critics. Forster says that study is
peripheral in the domain of art because it "teaches
us everything ... except the central thing, and between that and us it raises a circular barrier which
only the wings of spirit can cross. The study of
science, history, etc., is necessary and proper, for
they are subjects that belong to the domain of
information, but a creative subject like literature
- to study that is excessively dangerous." (8) The
notion that works of art should not be the subject
of study because study impairs spontaneity is ironic,
both because it comes from people who devoted so much
time to analysing and discussing art, and because it
was forgotten by them that only people who have already been properly educated can respond ' sponta-
neously' to works of art.

It is, however, possible to interpret Forster
more charitably because his basic endeavour is not

so much to denigrate criticism as to insist that criticism should not be allowed precedence over art. While Forster seems to adopt a generally hostile attitude to critics, he does at other times acknowledge some of the virtues of criticism. He realizes that reading criticism can lead towards a better understanding of art than is possible simply through sheer personal enthusiasm. His own practice as a critic also shows that he attaches to criticism considerable importance as propaganda for art. The innate but simple "desire to love (art)" is not enough because "we shall tend to slip about on the surface of masterpieces, exclaiming with joy, but never penetrating." (9) Untrained appreciation is naive and may lead to a complacent satisfaction with a very imprecise understanding of art. Good criticism trains the individual to be sensitive and is a corrective to impressionistic looseness. It is "desirable to know why we like a work, and to be able to defend our preference by argument" and, "Besides learning about the work one increases one's powers. Criticism's central job seems to be education through precision." (10) It can perform this function if the critic is sensitive and tries to grasp the imaginative logic of the work and does not try to analyse it with the logic of a scientist. All too often "the subject matter is apt to retire while it is being discussed, like an ebbing tide, and the critics are left in a row on the beach, in the form of seaweeds and odds and ends of cork." (11) Coleridge is one of Forster's examples of a good critic who knew after the 'Dejection' ode that "The feeling of being outside things is a feeling which the critic has or ought to have: he ought to be an imaginative outsider ..." (12)

Criticism is also allowed some value as an emotional exercise by Forster. He defends impressionistic criticism, not as good interpretative criticism, but as a method of stimulating interest in the original from which it derives. Like T.S. Eliot in 'The Perfect Critic', Forster acknowledges that impressionistic criticism is probably an outlet for a suppressed creative wish, but unlike Eliot he does not consider this any reason to disparage its production. (13) He merely suggests that 'criticism' is the wrong word with which to describe the activity. This view appears during a discussion of Oscar Wilde's 'The Critic as Artist' in the 1931 lectures. Forster says that Wilde's essay makes three points - first, that "There is no art without self-consciousness and selfconsciousness and the critical spirit are one", second, that "criticism should regard art, good or bad, as an opportunity to create ...", and third, that "as art springs from personality so it is only to personality that it can be revealed, and from the meeting of the two comes right interpretative criticism." (14) With regard to the first point, Forster says that both the artist and the critic may be self-conscious, but this hardly proves that they are indistinguishable from each other. He finds the second and third points more interesting because "they both rest on the assumption that the work of art has no fixed meaning but varies according to the attitude of the observer." (15) Forster says this is a wrong assumption. He does not deny a reader the right to "use a work as a kick off for work of one's own ... Pater was justified in misdecribing Mona Lisa, Fitzgerald in mistranslating Omar Khayyam, and Shakespeare in mishandling the legend of Macbeth." (16) But these works should be categorized under creation and not criticism. Wilde is simply using the wrong word to describe this kind of writing. The critic requires imagination, but "his imagination must be disciplined and canalized ... He has to re-create what the poet has created, and if he moves in a direction other than the poet's, he has failed, because he interprets something that hasn't existed." (17) The 'intentional fallacy' is therefore an important element in Forster's own criticism, and he tries to re-create the original emotional and intellectual processes by which a work of art is created. Consequently, though he finds impressionistic criticism interesting, this is because he sees it as a form of creativity and not, strictly speaking, as criticism. It is interesting as an activity which leads to quasi-creative work that is enjoyable for its own sake, and because such work draws attention to the original from which it derives.

From this it follows that Forster disagrees with Wilde's view that a work of art means whatever the critic interprets it to mean. He feels that "A book does mean one thing rather than another, and so the judgements passed on it can be less true or more true ... no critic may be able to hit it exactly. But there is something to hit. There is such a thing as a final interpretation of 'Hamlet', as apart from the responses 'Hamlet' has evoked through the ages ..." (18) Forster feels that when a creative artist turns to criticism he often forgets that the works of art have an objective identity of their own. The habit of 'self-extension', of discovering

FORSTER ON CRITICISM AND AS A CRITIC

"poetic or emotional kinship" (19) impairs much of the 'criticism' written by creative artists. "Dante had this feeling for Virgil, Keats for Burns, Matthew Arnold for de Senancour, D.H. Lawrence for Fenimore Cooper, James Joyce for Shakespeare, Edith Sitwell for Pope. The feeling may incidentally produce flashes of wonderful criticism, but it is not a critical feeling; the creator ... is seeking for his peers ... and often encountering his own image instead." (20) On the other hand, when the artist does manage to look at the work of other people disinterestedly, his "general sensitiveness and vitality" (21) helps to make his interpretations interesting and valuable.

Forster does not feel that criticism is of much help to the artist. "The truth is that good writing can only be learned from good writing" he says in <u>Aspects</u>. (22) Unlike Arnold who felt that criticism was vital for high cultural standards and for an ethos conducive to creative work, Forster is sceptical about the need for artists to be in touch with the finest ideas of their age. He feels that "only certain writers are capable of being in touch with their age, and if the critic brought first aid to the others, he would merely make them unreadable. A balanced Byron, a sophisticated Hardy, wouldn't be Byron or Hardy." (23) Arnold did not think of the critic as someone who brought 'first aid' to artists as mechanically as Forster seems to think, for he used 'criticism' in a wide sense to denote the intellectual and cultural ethos. In 'The Function of Criticism at the Present Time' (1864) he criticized Romantic isolationism because it divorced poetry from other contemporaneous intellectual currents. Forster diminishes Arnold's argument because of his thorough-going Romanticism. This is clear both from his feeling that artists are more likely to be impaired than improved by criticism of any kind and from the fact that his own interest as a critic is in those aspects which are unique and peculiar to artists over those which make them typical of their age. This is reiterated with only a slightly different emphasis in 'The Raison d'Etre of Criticism' - "To be alone may be best - to be alone was what Fate reserved for Beethoven. But if he (the artist) wishes to consort with ideas and standards and the work of his fellows ... he must beware of the second rate ... The lowering of critical standards ... may lead to inferior work. That is all there seems to be to say about this vague assistance, and maybe it was not worth saying." (24)

FORSTER ON CRITICISM AND AS A CRITIC

Some of Forster's reviews of critical books further illustrate his view of criticism. A joint review of Middleton Murry's Aspects of Literature, Robert Lynd's The Art of Letters and Clutton Brock's Essays on Books, titled 'In the Temple of Criticism', begins with a general castigation of critics "who have neither instinct nor education to guide them." (25) One section of the temple of criticism is inhabited by surgical critics who dissect books, another by a confused rabble which does not know what to make of books. No one within this Laputan scenario can reply to the common reader's request for good books. Within this context Forster finds Murry and Lynd exceptional in their desire to answer elementary questions and communicate opinions, but also feels they are prone to sail into the shallower waters of academic debate. Murry, in particular, tends to use his aesthetic apparatus like a scientist and forget his audience - "When his apparatus is in his hands, it sometimes masters him, like the machinery of a Government office ..." (26)

Caudwell's work typifies the kind of literary criticism which does not consider art as art, but as good or bad politics. In his review of Studies in a Dying Culture Forster says that while Caudwell brilliantly analyses the malaise of bourgeois writers, "he has not faced the fact that books do give pleasure; he has not discussed art at all ... For him a book is only good if it stands in a sound social relation to its age, and consequently no book can be good unless it is Communist. 'Kipps', 'The Plumed Serpent', 'Seven Pillars of Wisdom' need re-writing, and what matter if, when re-written, they are unreadable? Literature has nothing to do with enjoyment." (27) From Forster's liberal perspective ideology is wholly subsidiary, and aesthetic value cannot be naively inferred from the social value of art. Forster himself does not sympathize with the political views of Lawrence, Eliot, D'Annunzio and Kipling, and yet values their art because he perceives it as the transformation of data deriving from socio-historical roots into something which transcends these.

Forster's hostility to criticism vanishes when the critics he writes about happen to be his own friends or acquaintances. In Aspects he is less critical of Lubbock's The Craft of Fiction than he might have been, and Stallybrass's observation that "Forster never hesitated to subordinate criticism to friendship" (28) is entirely true if one looks at Forster's combined review of Ford Madox Ford's The

FORSTER ON CRITICISM AND AS A CRITIC

English Novel and Ernest Baker's History of the English Novel, Vol.I. Ford's book is a rambling story of the novel told in a haphazard and avuncular style. Baker's book, on the other hand, is incredibly detailed and scholarly. The first volume only covers the period from Anglo-Saxon fiction to the Renaissance. In his review of Ford and Baker, the only criterion of assessment that Forster uses is 'readability'. On this basis he compliments Ford's book as a fine effort and at the same time flays Baker's book with such gratuitous and unjust harshness that Baker wrote a letter of complaint to the editor. (29) Forster's review of Baker's book is not, fortunately, characteristic of his style as a reviewer. But he felt that over-detailed scholarship is pedantic and pointless for it contributes nothing to the enjoyment of literature. This kind of criticism certainly seems to have infuriated him more than any other, and in this respect the review is reminiscent of his hatchet job on Clayton Hamilton in 'The Fiction Factory'.

Taken collectively, Forster's remarks about criticism are concerned more with pointing out what criticism cannot and should not do rather than with what it can and should do. What he really offers is a criticism of criticism, not a theory which can be of much use to the practising critic. The only positive value within his view of criticism is the vehement conviction that criticism must not, as it tends to, be given an importance greater than literature itself. In an era which saw the birth of modern literary criticism with I.A. Richards and its consolidation as an academic discipline thereafter - an era in which students of literature sometimes read more criticism of literary texts than texts themselves, Forster's view of criticism serves as a reminder that literature is more important than criticism.

II

Before providing a documentary account of some of Forster's literary criticism it would be useful to summarize the chief theoretical principles which link his essays with each other. It is necessary to stress, once again, that Forster's approach is always eclectic, and that these 'theoretical principles' are just loose strands which are usually, but not always, visible in the body of Forster's literary criticism.

The most obvious linking feature is that

FORSTER ON CRITICISM AND AS A CRITIC

Forster tends to deprecate influences and historical context, and prefers to examine literary texts as separate entities with which readers interact in different ways - as they would with different friends. Forster is interested in the separate 'life' of every text - this is one of the things implied in his use of the phrase 'art for art's sake'. His criticism provides a general impression of what is unique within each of the little ordered worlds made by artists. This might suggest that Forster follows I.A. Richards's and William Empson's method of close textual analysis and belongs with New Criticism, but irony, ambiguity and poetic tension do not interest Forster. Though he regards each text as an autotelic entity he never goes to any great length to explain how the units within a text cohere into an order. There are no references to New Criticism in Forster's writing, but it is likely that he would have thought it the kind of criticism which attracts attention to its own ingenuity rather than to the texts it recommends. Forster assumes that like the unique personality of the individual, the literary text is a spiritual and ultimately un-analysable order.

For this reason Forster's criticism tends to be impressionistic. It is impressionistic not in the sense that Forster uses texts as starting points for rhapsodic, creative utterances, but in the sense that he stimulates interest in literature by enthusiastic communication of personal impressions rather than by systematic and dispassionate analysis. If there is a single unifying feature in Forster's criticism it is that one is always aware that Forster, and no one else, could have written it. His criticism is interesting partly because his impressions of literary texts are so subjective and because these impressions are communicated with a zest that vivifies what is being scrutinized. In fact it is ironic that while Forster believes that the function of criticism is simply to draw attention to literature, his own sensitivity and peculiarly personal outlook make many of his essays in criticism readable because they are written by <u>him</u>. They do not seek to attract attention to themselves, but because they reveal an unusually subtle imagination and a cultivated mind they take on the quality of autonomous literary essays even when they were intended as interpretations of other writers. At the same time, these qualities make for criticism which is often acutely perceptive because it illuminates literature from an unusual angle. Furbank sums up

FORSTER ON CRITICISM AND AS A CRITIC

Forster's method when he says that "As a critic he <u>looked</u>, he scrutinized the object as if nothing like <u>it had</u> ever existed, and he emerged with a brand new, freshly-minted formula, fitting not only the work in question but, potentially, a whole new class of works." (30) Forster's essays are thus impressionistic in the best sense of the word. They are not, like the essays of Wilde, Pater and Symons, written to fulfil suppressed creative desires, but they are unmistakably the essays of an artist.

Neither Forster's view of art as something transcendent nor his impressionism as a critic implies unconcern for society and humanity. The analysis of his world-view and aesthetics has already shown that Forster spans the gap between Wilde and Arnold. Art is not recommended purely for its hedonistic and narrowly personal appeal, nor merely because it embodies morally or socially desirable values. Forster's criticism is concerned both with the personal pleasure that can be derived from literary texts, as well as the larger spiritual and human (and thereby indirectly social) value of literature. Art for art's sake is inextricably tied up with Forster's concern with the preservation of human values and civilization. If he can be linked with the formalism of Richards, Bell and Fry, he can also, alongside other artist-critics like George Orwell, Virginia Woolf and D.H. Lawrence, be linked to the humanist tradition of criticism with its concern for human values - the tradition associated in contemporary criticism with Leavis and Trilling. This aspect is not always obvious, particularly in the pre-thirties essays (though it is, in the 1907 essay on Dante, for instance), but it does underlie all of Forster's criticism and surfaces in the essays of the thirties and after. In these later essays the moral concern behind the enjoyment being recommended is spelled out and one is left in no doubt that art is being revealed as both pleasurable and valuable.

While Forster's critical method is eclectic and not part of any school of professional criticism, he favours a broadly biographical approach. He uses biographical details and also analyses the author's subconscious self when explaining a text or when giving a general description of the work of an author. "The interpretations of Freud miss the values of art as infallibly as do those of Marx ...they cannot show us how a work of art is good or how it became good. But ... they can indicate the condition of the artist's mind" - Forster writes. (31) Forster's criticism tries to reveal the uniqueness of every author's mind, and he usually interprets texts as mediums which imply or reveal the author's personal values and philosophy of life. Patrick Parrinder has traced a tradition of criticism from Carlyle to Leslie Stephen, a tradition which draws up "a carefully chosen gallery of writers from the past whose personalities stood out against their times." (32) Forster's criticism is broadly consistent with this tradition. The artists he discusses are not carefully chosen, but in discussing their personally unique rather than historically typical qualities he sets them up as a part of the aristocracy of spirit which preserves the human tradition. One of the characteristics of the people within this aristocracy is to stand out like beacons of light within the general darkness of the public life of their times, and Forster's criticism makes evident his liking for subversive or dissenting writers. In fact ivory tower detachment from, or active opposition to, the currents of feeling which debase 'human' faculties, is one of the defining characteristics of the notion of literature in Forster's criticism.

When discussing an author or a text Forster is fairly consistent with his view that art draws from the author's subconscious or 'anonymous' self. His criticism is marked by the 'intentional fallacy', and even more specifically by what Fishman has called a "genetic fallacy". (33) He traces literature to the author's intention, and even more closely to specific sources of inspiration in the author's subconscious mind. These sources may be literary, for example the voyage books which Coleridge read before he wrote <u>The Ancient Mariner</u>, but Forster has a predilection for geographical or topographical sources of inspiration. While he is conscious of a writer's historical context (evident in the essays on Dante, Skelton and Proust), he is much more interested in the author's local habitation, his feeling for place, his childhood experiences, and the repository of details in his subconscious mind. He says that "The early impressions of poets have not yet been properly studied, and perhaps we tend to be sentimental about them and overrate their value. But of their strength there can be no question; they persist even when the poet is looking at something new and describing themes where they do not apply." (34) Thus Chekhov and Tolstoy are associated in Forster's criticism with the vastness of Russia and with a Russian spirit rather than with periods in Russian history, while the essays on Ibsen, Kipling, Forrest Reid, Wordsworth and T.S. Eliot similarly search for

FORSTER ON CRITICISM AND AS A CRITIC

the seminal and poignant experiences - always connected with geographical locations - which inspire creativity. Ibsen is connected with Norwegian forests, Kipling with the spirit of India, Reid with Belfast, Wordsworth with the Lakes and Eliot with English traditions and English stability. This aspect of Forster's criticism is again coloured by his Romantic temperament, for literature is traced back to its emotional origins. Forster is manifestly the creator turned critic, inferring from his own feeling for the countryside and his own experience of inspiration in particular locations that the same thing holds good for other writers. Parrinder has shown that Ruskin's criticism does something similar, for it "is concerned with art as the expression of man's history, which he traces in its social, psychological, religious and topographical aspects." (35) In the 'Mountain Glory' chapter of Modern Painters Ruskin connects Shakespeare's vision to the topography around Stratford, and Dante's to the topography around Florence. (36) This shows a Wordsworthian awareness in his criticism of the influence upon sensitive minds of the beautiful and permanent forms of nature - an awareness which seems to be evident in Forster's essays as well. Such awareness may lead only to commonplace discussion of a poet like Wordsworth since most critics link Wordsworth to the Lake District, but at other times, very specially in the essays on Ibsen and Kipling, it can produce the most penetrating and unusual insights.

Forster seems the type of critic denominated by T.S. Eliot as "the critic with Gusto". This type, Eliot says, "is not called to the seat of judgment; he is rather the advocate of the authors whose work he expounds, authors who are sometimes the forgotten or unduly despised. He calls our attention to such writers, helps us to see merit which we had overlooked and to find charm where we had only expected boredom ... (a critic with) the flair for discovering the excellence which is often to be found in the second rate." (37) Unlike Leavis, Forster is more a propagandist of art than a critic who demarcates and discusses the 'best' literature. He has a greater concern with highlighting the excellence that is to be discovered in minor writers. In a criticism of Leavis's The Great Tradition Trilling remarks that Leavis "takes no proper account ... of the art that delights - and enlightens - by the intentional relaxation of moral awareness ... Nor does he take any account of the impulse of sheer performance, even of virtuosity, which ... is of enormous human significance." (38) He traces this excessively puritanical seriousness to Leavis's antagonism towards the Bloomsbury group which did value the irreverent, the virtuoso and the fantastic in art. (39) If one looks at Forster's criticism, one finds something like the rounded sensibility which Trilling desires in critics, a sensibility which attaches importance to the moral function of art but also to its lighter and more casually pleasurable function. This is not to suggest that Forster is a greater or better critic than Leavis - he is quite obviously not - but only to point out that personal appreciation and a desire to recommend what he finds valuable or what others may have overlooked counts for more in Forster's criticism than interpretation and judgment of the greatest writers. However, when Forster does discuss the more established figures such as Scott, Meredith, Ibsen, James and Joyce, his response is individualistic enough to provide a fresh perspective and produce ideas that are different from prevailing opinions. Apart from stimulating interest in minor British writers, Forster tries to popularize foreign literature. The great tradition of the novel, in his interpretation, is not specifically English. On the contrary, Tolstoy, Dostoevsky, Proust and Melville seem to him much more visionary and profound in their outlook than George Eliot, Conrad and James. Forster also wrote about Iqbal, Tagore and Kalidasa, Gide and Rolland, Mark Twain, Sinclair Lewis and Howard Overing Sturgis, drew attention to English translations of Chinese, Japanese and Slav poetry, and made Cavafy famous in the West. In keeping with his liberal eclecticism, Forster's criticism is wide ranging.

In detailing these features, which in a loose sense bind together Forster's essays in criticism, some of Forster's limitations as a critic have been implied. The impressionism can lead to unnecessary idiosyncratic digressions, as in the opening paragraph of the essay on Virginia Woolf in <u>Abinger Harvest</u> (40) or triviality - in the essay on Jane Austen in the same volume. Almost everyone who has commented on Forster's criticism has complained of his whimsical and eccentric attitude, of something like a cultivated dilettantism. There is no doubt that Forster's essays are whimsical and chatty, sometimes tiresomely so. Their author is, as Trilling puts it, "a critic with no drive to consistency, no desire to find an architectonic for his impressions" (41) and this is partly because literary criticism is not, in his view, a serious cultural activity. If the all too serious preoccupation with barriers that separate the best from the second best is a flaw in Leavis's criticism, excessive relaxation and informality is Forster's failing. Trilling points out that this is consistent with Forster's "glorification of mess and relaxation, of the mind that does not precisely distinguish" (42) and Forster himself implies as much when he accuses Arnold of "confining greatness to five writers, instead of seeing it is sporadic, and can desert Shakespeare for Drayton."(43) Nonetheless, Forster's criticism could only have benefited by a less casually appreciative approach, and by greater rigour and seriousness.

The disregard of history in favour of a personal, ahistorical aesthetic scheme in Aspects is another flaw for it limits Forster's view of Scott, Swift and Joyce. These writers are presented as considerably inferior in imagination to novelists like Melville, Emily Bronte and D.H. Lawrence simply because they do not write the kind of fiction that appeals to Forster. To these flaws may be added another. This is Forster's suspicion of all writers whose work is produced or controlled by a theory of art rather than allowed to spring from untrammelled inspiration. Furbank points out that Forster's weakness as a critic is his radical distrust of all systems, his inability to enter into the frame of mind of artists to whom system matters. (44) This explains, in part, his failure to recognize the merits of James, and also his ambivalence towards Joyce and Virginia Woolf. This failing was unavoidable given the fact that for Forster the only thing that matters in the novel is a sense of unfettered life, of passion and vision which transcend the logic and intellectualism of a literary method.

It would be misleading to suggest that there are any more than these tenuous links within Forster's literary criticism. Generalizations cannot, ultimately, describe Forster's criticism adequately for his essays, like the authors and texts they recommend, each require independent appreciation. They vary greatly in size and quality, many of them being slight and unimportant, or when written to be broadcast, excessively simple and full of mere paraphrase. But a large number are both enjoyable and relevant today, not only for the Forster devotee but also for the common reader. They deserve to be read because they are well written and because they enrich our knowledge of literature, of Forster himself, and of what he represents - the value of a humane and civilized life.

NOTES

(1) 'Fragments', King's College Mss.
(2) Aspects, p.15
(3) 'The Enjoyment of English Literature', King's College Ms., vol. 15 (op.cit.) pp. 118-29 (pp. 125, 127).
(4) 'The Creator as Critic', King's College Ms. (op.cit.), p.69.
(5) TCD (pp.112-13).
(6) Art, p.262.
(7) Aesthetics and Psychology, p.87
(8) 'Anonymity', TCD (p.84).
(9) 'The Raison d'Etre of Criticism', TCD (p.105).
(10) ibid. (pp.106,107).
(11) 'Creation and Criticism', p.84.
(12) 'Death of a Poet: Birth of a Critic', The Listener, 26 August 1931, p.333 (p.333).
(13) Eliot's essay is in The Sacred Wood: Essays on Poetry and Criticism (London: Methuen, 1920) pp.1-14.
(14) 'The Creator as Critic', p.69.
(15) ibid.
(16) ibid.
(17) ibid. p.70.
(18) ibid. pp.70-1.
(19) ibid. p.91.
(20) ibid.,
(21) ibid., p.95.
(22) Aspects, pp.138-9.
(23) 'Creation and Criticism', p.101.
(24) TCD (p.117-8).
(25) Nation, 8 January 1921, pp. 512, 514 (p.512).
(26) ibid., (p.514).
(27) 'The Long Run' (p.971)..
(28) 'Introduction', Aspects, pp.VII-XVI (p.XIII).
(29) Forster's review is 'The Hat Case', Spectator, 28 June 1930, p.1055. Baker's letter and a half-grudging apology from Forster exist in Spectator, 12 July 1930, p.54.
(30) 'The Personality of E.M. Forster', (p.66).
(31) 'George Crabbe and Peter Grimes', a lecture given at the Aldeburgh Festival of 1948. Rpt. TCD, pp.166-80 (p.176).
(32) Authors and Authority: A Study of English Literary Criticism and its relation to culture (London: Routledge and Kegan Paul, 1977) p.112.
(33) "... Ruskin is guilty of the 'genetic fallacy', as are all critics who devote themselves to the psychology of the artist or to his social milieu. Inasmuch as Pater's studies are an

enquiry into the personalities of the Renaissance painters, he is also culpable." The Interpretation of Art, p.52.
(34) 'Introduction' in The Life of George Crabbe By His Son (London: World's Classics, 1932) pp. VII-XIX (p.XVIII).
(35) Authors and Authority, p.117.
(36) See 'The Mountain Glory', in Modern Painters, (1857; rpt. London: Smith, Elder and Co., 1873), vol. IV, pp. 353-93 (pp. 370-383). In his last year at school, Forster wrote a Ruskinian essay on 'The Influence of Climate and Physical Conditions upon National Character'. See Furbank I, pp. 47-8.
(37) 'To Criticize the Critic', To Criticize the Critic and other essays (1965; rpt. London: Faber, 1978) pp. 11-26 (p.12).
(38) 'Dr. Leavis and the Moral Tradition', A Gathering of Fugitives (London: Secker and Warburg, 1957) pp. 101-6 (pp.104-5).
(39) Examples of this antagonism exist in Leavis's review of Trilling's book on Forster - 'Meet Mr. Forster', Scrutiny, Autumn 1944, vol. 12, No. 4, pp. 308-9, and in Q.D. Leavis's attack on Desmond MacCarthy in 'Leslie Stephen, Cambridge Critic', Scrutiny, March 1939, vol. 7, pp. 404-15. An analysis of the differences between Bloomsbury and Scrutiny criticism exists in Noel Annan's Leslie Stephen, pp. 249-55.
(40) Forster's Rede Lecture on Virginia Woolf in TCD is also full of digressions. These are perhaps a symptom of his ambivalent attitude to her. Forster's hesitations about Virginia Woolf have been discussed in Harish Trivedi, 'Forster and Virginia Woolf: The Critical Friends', in E.M. Forster: A Human Exploration, pp. 216-30.
(41) E.M. Fortser: A Study (1944; rpt. London: Hogarth, 1967) p.141.
(42) ibid., p.148.
(43) 'The Creator as Critic', p.99.
(44) 'The Personality of E.M.Forster' (p.66).

CHAPTER SEVEN

FORSTER'S LITERARY CRITICISM

Though Forster is interested in the literature of all ages and cultures, most of his serious literary criticism is of English literature of the Augustan period and after. There are only six interesting pieces on pre-Augustan literature - 'Dante' (1907), 'Skelton' (1950), 'Shakespeare and Egypt' (1916), 'Peeping at Elizabeth' (1925), 'Julius Caesar' (1943) and 'The Tercentenary of Milton's Areopagitica' (1944). All these are concerned either with the personality of the writer who is discussed or with the strength and weakness of the moral values that can be inferred from his work. None of these are fine examples of literary criticism, but they are interesting because they show how Forster uses criticism to propagate a personal moral outlook.

The paper on Dante was delivered at the Working Men's College in London. It is based on the premise that in his poetry, Dante was a man talking to men. He was trying to answer the three fundamental questions of life - "How shall I behave to the people I know ... How shall I behave ... to the government, to society as a whole, to humanity as a whole ... How shall I behave to the Unknowable ... the invisible power that lies behind the world?" (1) These questions are seen as the themes of three of Dante's works. The New Life, which describes Dante's relationship with Beatrice, deals with personal relations. In it Beatrice is sometimes a woman but most often an ideal, and this does not appeal to Forster. He says that in contrast to Shakespeare's sonnets and plays, where the beloved is vividly realized, Dante's work gives no hint of Beatrice's personality. Such idealizing otherworldliness, in Forster's view, is the quintessence of medievalism. It implies an asceticism and disregard for earthly intercourse which he finds distasteful. Forster knows that the courtly love tradition, in which the beloved is a rarefied ideal, was a literary device, but he also feels that

> ... such a tradition shows a real defect in the minds of the men who adopted it ... Dante, in The New Life, looked through people; and through most of them he saw God. Why should he trouble over the dull majority. Those sublime visions of his, to which none of us can attain, seem to entail these unmanly lapses, to which none of us, I hope, will sink. (2)

While Dante's view of personal relations is found reprehensible, Forster commends his attitude to humanity as a whole. Like Milton who bullied his daughter's but wrote the Areopagitica, Dante's social outlook compensated for his private failings. This is apparent to Forster from The Empire, which he interprets as a humanist document where Dante desires the sort of social harmony that is compatible with individual differences and variety. In contrast to the jingoism of Kipling, (3) Dante's imperialistic belief in the Holy Roman Empire is laudable because he thought it would bring peace and the leisure with which the human race would realize its latent potential. This was a very idealistic view considering the fact that the Empire was riddled with corruption, but from Forster's viewpoint political idealism is necessary, for it postulates the perfect order to which the real world must approximate. Dante's political outlook is defensible because Dante desired a harmony "between the bloodiness of Mr. Rudyard Kipling and the greyness of Mr. Sidney Webb." (4) Unlike socialists he could warn against greed without desiring a grey equality, but like them he was convinced "that things are not all right as they are ... (and that) the best would come when the divergent types of men acknowledge some element that makes them one." (5) Dante's Utopian ideals were out of touch with the reality of the political situation, but Forster admires them because they suggest that love and unselfishness are the only real methods of harmonizing personal and public life.

Forster's discussion of The Divine Comedy - Dante's answer to the third great question - is relatively brief. From the presence of Brutus and Cassius in Inferno he infers that Dante condemned those who rebel against the earthly Emperor as severely as those who resist God. He also finds 'authoritative' Dante's vision of "the love that lies behind the universe and moves the stars." (6)

In 1950 Forster delivered a lecture on Skelton, the early Tudor poet, at the Aldeburgh Festival.(7) The obvious reason for speaking on Skelton was that as an East Anglian he was a fitting subject for the Aldeburgh Festival, but one may speculate other reasons as well. Skelton was an Erasmian figure who, without abandoning his church, attacked the corruption within it. He remained anti-dogmatic and sturdily independent of both court and church, yet combined his private existence with a strong social conscience. His early poetry is lyrical but became more and more satirical and critical as he became aware of ecclesiastical corruption. This corruption is symbolized in his poetry by Wolsey whom he attacked fearlessly. Furthermore, his poetry shows a robust and high-spirited temperament, a character both shrewd and impish. Though a parish priest, Skelton (like Crabbe - another of Forster's favourites) was a keen observer of life and never otherworldly in his attitudes. His poetry reflects the harmonization of self-cultivation, personal enjoyment and wider critical involvement in the serious social issues of his time - values that are wholly compatible with Forster's liberal humanism. Like the essay on Dante, this lecture places the poet in his historical context but then searches for the values that make him, in a sense, a contemporary. The questions asked are broadly the same - what was Skelton's private life like, what did he value, and how did he respond to social and political issues. Forster is really interested in revealing the man who speaks in his poetry, and his lecture is an excellent short introduction which summarizes and relates the main qualities of Skelton's poetry to his life. For instance, Forster finds that despite his boisterousness, Skelton is capable of tenderness. One of his poems 'Merry Margaret' shows that "Women could touch his violent and rugged heart and make it gentle and smooth for a little time. It is not the dying tradition of chivalry, it is something personal." (8) Skelton's notion of personal love contrasts with Dante's and reflects his post-medievalism. Forster's remark also reveals his own penetrating ability to recognize the connection between a writer's sensibility and his historical period.

The article 'Shakespeare and Egypt' was written thirty-four years before the piece on Skelton. Forster was in Egypt during the Shakespeare tercentenary celebrations of 1916 and probably wrote the piece for the Egyptian Mail. The essay shows how Shakespeare represents the transcendent and internationalist ethic of art. It also contains a short but subtle analysis of Antony and Cleopatra.

Writing in the context of the First War, Forster finds it ironic that a poet whose deep interest in human life transcends politics and nationalism is interpreted in twisted ways to subserve political ends -

> ...he is so universal in his appeal that the nations of the world might well have drawn together to worship him... (yet) Shakespeare is to be celebrated locally and for fugitive reasons. In England, for instance, too much stress will be laid on 'Henry V', because of its recruiting quality ... Italy will concentrate on 'Othello', Denmark on 'Hamlet' ...(9)

Egypt, Forster says, will naturally focus on Antony and Cleopatra, even though Shakespeare's imagination grasped the country very imperfectly. Forster finds little that is intrinsically Egyptian in the play because he feels that Shakespeare was mainly interested in the fate of his two protagonists. Shakespeare used Egypt as a backdrop, as a contrast to the sober, martial civilization of Rome, but did not really penetrate beyond the exotic facade of Egyptian history which he discovered in Plutarch, and he never got the feeling of Egypt as a real place:

> In his account of Actium, he could have followed Virgil and Horace to whom Egyptian religion was a real and a very disgusting thing. Virgil and Horace saw its monstrous gods fighting at Actium with the clear-browed deities of Rome; Shakespeare sees only the triple-turned whore whose flight brings disaster to her lover and herself. It is surely remarkable that the only god who crosses the action is the classical Hercules ... remarkable that in the supreme scene no voice but Charmian's should haunt the monument. (10)

Shakespeare, in other words, did not have Egyptian history in his bones when he wrote the play. His interest in the human dimension, evident from his undeviating focus on the lives of his characters, prevented him from recording anything authentic about the culture of ancient Egypt. This makes his play a tragedy more than a history.

Forster finds one exciting exception in Shakespeare's inability to convey the spirit of Egypt. This is the use of the image of the Nile, which Forster sees as a sort of Wagnerian or Proustian rhythmic thread which beautifully binds the play and makes it recognizably Egyptian -

> Cleopatra swears by the "fire that quickens Nilus' slime", and is the "serpent of old Nile" herself; the flies and gnats of the river shall bury her ill-starred people. And just as 'King Lear' is full of storm and 'Macbeth' of sleeplessness, so some tardy and ominous power slides through the brilliancy of 'Antony and Cleopatra' through the banquetings and the quarrellings and the reconciliations and the lust until the final words, simple as they are, seem to bear incredible meanings -
>
> > "This is an aspic's trail: and these fig leaves/ Have slime upon them, such as the aspic leaves/ Upon the caves of Nile."
>
> Of course, one must not press symbolism; to symbolize is to destroy him. Yet perhaps this mud of Egypt was working in his mind, and but for Egypt would not have been in it. (11)

This article is a typically Forsterian piece in three distinct ways: it is concerned with the nature of the poetic process in the author's mind and traces the work of art to its sources of inspiration; it says something about the writer's outlook and values - Shakespeare's overriding interest in the emotional life and tragic fate of his protagonists is taken as evidence of his humanism; there is the perceptive observation of a recurrent topographical image - the Nile. Forster's penchant for discovering poetic unity of this sort could only have come about because of his unusually keen ear for 'rhythms' of this kind, (12) while his great sensitivity to region and local geography springs from his Romantic feeling for nature.

While this criticism of <u>Antony and Cleopatra</u> suggests that Shakespeare did not absorb as much as he could have from the available historical literature, one of Forster's reviews of a book about everyday life in Elizabethan England expands this criticism into a general accusation of the inadequacy of the Elizabethan intellectual outlook -

> There was very little thought in these spacious
> times, just as there was little unashamed or
> uncontorted passion. Socrates, Cleopatra - no,
> they do not occur. Continents were discovered,
> beards singed, bowls bowled, but for all its
> bravery life had retreated to the muscles and
> will, and even Shakespeare, who could have con-
> tained so much, suffered from the surrounding
> impoverishment as he pegged away at his thirty-
> seven plays. (13)

Forster seems to have forgotten about Bacon and the scientific revolution, but even from a purely literary standpoint this is an astonishing verdict upon what is generally recognized as the most creative epoch in English history. It can only be ascribed to Forster's interpretation of the Elizabethan age as one dominated by the spirit of aggressive imperialism, a spirit of which he had been severely critical only the year before in *A Passage to India*:

> There was a vigour and swagger about them (the
> Elizabethans) which all must admire and some
> would adore. Epics, treatises, hundreds of
> plays, thousands of sonnets bounce about ...
> but most of them have proved less permanent
> than the British Empire. Oblivion engulfed
> them because they had not spiritual sincerity.
> Freshness and vitality were not enough ...Quite
> what was amiss we can see when we come to a
> less confident age, and read the poems of Donne.
> Donne tried to be straight about love and about
> other things also: he attempted the process
> known as thought. And though thought may betray
> a man individually and bring Empire to ruin, it
> is nevertheless the only known preservative,
> the only earnest of immortality. The Elizabeth-
> ans, even the greatest of them, plumped for
> the native hue of resolution ... they increased
> our political power and glorified our race, and
> are rightly commended on public occasions. But
> they were at once too violent and too hazy to
> contribute much towards the development of the
> human mind ... (14)

Forster's anti-imperialism, in this case, causes a colossal misjudgment, for it prevents him from seeing that thought and deep feeling are as much a part of Elizabethan drama as they are of the introspective verse of Donne. Forster's dislike of commercialism, warfare, imperialism and physical heroism of the swashbuckling sort interfere more with his critical judgment in this essay than in any other. The essay also contradicts the tentative generalization made earlier that Forster sees writers and literary texts outside their historical context. It is a reminder that consistency is not a strong point in Forster's opinions and that it is futile to make blanket generalizations about hs critical method.

Forster spoke on Shakespeare on two other occasions, in 1943 on Julius Caesar and in 1944 on the nature of the chronicle plays. Both are broadcasts intended for student audiences and therefore of a very introductory nature. Little needs to be said about them, or about the essay on Areopagitica which is a simple defence of free speech.

Forster's view of the medieval and Renaissance periods, evident from his Italian novels and the Abinger Harvest essays on Gemistus Pletho and Girolamo Cardano, is further illustrated by the essays that have been discussed above. Dante's mystical and idealising nature suggests some of the tendencies from which Forster recoils when he writes about Christianity or when he creates characters like Mr. Beebe and Cecil Vyse. Skelton and Shakespeare, in contrast, represent the humanistic direction of the Renaissance. In the ultimate analysis, however, Forster examines each writer as unique rather than typical, as a person who contains multitudes rather than as one who represents a historical period. Dante is medieval in his attitude to personal relations, but in his public life he stands out against his times as much as Skelton and Milton. Shakespeare cares above everything else about human destiny and yet does not shine out as a dissenting voice against the aggressive, imperialistic fervour of his age. Forster can see the links between writers and their historical situations, but his criticism is less an overview of historical periods than an atomized view of the various personalities that make them up. As a liberal and an artist he is too conscious of individual differences, and therefore stresses autonomous uniqueness above socio-historical typicality. Dante and Shakespeare are both recommended because both are great artists who transcend history by creating the emotionally structured worlds to which Forster, as a human being, can respond.

II

Forster's criticism is generally nostalgic

about eighteenth century Europe, for it represents an era of pre-revolutionary stability during which industrialism had not despoiled the countryside, an age which favoured the kind of creativity which is only possible through a life of detachment and cultivation. "Later historians, such as Macaulay or Carlyle, are always fussing about something or other - worrying about the underdog or preaching the gospel of work. Gibbon never fusses. He is an aristocrat. The underdog never unduly distresses him ..." (15) Even more than Gibbon, the figure who symbolizes the eighteenth century for Forster is Voltaire. "If I had to name two people to speak for Europe at the Last Judgment I should choose Shakespeare and Voltaire - Shakespeare for his creative genius, Voltaire for his critical genius and humanity" (16) Forster writes. And on another occasion he notes - "Voltaire and I do speak the same language; vast though be the difference in our vocabularies, we are both civilized ... we belong to the cultural interlude which came between the fall of barbarism and the rise of universal 'education' ... We believe in reason, in pity, and in not always coming out right." (17) There are other similarities. Voltaire was less concerned with political theory than with the remedy of concrete wrongs. Consistency and system building did not interest him and passion and disinterestedness were more important in his philosophy than logic. According to Laski - "Tolerant, invincibly liberal, eclectic, there was something in him which warned him always that politics is a philosophy of the second best."(18) If one adds to this Voltaire's hatred for religious fanaticism and passionate defence of civil liberty, the reasons for Forster's admiration are clear. This similarity of values is explored in six short pieces written between 1931 and 1958. The first two, collectively titled 'Voltaire's Laboratory' (1931) and reprinted in Abinger Harvest, see Voltaire as a precursor of popularizers of science like Samuel Butler, Aldous Huxley and Gerald Heard. Voltaire's efforts, though absurd in the light of modern knowledge, are seen as one individual's attempt to free man from Authority and to make him aware of a world larger than that envisaged by the Church. The third piece describes a visit to Ferney just before the Second War. The house, as so often in Forster's writing, is seen as a symbol of the spirit of its master - "Civilization, Humanity, Enjoyment. That was what the agreeable white building said to us ..." (19) Both here and in the other three pieces, Voltaire is seen as the epitome of the values which Fascism despises - "... if a man believes in liberty and variety and tolerance and sympathy he cannot breathe the air of the totalitarian state ... Voltaire kept faith with the human spirit. He fought its battle against German dictatorship two hundred years before our time." (20)

The only English Augustan discussed by Forster is Dryden, in his fifth lecture in the 'Creator as Critic' series. The lecture is briefer than the other lectures and it is possible that Forster used quotation extensively. Dryden's career as a critic is divided into three categories - defensive, didactic and interpretative. The defensive criticism consists of all that Dryden wrote in connection with his own plays, the didactic of Dryden's remarks on aesthetic issues like translation, and the interpretative of what Dryden had to say about other writers. Forster briefly discusses each category and finds that though Dryden shows insularity in his view of Racine ("The exquisite and exotic art of Racine meant nothing to him at all"), he is interesting on Shakespeare and Chaucer. He was the first to demonstrate the many-sidedness of Shakespeare's characters and perceptive in recognizing Chaucer's feeling for place - "he instantly catches the general atmosphere of the Tales - the background of Inns and Roads ..." (21) In his conclusion to this lecture Forster expresses his own opinion of Dryden as a creator and as a critic. He says that despite Dryden's sensitivity, there is a lack of human warmth in his poetry. Dryden does not come across as a man speaking to men -

> He was a great man of letters, versatile, vigorous and intelligent, but ... we can't get into personal contact with him, we wouldn't recognize him if he came into this room. It isn't his greatness that removes him from us .. It's as if the centre of him, the space where a man says 'I am I' is a void ... You may say one doesn't commune with Shakespeare ... but in Shakespeare and other remote writers one feels they are remote from some decision of their own; they did not choose to receive us. Dryden's ... not elusive or reticent. It is that the central spot isn't there. (22)

But this central vacuum which leaves Forster vaguely dissatisfied with Dryden's creative work does, he feels, make Dryden a good critic. Because he lacks the usually passionate nature of the artist and is all "jokiness and decentralization", Dryden is never dogmatic in his approach to other writers.

It is even more difficult to suggest from these scattered observations on eighteenth century writers that Forster has any more coherent a view of this period than he does of the medieval and Renaissance worlds. In a general sense he seems to admire the pre-revolutionary and pre-industrial stability of the age as well as the civilized values he finds expressed in the work of Gibbon and Voltaire. But he has little of consequence to say about English writers of the period. His preference for Romantic passion, the countryside and personal relations perhaps makes him less enthusiastic about writers whose chief concerns were social and whose chief literary method was satire.

III

Forster's real insights into literature and his ability to illuminate authors and texts in new and perceptive ways are to be found in what he has to say about the literature of the nineteenth century.

Forster's favourite nineteenth century novelist is Jane Austen, but his remarks on her are not very illuminating. If Butler, with his iconoclastic view of Victorian morality was a directly personal influence on Forster's outlook and Proust the novelist who helped Forster understand the modern zeitgeist, Jane Austen helped Forster to understand that delicate social comedy could radiate psychological depth. (23) There is an obvious affinity of interests between Forster and Jane Austen, both being concerned with the imaginative limitations of the middle class, with understanding, sympathy and art rather than power and politics, with the moral quality of inner life behind the social facade. Forster feels that criticism can never adequately describe the peculiar English charm which only Austen's novels contain - "When the humour has been absorbed and the cynicism and moral earnestness both discounted, something remains which is easily called Life, but does not thus become more approachable ... something as impalpable as stardust, yet it is part of the soil of England." (24) In the following year (1925) _Sanditon_ was published. Forster found it of small merit, but the locale - the topography of Sanditon as a place - interested him, and he thought it showed Jane Austen's feeling for place. Whereas the earlier novels seemed to have been dominated by ebony cabinets and massive chests, "Sanditon gives out an atmosphere, and also exists as a geographic and economic force." (25) Forster detects this as an upsurge of a latent Romanticism in Jane Austen's temperament. He attributes the upsurge to a need for the open air because of Austen's ill-health and weariness with her enclosed world. Two years later, in Aspects, Forster drew attention to the subtlety of Jane Austen's characterization by demonstrating that the apparently 'flat' and dull Lady Bertram of Mansfield Park did have a mind of her own. This is really the only occasion when Forster analyses a scene from a Jane Austen novel. His 1932 review of Chapman's edition of Jane Austen's letters is uninteresting and undeserving of a place in Abinger Harvest. A 1944 broadcast on Sense and Sensibility is only marginally more interesting. Written in the Second War context, it stresses that Jane Austen's aloofness from the Napoleonic Wars must not be held against her, for the world of her fiction has an equal if not greater significance than the world of Napoleon. Only Forster's unusual perception of life could produce this - "(If) She cared nothing for Napoleon ... Napoleon no doubt returned the compliment, cared nothing for her, and probably never heard her name." (26) Forster's sympathy is with Napoleon for what he missed!

Apart from the observations in Aspects, Forster wrote nothing of importance on Dickens, George Eliot and Thackeray. There is a short descriptive essay on Mrs. Gaskell in which Forster says that Wives and Daughters, not Cranford, is Mrs. Gaskell's masterpiece. He admires the novel partly because it has a loose, symphonic construction. (27) But Forster does have some interesting things to say about Meredith, Butler and Hardy.

After the First War it was impossible to look towards Meredith with the sense of awe with which he had been regarded before it. His optimistic philosophy, his lofty sentiments and his generally narrow focus upon England's country life made him seem too limited and insular in outlook. Forster was among the first to point out that Meredith's novels "do not endure like Hardy's, there is too much Surrey about them..." (28) But in 'Three Generations' Meredith is seen from a historical perspective and shown to be the finest representative of the pre-war period of stability.

In his conclusion to this paper Forster says his aim has been to analyse the three civilizations through which he has lived. The three 'acts' of

FORSTER'S LITERARY CRITICISM

English history are roughly 1900-14, 1918-33 and 1933-9. Meredith represents the first period, Proust the second, and Auden (in a tentative way) the third. Forster's view of the first period has been outlined earlier and is summed up by him as the age of 'hope without faith'. The idea that human personality and human society are not as solid as they appear could not have struck Meredith, "living as he did through a period of peace diversified by a few picturesque little wars." (29) As the future seemed bound to get brighter, "the noble men and women whom he delighted to create found their highest activity in speeding the future up, so that it brightened ahead of schedule. Vittoria hurries up the unification of Italy, Clara Middleton the emancipation of women."(30) In England it was Meredith rather than Ibsen who helped prepare the way for the suffragettes, for though he died before their struggle began, The Egoist was prophetic in suggesting "that though an Englishman's home is indeed his castle, he shouldn't keep his wife in the dungeon. Clara Middleton escapes from a prospective dungeon ..."(31) Meredith's fiction also embodies the enormous importance once attached to witty conversation - "D.H. Lawrence killed it though you can still find its corpse weekly in Punch - this fetish is enthroned in Meredith's novels, and at the time we all bowed our knees there too." (32) Finally, Meredith documents the shallowness with which science was regarded up to the first decade of the twentieth century: "Science was something which made smells in laboratories, and we never dreamed that those smells would one day escape, poison cities, and be used as blackmail by tyrants." (33) Forster observes that Sir Willoughby's laboratory in Patterne Park is supposed to suggest the egoist's stupidity.

Forster's remarks on Meredith are an example of his capacity for perceptive 'sociological' criticism. The weakness of the paper is (typically) that there is no attempt to build on the insights or follow them up with textual demonstration. Consequently this remains a finely written and patchily brilliant essay rather than, as it might have been, a thorough piece of literary criticism.

As a satirist of the narrowness of the English vision of life Forster felt an affinity with Samuel Butler, and like Bernard Shaw, he did his best to propagate Butler. Butler's radical outlook is not savage like Swift's and Joyce's, but stems from an idiosyncratic irreverence. His writing is not marked by saeva indignatio, but by a gentler and curious combination of satire, humour, fantasy and whimsy - a combination noticeable in much of Forster's writing. (34) Butler's common sense attitude to money, his immense variety of interests, his Voltairean desire to experiment and discover things for himself and his curiosity about how he would be thought of by posterity, are features which link him to Forster. (35) At one stage Forster even had a contract to write a book about Butler (36) but he never saw this project through, and what remains is one unpublished talk to the Weybridge Literary Society (c.1910), a broadcast talk on *Erewhon* (1944) which was reprinted in TCD, an uncollected review of his own biographer's study of Butler (1948) and an article in *The Listener* on 'The Legacy of Samuel Butler' (1952). Each of these essays says more or less the same things about Butler, and only the first two need be discussed here.

The Weybridge talk begins in a semi-allegorical fashion. A vast edifice (English literature) is being constructed by workmen (writers) and is supported by central columns (Shakespeare's plays). The work is overseen by John Bull (the average Englishman) who notices that one of his workers (Butler) never works to rule (he produces literature but also dabbles in science, evolution, theology, travel books, painting, music, criticism and sheep farming). John Bull makes enquiries about Butler and is told that Butler admires him, but for the oddest reasons. Butler is discovered to be a materialist who dislikes idealism and saintliness - he likes the worldliness of John Bull. He also likes Bull's unselfconscious and muddleheaded character, his good breeding, good health and good looks, for he thinks of these as great gifts that humanity has acquired during the evolutionary process. John Bull, however, is suspicious and alarmed by this exposure of his character. Butler's salary is cut off and he departs (leaves for New Zealand). This is precisely the kind of materialism which Forster criticizes in 'Notes on the English Character' and it may be wondered why he admires Butler. The answer is in the second part of the essay, where Forster shows that Butler's conservatism was derived from his eccentric research into evolution and has no further relevance. Butler's real significance, he feels, lies in puncturing and exposing English complacence.

'Books That Influenced Me' discusses *Erewhon* because, Forster says, this is a book he might have written himself. One of Leonard Woolf's remarks about the nature of Butler's satire also helps to clarify why Forster should have picked Erewhon. Woolf says that unlike Swift, whose inverted Utopia is animated by anger, indignation or mere pity, "when Butler describes the Musical Banks or the Erewhonians' attitude towards disease, it is impossible to detect the least flicker of emotion." (37) There is an aesthetic detachment in Erewhon which is rare in social satire. The satire operates without preventing delight in the autonomous fantasy universe of Erewhon, and this appeals to Forster. He feels that as Blake's humanism is the opposite of St Augustine's asceticism, Voltaire's philosophy of Machiavelli's, the moral in Antigone of Carlyle's Of Heroes, Hero-Worship and the Heroic in History, so Erewhon is the aesthetic antithesis of Gulliver's Travels.

In Aspects Forster says that Hardy cannot construct good plots and convincing characters but that he has a poet's intense vision which makes his novels poignant and beautiful. This view is elaborated in a 1942 broadcast on The Return of the Native. The richness of local detail in the novel is traced to the region which inspired Hardy - "Hardy is a little corner of England. He is something else as well, and something greater, for he moves in the vast region of ideas which is shared by the whole of the human race. But geographically he is merely Dorsetshire and the counties bordering it..." (38) The reader is asked to concentrate on the feelings which suffuse the topographical details and to look for the connections between man and the soil. Another seminal source of inspiration is shown to be Hardy's rustic origin and nostalgia for the lost innocence of childhood, for it was always "as a gentle country boy that he confronted the irony of circumstances and the cruelty of man." (39) Forster also believes that Hardy's novels can only be understood in relation to his poetry, because Hardy was essentially a poet. His greatest poetic achievement is The Dynasts and the best scenes in The Native anticipate the later work - "the conversation round the bonfire, on Rainbarrow for instance, and the philosophy which was to develop from the deification of Egdon Heath to the doctrine of the Immanent Will." (40) These show Hardy for what he really was - "a poet and a brooder, who looked through the smooth surface of civilization into something disquieting." (41) The plot of The Native is ridiculous and the characters are magnificently described but unconvincing as people. Hardy's success qua novelist lies mainly in his creation of minor characters. Granfer Cantle is so good because Hardy had such deep feeling for old-fashioned characters and local customs. The rustic scenes - the mumming, the frying of adders, the voodooism, the Sunday haircutting in village streets - delight Forster the most because they re-create a rural England which had not lost its precious connection with its past. Despite his failure with plot and character, Hardy remains among Forster's favourite writers because of his values and Romantic sensibility.

Forster's fiction - which places a high value upon passion, vitality and the spirit of rural England - has aesthetics, which is based on Romantic premises - and his literary criticism, which is interested in the writer's personality, sources of inspiration and geographical roots - are all evidence of his fondness for the English Romantic poets. But despite this emotional kinship, Forster said relatively little about the Romantics. There are three short pieces on Coleridge, one on Wordsworth, and a review essay on Blake. Keats is scarcely the subject of the enigmatic 'Mr. and Mrs. Abbey's Difficulties' in Abinger Harvest. Byron is never mentioned, and Shelley only crops up in passing in some of Forser's essays. (42) Forster might have felt that the Romantics were not in need of propaganda, because if one looks at one of the pre-Romantics, Crabbe, one finds Forster making a considerable popularizing effort. (43) Although chronologically Crabbe and Blake belong more to the eighteenth century than to the nineteenth, within the terms of literary history they prefigure the Romantics and it is convenient to discuss them here.

One of Forster's favourite biographies was the one of Crabbe by his son and in 1932, the centenary year of Crabbe's death, Forster wrote an introduction to the World's Classics Edition of that book. This introduction summarizes Crabbe's career and provides some typically Forsterian insights into his poetry. Crabbe's work is not difficult, but it is unique. The uniqueness is traced to an unattractive feature of the poet's personality - his reproving nature - "Wherever he looked, he saw human beings taking the wrong turning ... analysis and censure is a speciality of Crabbe's ... To all his characters and to their weakness Crabbe extends a little pity, a little contempt, a little cynicism, but a much larger measure of reproof ..." (44) Crabbe's fondness for reproof is shown to have been the result of his miserable childhood in Aldeburgh. Had he continued to suffer in later life he might, like Hardy, have written tragic verse, but he gained the patronage of Burke, and this "though it never sweetened, softened, and he disapproved where once he would have denounced or recoiled." (45) This gives Crabbe's poetry a rare flavour unobtainable elsewhere in literature. Despite the moralizing tone, Forster likes Crabbe's poetry because the poet does not hesitate to reprove his own failings and because the atmosphere of his work is "...so to speak, sub-Christian; there is an implication throughout of positive ideals, such as self-sacrifice and ascetism, but they are rarely pressed..."(46) Forster also enjoys another unique feature in the poetry of Crabbe - its feeling for the topography of the Suffolk coast - "Into the work of Crabbe there steals again and again the sea, the flat coast, the local meannesses, and an odour of brine and dirt - tempered occasionally with the scent of flowers." (47) Forster believes that though Crabbe hated the region, spiritually he could never escape it, and subconsciously it attracted him and inspired his best poetry. These same ideas are the substance of Forster's 1941 article 'George Crabbe: The Poet and the Man' (48) where topographical features are linked to the soul of the warped Peter Grimes, as well as the 1948 Aldeburgh Festival address reprinted in Two Cheers for Democracy. In 1955 Lilian Haddakin's The Poetry of Crabbe was reviewed very briefly by Forster. He says that criticism is ultimately futile because the essence of Crabbe is uncommunicable in prose and may only be obtained by reading his poems. (49)

Blake is yet another example of a poet who, in Forster's view, could do without critics. "The cry that is raised by all literature - the cry of 'Read me, do not write about me..' rings with particular force through Blake" says Forster in his review of Laurence Binyon's 1932 edition of Blake's verse.(50) Forster is critical of Blake's poetry when it is excessively mystical and obscure, yet admires the Blake who voiced the important truth that salvation is not something external but lies within man, in the creative potential of the human imagination.

Forster's discussion of Wordsworth is even briefer and less remarkable. It consists of a broadcast to India in 1944. The poet is connected to his soil - "He belonged to his soil, not someone else's, to his rocks, not to the Himalayas, to his own sky and his own flowers", (51) and discussed as a writer who celebrated the world of nature and the human spirit against the materialism of industrial civilization.

FORSTER'S LITERARY CRITICISM

Forster wrote with a little more detail on Coleridge. He saw that Coleridge's literary career was divisible into two halves, the first half as poet, the second as critic. It was probably personally comforting for Forster to observe that the second half of Coleridge's life was as fruitful, in a different way, as the first. In the second 'Creator as Critic' lecture titled 'Self-Defence', Forster notices two peaks in Coleridge's achievement - 1797 when he produced his best poetry, and 1817 when he wrote the Biographia. The passage from 1797 to 1817, he says, is "from sleep to alertness, from the unconscious to the conscious life." (52) 'The Destiny of Nations' with its icy landscapes and spectral lights is less successful than 'The Ancient Mariner' because Coleridge was less 'unconscious' when he wrote the earlier poem. With regard to Coleridge's criticism, Forster thinks highly of his Shakespeare lectures, not for their analysis but because of their enthusiasm - "We feel him (Coleridge) vibrating all the time and there are moments when he seems to connect us physically with the movements and characters of the drama." (53) Forster is impressed by the sections of the Biographia which discuss Wordsworth's poetry, but evinces little interest in Coleridge's theoretical speculations about the nature of poetry.

Later the same year Forster reviewed a new edition of Coleridge's poems, merely abbreviating what he had already said in his Cambridge lecture.(54) Another 1931 essay, 'Trooper Silas Tomkyn Comberbacke', fits well into Abinger Harvest, for it is a speculative reconstruction of Coleridge's brief tenure in the dragoons. It is concerned with Coleridge's boyhood memories and, like the essays on Keats and Gibbon in the same volume, with showing how ill the artist fits into a regimented existence. Finally, in a 1932 review of E.L. Griggs's two volume edition of Coleridge's unpublished letters, Forster shows that the poet was a complex and contradictory character, and that his letters increase rather than explain his complexity. (55) The review reaffirms Forster's aversion for criticism which seeks to explain genius. He prefers genius to be recognized for what he believes it is - complex, mysterious and unique.

The last of the nineteenth century writers discussed in Forster's criticism is Matthew Arnold. The importance of Arnoldian liberalism for Forster's outlook has already been discussed. One of the basic arguments of Culture and Anarchy is - "Religion says: The Kingdom of God is within you; and culture in like manner, places human perfection in an inner condition, in the growth of predominance of our humanity proper, as distinguished from our animality." (56) Forster's criticism argues with similar religious zeal about the importance of culture as inner, enlightening experience in a world swamped by the outer life of commerce, machinery and politics - even though Forster is more sceptical than Arnold that the cultural gospel can effect any major social transformation. Arnold, says Forster, could be rather naively optimistic about the relation between literature and life. He believed that the evil of life was man's "fever, restlessness, irritability", and the function of literature was therapeutic, to "allay that fever and restore us to our true selves." (57) With regard to his criticism, Forster says that Arnold's judgments on other writers "aren't always acceptable", but his importance as a critic is justified because "what he's so good at is asserting that literature is important, and asserting it emotionally ... without didacticism." (58)

As a writer who felt strongly about the spiritual value of art, natural beauty and the development of the inner life, Forster is part of mainstream nineteenth century literary theory which criticized the dehumanizing effects of industrialism. While his essays are more a conglomeration of isolated opinions about unique authors, something like an overview of nineteenth century writing can be inferred from 'Notes on the English Character' (1920). This essay is an exposure of the phlegmatic, complacent and unimaginative character of the English middle class in the nineteenth century. Like 'Peeping at Elizabeth', it sees little good in the social temper of the age it discusses. Whenever Forster surveys mankind in the mass, or examines the quality of public life, he finds little to approve of. But as a generalization about an epoch 'Notes on the English Character' is less severe than 'Peeping at Elizabeth' for the reason that the literature of the period does not share in Forster's general disapproval. The radical split between culture and industrial society in the nineteenth century (as Raymond Williams has shown) makes possible a clear cut distinction between the private or spiritual or human values upheld by artists on the one hand, and the materialistic public character of the period on the other. Whereas, in Forster's view, Elizabethan writing loses in value by sharing the aggressive, commercial and militaristic character of its community, writers like Jane Austen, Blake, Coleridge and Wordsworth gain in value because by their relative detachment from society they represent the personal and transcendentally human values which oppose social decay. Their writing reflects the 'wobble' which occurs when private, ivory tower creativity is consistent with a critical, social concern.

IV

The bulk of Forster's literary criticism is about modern writers. The word 'modern' is used loosely here and covers writers like Tolstoy, Dostoevsky, Chekhov and Ibsen (who were translated into English and became known in England around the turn of the century) as well as Kipling, Wells, Conrad, James, Proust, Joyce, Yeats, T.S. Eliot, D.H. Lawrence and Virginia Woolf. Forster has something to say about all these writers, and also about relatively minor writers like Forrest Reid, Sinclair Lewis, Lytton Strachey, Andre Gide, Romain Rolland, Ronald Firbank, C.P. Cavafy, T.E. Lawrence, George Orwell, Howard Overing Sturgis, Tagore and Iqbal. Most of this criticism is accessible in Abinger Harvest, Two Cheers for Democracy and Aspects, or has been the subject of critical discussion elsewhere. The emphasis in this section will therefore, once again, be upon those of Forster's criticisms which are hitherto unpublished or uncollected or undiscussed.

One of the best critical essays that Forster ever wrote is 'Ibsen the Romantic' (1928). Forster defines the central source of Ibsen's inspiration as a Romantic feeling for place as well as a passionate and contorted perception of life. The essay is a reaction against Shaw's The Quintessence of Ibsenism (1891). Shaw's Ibsen is a campaigner for moral and social reform, and is made nearly identical with Shaw himself. Forster argues that the quintessence of Ibsen is not any moral or social message, but intense Romantic passion and a unique subterranean atmosphere. Ibsen has the air of a preacher, but is really a prophet. His moral messages always rest "on passing irritabilities, and not on any permanent view of conduct or the universe", (59) whereas the essential Ibsen is the poet. Ibsen's value as an artist is connected only incidentally with his criticism of society and primarily with his capacity to connect with the universal 'unseen'. "It is proper", Forster says, "that we should ask such

FORSTER'S LITERARY CRITICISM

questions ... (about) the moral and social aspect of his work ... But as soon as we shift the focus ... the reformer becomes a dramatist ... we shift again and the dramatist becomes a lyric poet ..." (60) Forster's essay also reveals the 'genetic fallacy', for Ibsen's imagery is traced to his "experiences of passionate intensity" among the mountains of south-western Norway.

While Forster's analysis of Ibsen is reasonably well known, one of the most important (and certainly the most detailed) critical essays he ever wrote is unpublished and remains unknown. This is Forster's essay on Kipling which was probably presented to the Weybridge Literary Society in 1908. (61)

In Kipling's poem 'The <u>Mary Gloster</u>', Sir Anthony says to his son - "Harrer an' Trinity College! I ought to ha' sent you to sea - / But I stood you an education, an' what have you done for me? / The things I knew was proper you wouldn't thank me to give, / And the things I knew was rotten you said was the way to live." If Sir Anthony is roughly the embodiment of Kipling's personal beliefs, the son who is berated for his softness can be seen to represent the world to which Forster belongs. The outlook of the two writers is antithetical. Kipling values imperialism, class, conquest, self-abnegation and practical science. He upholds, as Samuel Hynes puts it, "a world governed by white men with machines." (62) Forster values social equality, culture, Epicurean enjoyment, disinterested knowledge and a world inhabited by racially hybrid men without machines. As a person, therefore, Forster finds Kipling distasteful, and feels that many of Kipling's uglier ideals discolour his poems. But Forster also recognizes that Kipling's work reveals a deeper aesthetic or impersonal level which enables it to transcend the political conservatism of his surface personality. (63) Although 'man' and 'artist' are never very separate in Forster's criticism, this essay offers starkly contrasting opinions on the personal character and aesthetic merit of Kipling. It briefly demolishes Kipling the reactionary but also affirms Wilde's judgment that Kipling "knows vulgarity better than anyone has ever known it. Dickens knew its clothes and its comedy. Mr. Kipling knows its essence and its seriousness. He is our first authority on the second rate..." (64) In fact Forster goes further, identifying a Romantic spiritualism and feeling for place which raises some of Kipling's work to the most transcendent aesthetic level.

FORSTER'S LITERARY CRITICISM

The first section of the essay reveals the intermingling of doctrinal vulgarity and emotional force in Kipling's poems - "Kipling is vulgar. He does brag. He is at times the bounder ... (but) if Kipling was what Kipling seems, if he really was putty, brass and paint - how quick we'd drop him, how remote he would be from literature ..." (65) The whole truth is more complex, for the 'putty, brass and paint' "is fused, at times inextricably, with a precious metal ... Words that move the reader so deeply, that have an almost physical effect upon him, cannot be the words of a charlatan." (66) Kipling's superabundant vitality, his power to 'bounce' the reader, is a quality that Forster greatly admires. At the same time he warns that this sense of life (an aesthetic quality) should not be confused with an ideal of life that is often repugnant -

> How magnificent (we think) to lead a lawless roving life somewhere East of Suez ... Armed with a sword instead of an umbrella and a revolver instead of a tram ticket, how magnificent to meet some other strong man face to face ... we are too apt to exclaim 'Oh this is reality. This is life' ...too apt to regard him (Kipling) as a sort of inspired buccaneer and not as a complex poet, who, like most poets, touches the facts of existence at one moment, and fails to touch them at the next.(67)

For a true estimate of Kipling, the critic must steer between the two extremes of Art for Art's Sake and Life for Life's Sake, for "if we go too near (the first) ... we shall undervalue Kipling ... and if we go too near (the second) ... we shall overvalue him." (68) The point is to discover the aesthetic core buried below the surface morality (or immorality) of Kipling's poetry. This is the purpose of the rest of Forster's essay. Kipling's poems are divided into five categories and each category is discussed through analysis of two or three representative poems.

The first category comprises the narrative poems which Forster considers the best work that Kipling produced. 'The Ballad of East and West', 'Tomlinson', 'The <u>Mary Gloster</u>' and 'McAndrew's Hymn' show, first of all, a superb control of narrative - "All of them ... grip our attention in the opening lines, proceed without effort to a climax, and leave no loose threads at the conclusion ... The incidents are simple and striking, the characters firmly contrasted: regarded merely as craftsmanship they are worthy of high praise." (69) But technical merit is in itself insufficient in accounting for aesthetic merit. Like Forster's other criticism, this essay affirms that aesthetic value has less to do with the artist's ability to shape material into a pattern than with his power to infuse his subject with intense passion. This, he believes, lifts Kipling's narrative poems from journalism into literature. 'The Mary Gloster' is called the greatest triumph of what Forster pithily terms a "mixture of slang and bluff and scriptural reminiscences - the Kipling amalgam." (70) It represents a radically new use of the ballad form, for "to express the heights of emotion in the dregs of our common speech is absolutely new in literature." (71)

The second category of poems comprises those that deal with military matters - chiefly the Barrack Room Ballads. For many readers these are the essential Kipling. Forster thinks that Kipling's depiction of the variety and depth of life in the ranks is superb, but says that the 'amalgam' tends to crack when Kipling puts more into the mouths of his simple characters than they can credibly hold:

> Tommy Atkins may be as artificial, as 'literary' as were ever the Strephons and Silvios of the eighteenth century, and may equally fetter the poet in the expression of truth. The Barrack Room is not a large place: it is larger than we civilians thought, but it is not the whole world. And the ballads sung therein must keep to their own subjects: when they venture into high tragedy or romance they become either painful or insincere. (72)

The third category consists of those poems suggested by residence in India. These are thought poor. India, says Forster, inspired Kipling's prose, not his poetry, for the Departmental Ditties with their "jumble of girls and subs and rickshaws are not India" -

> The real India, that has its capital not at Simla, nor at any city built by men, the India of Buddha and of Brahm, that desires not government appointments, but unity with the divine, the India that the Bridge Builders saw when the Ganges came down in flood, and the lama saw when he found the River of the Arrow and rescued Kim

> from the tyranny of the wheel - that India -
> only by chance I think - scarcely finds expres-
> sion in the poems at all. (73)

The only reason why Forster reads these poems is because they remind him that the deepest source of Kipling's inspiration was India -

> India is the most important religious influence
> that Kipling has ever felt. Of religion as it
> has presented itself to the finer minds of the
> West he has little comprehension ... The God of
> his celebrated 'Recessional' is a Hebrew deity
> who has given us dominion over palm and pine,
> and who may take the dominion away if we do not
> keep the law: the spirit is not mentioned. It
> is to Jehovah of the Thunders that we are to
> pray in the 'Hymn Before Action' ... The New
> Testament exists for him scarcely more than it
> did for the Ironsides of Cromwell; all his
> sympathies are for the Old. It is true that
> Calvinism (approaching as it does to the idea of
> a Jewish theocracy) finds him sympathetic ... To
> admire Calvinism and to admire Buddhism as well
> might seem impossible. But life is always more
> wonderful than one supposes ... behind it all
> (Kipling's work) there remains the mystic,
> passionless face of India and the lama saying
> to Kim 'Just is the Wheel! certain is our
> deliverance. Come!' (74)

The centrality of *The Dynasts* in Forster's inter-pretation of Hardy has a parallel in the importance given to *Kim* in this essay. *Kim* is seen as the climactic expression of the one predominant source of inspiration visible in nearly everything Kipling wrote -

> 'Kim' *is* Kipling. It is the one book that we
> must bear in mind when we are trying to estimate
> his genius, for it contains the spiritual stand-
> ard by which all his developments must be meas-
> ured. Mysticism may be a mistake, but ... if
> once a man shows traces of it, those traces must
> be carefully scanned by all those who are trying
> to understand him. To have felt, if only for a
> moment, that this visible world is an illusion -
> to have conceived, however faintly, that the
> real is the unseen, to have had even a passing
> desire for the One - is at once to be marked
> off from all who have not thus felt, thus

> conceived, thus desired. There is no explanation of the gift of mysticism ... only one thing is certain; it is the peculiar gift of India, and India has given it to Kipling, as she gave it to his boy hero, Kim. (75)

When seen in relation with Kim, the second rate quality of Kipling's Departmental Ditties becomes clear, for "they are thrown off by the superficial layers of Kipling's mind, while 'Kim' proceeds from the central core of it." (76) To a large extent, this is a reading into, rather than a reading of, Kipling's poetry. It is a very subjective interpretation because Forster is narcisstically finding his own nascent feeling for the spiritual India reflected in Kipling's work. But even if India was less responsible for Kipling's capacity to apprehend the unseen than Forster assumes, the crux of his argument is still valuable. This argument is that something spiritual permeates and underlies the Kiplingesque surface of 'putty, brass and paint', and that it is by being attuned to this dimension that one can enjoy and value even the less impressive poems of Kipling.

The fourth category of poems are those that are jingoistic celebrations of imperialism. Forster finds it impossible to like these because they show only the dogmatic, metallic and callow Kipling. He says that only those who believe that the Anglo-Saxon race is Chosen can like these poems, whereas "Those who, like myself, have a sneaking admiration for 'them furriners' and who hope that France, Italy and Germany, even Germany, will help to shape the civilizations of the future - we shall read these later poems with a feeling of tension ..." (77) In the South African songs Forster feels that the cheeriness of the Barrack Room Ballads has been replaced by brutality. The activity of the spirit is nowhere evident, and action is the only demand - "he (Kipling) cannot realize that all those men who do the work for which they draw the wage, must at the same time lead inner lives of their own and the state of these inner lives is the true measure of national progress." (78) The Kipling of these later poems has lost his balance and can only be admired as a craftsman. But does this then mean, Forster asks, that imperialism is a subject unfit for poetry? His answer is given in the form of an unusual and interesting comparison of Kipling with another poet of imperialism - Virgil:

> An Empire is a very difficult subject for
> poetry. Unless the poet possesses exquisite
> taste and deep inspiration, he will fall into
> Kipling's error, and praise it because it is
> big and can smash up its enemies. To celebrate
> a nation is easy enough: it demands a straight-
> forward patriotism which most of us can supply.
> But an Empire, with its claims to world-wide
> dominion demands something more profound - that
> instinctive reverence for all humanity possess-
> ed by Virgil ... Kipling's task is more diff-
> icult than Virgil's, for the British Empire,
> unlike the Roman, cannot claim a monopoly of
> civilization. And needless to add, he lacks
> the Virgilian qualities: he would scorn them as
> un-British. The results are depressing. For
> one thing the colonies are exalted beyond all
> proportion, because being young communities,
> (they) are therefore still engaged in the
> physical struggle with nature ... whereas
> England, aged 1000 years, and occupied in the
> effeminate problems of education and social re-
> form, rouses his soul to loathing. For another
> thing the foreigner is, beyond all proportion,
> insulted. Kipling's big vital empire must <u>do</u>
> something. Fortunately there are the foreign-
> ers, whom he regards as a sort of moral foot-
> ball, designed by providence for the purpose of
> keeping the Chosen Race in good condition. (79)

This shows a very perceptive and mature understanding of the historical difference between Roman and
British imperialism. Virgil's sentiments are acceptable because within his historical context it was
possible to maintain that Rome was civilized and
imperialism a method by which civilization was
extended. But Kipling's intellectual confusion - on
the one hand his respect for the heathen's primitive
contact with nature and on the other his justifica-
tion of empire as a civilizing agency - is contrariwise shown up by Forster both as evidence of a ridiculous mentality, and of the moral hypocrisy of
British imperialism of which Kipling's jingoistic
poetry is representative.

The last category of poems contains those
written for children. These are not uniformly good,
but all of them contain "the wings of Romance" and
are unmistakably the work of the man who was "awak-
ened into life by India." (80) In these poems
Kipling "is half a child himself. He too loves puns
and catchwords and vain repetitions, like the

younger heathen." (81) The rule of Law gives way
to the gentler rule of spirit. In the poem 'Merrow
Down', for instance, the essential Kipling is heard
again, as he ...

> ...joins the world together link by link, not
> by the tinkle of the banjo - but by a nobler
> bond: the thread of paternal love that has
> descended unbroken through the centuries ...
> Words like these will never be widely popular.
> They will never be shouted from the platforms
> at elections, or quoted as headlines by the
> halfpenny press. They are too melodious, too
> tender, too wise, they only deal with what is
> permanent and noble in our humanity. They
> speak to us of the past: they may speak about
> us to the future, in days when our politics are
> forgotten and our newspapers undecipher-
> able. (82)

The importance of this essay is self-evident. It
offers very valuable insights into Kipling and is
simultaneously interesting for what it reveals about
Forster - especially his attitude to India, imperialism, and the way in which these two subjects
ought to be treated in literature. The essay is
also distinctively Forsterian in other ways. It
discovers in Kipling (perhaps imposes upon him) a
Romantic feeling for the unseen which derives from a
specific geographical location - India. It values
those aspects of Kipling's poetry which Forster himself is impelled towards - passion, tenderness, the
vivid re-creation of intense private experience,
spiritual awareness, and sympathetic curiosity about
the vast variety of human life. It is also, as some
of the quotations may have revealed, an extremely
well written essay with many aphoristic turns of
phrase. It is uncharacteristic in only one respect,
and this is to its credit: it is more empirical and
less impressionistic than Forster's other essays,
for its conclusions are demonstrated by textual evidence. Of all of Forster's unpublished criticism,
this essay on Kipling (along with 'Three Generations') most deserves publication.

It is interesting to see how Forster's view of
Kipling, though it did not fundamentally alter, is
modified by the historical context of his later notices. As the situation became more politicized,
Kipling's philosophy began to seem even more obviously crude. Reviewing Kipling's <u>Letters of Travel</u> in
1920, Forster says that the letters show an immature

school-boy who never outgrew his ardour for king and country - "Few men have seen as much as Kipling; few have experienced so little in the true sense ... he inspects civilization from the window of the Fifth form room ... whooping, and blustering, and tomahawking, and sniggering, and throwing up his cap for the Chosen Race ..." (83) This is an attitude which Forster finds particularly reprehensible in the context of the Amritsar massacre. Then in 1937 Forster reviewed Kipling's autobiography, <u>Something of Myself</u>, and said that Kipling anticipates the concept of a Fascist guild-state in which men work unquestioningly and unceasingly like machines. (84) At the same time, Forster asserts that Kipling exemplifies a schizophrenic split between the callow ideologue and the great artist, between the surface and the lower personality. Forster is here implicitly rebutting the notion of the shallower thirties Marxists that political conservatism precludes the creation of great literature. Finally, when T.S. Eliot's edition of Kipling's verse appeared in 1941, Forster agreed with Eliot that Kipling was an exquisite craftsman, but also warns that "No amount of sympathetic pleading will conceal the fact that Mr. Kipling was a bully and a vulgarian and rotten with racial consciousness ... he saw everything and everyone with racial consciousness." (85)

Kipling's contemporary Henry James is, both as man and artist, his antithesis. Kipling believes in strength, courage, manliness, endurance and the vigorously physical (and relatively mindless) outdoor life. His writing is intellectually uncomplicated and easily understood. James, on the other hand, believes in urbanity, the arts and the indoor life of self-cultivation. His writing is contorted, and when he describes emotional nuances and fine shades of feeling, often extremely obscure. Although Forster's Bloomsbury connections - his upbringing, his belief in inner cultivation and personal relations, and his idea of art for art's sake - suggest kinship with James, his admiration of vitality, tenderness and passion - all that distances him from Bloomsbury and connects him with Lawrence - show that his sympathies lie somewhere between the extremes of Art and Life represented by James and Kipling. Forster met James once, in January 1908, and seemed to sense immediately that James (in Furbank's words) "could never mean much to him personally. There was something stuffy and pompous in the Lamb House atmosphere; it was not his road."(86) He identified James with a drawing room world, (87) whereas his own sympathies, he says recollecting the visit, were with "the darkness, the social vastness and the human warmth of the world outside" (88) - the world of Lawrence, Dostoevsky, Melville and Emily Bronte. This is obvious in Forster's criticism of James.

One of Forster's earliest references to James is in a letter from Alexandria to his friend Bob Trevelyan -

> I am already deep in The Piddle Years (sic). I never find Henry James difficult to understand, though it is difficult to throw off the interests of one's larger life, and flatten oneself - flat flatter flattest - to crawl down his slots. Intellectually the exertion is slight. Bring muscle or blood to bear, and you stick at once, and put down your failure to deficiency of brain. (89)

This criticism of James's narrow interests and of the lack of physical vitality in his work is repeated in Aspects, and again in the 'Creator as Critic' lectures. James is discussed here as a 'self-critical critic' who theorized too much about his own work. This kind of critic has integrity, but is also "over anxious about personal salvation, which may be as paralysing in the aesthetic world as it is in the moral." (90) Forster then provides an unsympathetic paraphrase of James's idea of the novel which more or less duplicates the view presented in Aspects:

> A novel, for him was a very delicate fabric which can only be constructed out of very carefully selected material ... you might easily insert some(thing) heavy or coarse, and then the whole book would break. Consequently his characters fall into a few types and are constructed on meagre lines ... He seems to me our only perfect novelist, but alas, it isn't a very enthralling type of perfection. (91)

In 1956 Forster reviewed an anthology of James's art criticism, and the review suffers from the same early prejudices. Forster finds James perceptive, but does not feel that James fully enjoyed the pictures he looked at. The review begins by contrasting Forster's own idea of enjoyment - "I enjoy mooning about and looking at pictures" - with James's severely determined effort to understand pictures as aesthetic objects - "He did not moon; he was too well-trained and well contained to do that; he received impressions, came to conclusions, transmitted opinions." (92) James is found intelligent on Ruskin, Burne-Jones and Sargent, but Forster finds him too much of a polished gentleman to enjoy pictures that fall short of his narrow notion of good taste. The outdoor paintings of Winslow Homer, for instance, "hale the spectator (James) physically into the open air and send him down rapids in the Adirondacks where his top hat rolls off. The wilderness and the countrified places were slightly suspect to the neatly attired James." (93)

Forster has, in the end, a sort of moderated dislike for James. He likes some of James's novels (he praises <u>Portrait of a Lady</u> highly in 'Does Culture Matter'), and is often surprised to discover 'living' passages and characters in James's work, but these never quite compensate the general emotional barrenness, the arid intellectualism and the puristic concern with 'form' which Forster perceives as the essence of James.

I will conclude with Forster's view of two major writers of the twenties - Proust and Joyce. Forster did write about many other writers of the twenties and post-twenties, but his views on them will not be discussed partly because they are straightforward appreciative accounts (for example the essays on Gide and Orwell) available in published form, partly because some of them are about very minor writers and can be understood in the light of what has already been said about Forster's general critical method (for example the essays on Reid and Firbank), and partly because little more can be added to already existing discussion of Forster <u>vis a vis</u> D.H. Lawrence, T.E. Lawrence, T.S. Eliot and Virginia Woolf. (94)

In his 1929 essay on Proust, (95) Forster says that Proust's <u>A La Recherche du Temps Perdu</u> is the epic of the early twentieth century. The novel accurately reflects the modern mood, for its characters are not tragic but merely doomed to a process of slow decay. There is neither grandeur nor ultimate purpose in their lives, and they are only allowed a detached curiosity about the future. Proust's outlook is despairing, pessimistic and nearly cynical for unlike Dante who could pin his faith in a celestial future, Proust can only perceive a world in which illness and cruelty dominate, love is illusory or leads to jealousy, and where the only hint of permanence is to be found in works of art. Forster

FORSTER'S LITERARY CRITICISM

himself does not share Proust's profound pessimism and mistrust of love, but he believes that Proust's novel is unparalleled as a record of the temper of the times.

Forster's own account of the twenties, in which Proust figures as the representative writer, exists in the second section of 'Three Generations'. The period is summarized by the word 'curiosity' because ideals had been shattered by the war and men could only grope about in a fragmented universe. There was a sense of immense disillusionment and despair, but this gradually gave way to curiosity as well as a desire to enjoy life while it lasted -

> Even if you are disillusioned about the progress of society and the progress of the human race, even if you see no purpose in the universe, there are two important things you can do if you possess sufficient vitality: you can have a good time and you can try to understand. The post war people came out strongly in both these ways. (96)

The thirst for pleasure was pervasive. Exhausted by the war and cynical of ideals, particularly liberalism, people sought relief in immediate sensation. Amongst the more serious minded, the thirst for pleasure coincided with a disinterested curiosity about life. Unlike the writers of the thirties, the writers of the twenties were not trying to prove a theory, but only trying to record the truth about life as they saw it. In these two respects, enjoyment and disinterested curiosity, the twenties seem to Forster to have embodied two attitudes for which he has a high regard. Proust is the novelist of this age because he is self-centred, uninterested in the fate of civilization, yet curious about human beings:

> (He has an) exquisite in-turned vision ... which like a sea-anemone, gathers all that passes for its nutriment and never turns outward like a rose. The civilization Proust represents is self-centred, it retreats from public affairs. It doesn't however, retreat from reality: its curiosity saves it from that ... it believed in tolerance (while) scarcely anyone believes in tolerance today. (97)

Most students of English literature have come to accept that the fictional epic of modern times is

Ulysses. Forster, however, prefers Proust's novel to Joyce's as the 'book of the age' because he finds Ulysses far too cynical to be accurate about life and far too difficult to be read with pleasure. Along with Scott and James, Joyce is a writer Forster is often accused of underestimating. Forster's remarks on Joyce show that he was conscious of this and that he made a considerable effort to understand and enjoy Ulysses.

Forster reviewed Ulysses in 1926. He admires Joyce's ability to handle an immense variety of styles, but feels that this makes Ulysses more a novel for writers than readers. He also finds Joyce's world view excessively sour and therefore incomplete. Ulysses records only the bitterness and horror of life but is oblivious of its glory, for in it Joyce "tries to bespatter the universe with dirt and to make all our habits and ideals (art, religion and society in particular) seem ludicrous and repulsive ... a book that would fully express our age must take into account occasional beauty, strength and nobility." (98) Arnold's view that "culture has one great passion, the passion for sweetness and light" (99) seems to have been turned upside down. Forster finds that the novel suffers from an "inverted Victorianism" because its passion is only for "crossness and dirt". This is substantially the view of Joyce offered in Aspects the following year. Joyce is seen, alongside Swift, as a gratuitously savage satirist of life.

Two years later, in 1929, T.E. Lawrence tried to interest Forster in Joyce but Forster wrote back to him saying "I feel sure I haven't seen Joyce's greatness, but this may be due to my age, and therefore not worth worrying about." (100) Nonetheless, Forster did re-read Joyce at least twice in subsequent years. In his 1931 lectures Joyce is briefly discussed as a 'self-extensive' critic - the type of critic whose personality appears very strongly in his criticism.

Forster read Joyce again in 1943 for a broadcast of February 1944. In October 1943 he wrote to his P.E.N. friend Hsiao Chi'en - "People have blamed me for my lack of insight over it (Ulysses), so I am re-reading it, and certainly get much more than I did the first time, but must also be missing much ..." (101) Five weeks later Forster was still ploughing through the book and wrote again to Chi'en - "It is a very odd book, I now think it is about masturbation - surely the only epic ever to be built on that somewhat limited topic." (102) Before the broadcast Forster also read Harry Levin's newly published James Joyce: A Critical Introduction which helped him understand Joyce, though Forster asserts in the broadcast that "I shall never take him (Joyce) to my heart." (103) Forster's broadcast follows Levin's biographical interpretation, showing that Joyce was an exile in three interconnected ways. He was an exile from Ireland, from Catholicism and from the English language. He also became blind. This knowledge helps Forster to understand the bitterness in Joyce's writing, and he says -

> He abandoned a great deal, but what did he gain? Nothing by the world's judgment. A great deal if we seek the subtler judgment of art. Joyce managed to build up something which was unique, something which represents our troubled age more than our age likes to confess - something very disquieting, very unsatisfying, something which lacks the milk of human kindness and even dramatic movement, but it expresses our inmost writhings with an appropriateness which achieves beauty. (104)

It may have been that Joyce's bitterness seemed more true to Forster in 1944 because of the general torment of a war torn world, but the reason for this more sympathetic view is also that Forster turns a blind eye to the bleakness of Joyce's outlook and listens for the musical qualities of his prose. He feels that Joyce "is interested in events, in people ... but still more in the words which express them, and alternatively in words for their own sake. Joyce's work tends to twist away from fiction towards music ... even his condemnation of the human race is incidental ... what really interests him is words, their overtones, their undertones ..." (105) Joyce also appears here as one more in Forster's list of writers whose inspiration derives from one centrally potent source. This source is shown to be memories of youth - "After leaving Dublin he picked up thousands of new words, but no new impressions ... he was probably of the type to which Wordsworth, among others, belongs: the type which experiences acutely in youth and is afterwards dependent on memories and combinations." (106)

This last broadcast shows Forster realizing that in the twenties he had not distinguished clearly enough between Joyce's misanthropic outlook and his achievement as an artist. He is here more consistent with his essays on Kipling, Dante, Proust and Lawrence, because while he remains unsympathetic to Joyce's philosophy of life he is able to distinguish between the inadequacy of the philosophy and the aesthetic merit of the work. Forster sees that the anger and resentment which colour Joyce's outlook and memories are not in themselves the essence of his art, and sees that they are the speck of grit which led to the creation of his fiction. This is not to suggest that Joyce comes to be seen as a 'prophet' in this broadcast. Despite his praise, Forster still has reservations about Joyce because his unstinted admiration is only for those writers who are sensitive to both the pain, the evil and the horror of life as well as to the potential for creativity, beauty and goodness which exists in the human spirit.

To venture upon a discussion of a Forsterian overview of twentieth century literature is a less hazardous business than to discuss his general ideas about the writing of earlier periods because despite the vast variety of modern writers, Forster himself discovers points of homogeneity that connect these writers with each other. The unusual task of connecting up twentieth century writing into a general historical framework was, in fact, attempted by Forster on no less than three occasions. The first of these was in an article called 'Sovremennaya angliskaya literatura' (1927) in a Russian journal. (107) The English translation of this article begins - "I picture contemporary English literature as a large untidy room. Disorder is everywhere ..." Like the later 'Three Generations', this traces the disorder to the First War:

> The years 1914-18 left a deep impression in the heart of every writer, whether or not he speaks about them... (It caused) Disillusion with everything - but without any kind of tragic element. Duty, willpower, inner discipline devalued, mysticism and unselfish awareness suspect, and the ideal of younger writers (insofar as one can speak of an ideal with regard to them) an observant and refined idleness ... Read Norman Douglas, George Moore, Virginia Woolf, Stella Benson, Max Beerbohm, Lytton Strachey, David Garnett, the Sitwells: there are many points of difference, but on one thing they are all agreed - they have no intention of perfecting either themselves or the world.

FORSTER'S LITERARY CRITICISM

The essay then enumerates the writers who Forster feels are not affected by this general confusion and disorder and who do not, for that reason, reflect the age. These turn out to be Yeats, Bridges, Housman, D.H. Lawrence, Walter de la Mare, James Barrie, G.K. Chesterton, Hilaire Belloc, Naomi Mitchison, Forrest Reid and Lowes Dickinson. At a later point, Eliot and Joyce are mentioned as writers "who endeavour not only to use the surrounding chaos, but also to express and understand that chaos" - in other words they are a part of the first category of writers who reflect their age.

The only thing apparent from these two lists is that Forster identifies the spirit of the age as one of disorder, and lumps together all the writers whose disillusionment and Epicureanism (or 'refined idleness') are a consequence of this disorder. The historical generalization is inadequate because Forster tends to exaggerate the importance of the First War upon the literature of the twenties. When, for example, he reiterated in his 1929 essay on Eliot that 'The Waste Land' was a poetic expression of the effect of the First War on Eliot, the poet wrote back contradicting this idea. (108) Also, Forster's two categories are slightly suspect because it is not accurate to suggest that writers like Eliot, Joyce, Woolf etc. reflect their age whereas Lawrence, Yeats, Lowes Dickinson etc. do not. The trouble is that having isolated disillusionment and disinterested observation as the only symptoms of contemporary writing, Forster has to see Yeats and Lawrence in ahistorical terms - as writers whose private visions and myths overshadow their historical typicality. The fact is that these writers reflect their age in complex and indirect ways, for the construction of private mythologies is only a different response to, and reveals a different awareness of, the spirit of the age.

Proust is not mentioned here since the essay is on English writers, but he springs to mind in this context because in 'Three Generations', 'Our Curiosity and Despair' and 'Our Second Greatest Novel?' Forster discusses Proust as the literary paradigm of the post First War zeitgeist. 'Three Generations' is in fact Forster's second effort to generalize about modern writers, but as this essay has been discussed earlier, a glance at Forster's third attempt - in <u>The Development of English Prose Between 1918-1939</u> (1944) - will conclude this section.

Forster does not here make the dubious distinction between writers who reflect their age and those who do not. Instead, his perspective is consistently historical and the division he sees is between writers of the twenties and thirties. The twenties writers want to understand and enjoy life, the thirties writers want to understand life for the purpose of preserving civilization. Forster also perceives in contemporary writing influences other than the insecurity bred by warfare. He discusses socio-economic changes and he talks about scientific and psychological changes - Einstein and Freud. This is a more sensible and more credible way of generalizing about modern writing. The essay also has the advantage of concluding with a personal opinion of Forster's contemporaries -

> I do not agree with those numerous critics who ... scold mankind for enjoying itself too much in the twenties and theorizing too much in the thirties. (109) We are plunged in a terrific war, and our literary judgments are not at their best. All our criticism is or ought to be tentative. And tentatively I suggest that the long weekend did valuable work, and I ask you to pause before you yield to the prevalent tendency to censure it. (110)

Perhaps what appeals most about this kind of conclusion is that it does not attempt to be conclusive or authoritative. In this respect it typifies much of Forster's criticism - it offers personal opinions for consideration in lucid, persuasive and distinctive prose.

NOTES

(1) Working Men's College Journal, February-April 1908, vol.10, pp. 261-4, 281-286, 301-306. Rpt. Thomson (p.146).
(2) ibid. (p.153).
(3) Kipling was very much in the public eye at this time. He was awarded the Nobel Prize in 1907. Forster's paper on Kipling (discussed later) was probably written quite soon after the essay on Dante.
(4) ibid. (p.160).
(5) ibid. (p.162).
(6) ibid. (p.167). By the thirties Forster knew that love did not order the universe, though he affirmed that it was the only thing that could order human life. See Chapter One.

(7) Forster delivered a lecture titled 'George Crabbe and Peter Grimes' at the Festival of 1948. The Aldeburgh Festival was begun in 1947 by Benjamin Britten who, like Crabbe and Skelton, was an East Anglian.
(8) TCD, pp. 133-149 (p.142).
(9) 'Fragments', <u>King's College Mss</u>.
(10) ibid.
(11) ibid.
(12) Proust's novel was published later, but Wagner, and quite possibly Bergson, were familiar to Forster.
(13) 'Peeping at Elizabeth', <u>Nation and Athenaeum</u>, 8 August 1925, pp. 568-9 (p.568). Review of <u>The Elizabethan Home - discovered in two dialogues by Claudius Hollyband and Peter Erondell</u>, ed. M. St. Clare Byrne.
(14) ibid. (p.569).
(15) 'Edward Gibbon', in <u>Talking to India</u>, ed. George Orwell (London: Allen and Unwin, 1943) pp.11-16 (p.12). Rpt. (revised) as 'Gibbon and His Autobiography', TCD, pp. 157-61 (pp.158-9).
(16) 'But...', <u>The Listener</u>, 23 January 1941, pp. 120-1 (p.120). Rpt. as 'Voltaire and Frederick the Great', TCD (p.162).
(17) CB, c. 1935, p.103.
(18) <u>The Rise of European Liberalism</u>, p.211.
(19) 'Happy Ending', <u>New Statesman and Nation</u>, 2 November 1940, p.442 (p.442). Rpt. as 'Ferney', TCD (p.336).
(20) 'Voltaire and Frederick the Great', TCD (p.165). The two other pieces are 'Fog Over Ferney' and 'Uncle and Niece' (both 1958).
(21) 'The Creator as Critic', p.110.
(22) ibid., p.111.
(23) Forster acknowledges his debt to these three writers in 'The Legacy of Samuel Butler', <u>The Listener</u>, 12 June 1952, pp.955-6 (p.955).
(24) 'Jane, How Shall We Ever Recollect', <u>Nation and Athenaeum</u>, 5 January 1924, pp. 512-14 (p.514). Rpt. (revised) as 'Jane Austen, I: The Six Novels', AH (p.166).
(25) AH (pp. 169-70).
(26) 'Some Books', <u>King's College Ms.</u>, 11 April 1944, vol. 23, p.313. Virginia Woolf says much the same about Jane Austen in 'The Leaning Tower' (op.cit.).
(27) See 'The Charm and Strength of Mrs. Gaskell', <u>Sunday Times</u>, 7 April 1957, p.10.
(28) <u>Aspects</u>, p.62.
(29) 'Three Generations', <u>King's College Ms.</u>, vol.16

(op.cit.) p.190.
(30) ibid.
(31) ibid., p.191.
(32) ibid., p.192.
(33) ibid., p.183.
(34) Forster's fiction has been compared to Butler's by Lee Elbert Holt, 'E.M. Forster and Samuel Butler', P.M.L.A., September 1946, vol. LXI, pp.804-19.
(35) Butler's influence on Forster's attitude to money has been discussed in Wilfred Stone, 'Forster on Love and Money', in Aspects of E.M. Forster, ed. O. Stallybrass (London: Edward Arnold, 1969) pp. 107-21. Forster's fantasy 'My Own Centenary' in AH shows his curiosity about how he would be regarded by posterity.
(36) See Furbank II, pp.3-4.
(37) 'Samuel Butler', Essays on Literature, History, Politics, Etc. (London: Hogarth Press, 1927) pp.44-56 (p.47).
(38) 'Some Books', broadcast dated 24 February 1942, King's College Ms., Vol. 22, p.123.
(39) ibid., p.125.
(40) ibid., pp.125-6.
(41) ibid., p.126.
(42) Forster's Romanticism has been thoroughly discussed in J.B. Beer, The Achievement of E.M. Forster (London: Chatto and Windus, 1962). Beer has drawn attention to Forster's remark that he did not care for Plato, Shelley and Goethe. See GLD, pp. 28-9, and Beer, pp.35-6.
(43) Forster's 1941 essay on Crabbe gave Britten the idea of composing his opera Peter Grimes. See Furbank II, pp. 281-2, and Benjamin Britten, 'Some Notes on Forster and Music,' Aspects of E.M. Forster, pp. 81-6.
(44) 'Introduction' to The Life of George Crabbe by His Son (London: Oxford Univ. Press, 1933) pp. VII-XIX (pp.XVI-XVII).
(45) ibid., (p.XVII).
(46) ibid.
(47) ibid. (pp.XVIII-XIX).
(48) The Listener, 29 May 1941, pp. 769-70.
(49) 'Sidling After Crabbe', The Listener, 9 June 1955, pp. 1039, 1041.
(50) 'An Approach to Blake', Spectator, 2 April 1932, p. 474.
(51) Broadcast dated 9 May 1944, King's College Ms., vol. 23, p. 328.
(52) 'The Creator as Critic', p.79.
(53) ibid., p.80.

(54) 'Death of a Poet, Birth of a Critic', (op.cit.).
(55) 'Coleridge in His Letters', Spectator, 10 September 1932, pp. 309-10.
(56) Culture and Anarchy, p.11.
(57) 'The Creator as Critic', p.98.
(58) ibid., pp. 98-9.
(59) Nation and Athenaeum, 17 March 1928, pp. 902-3 (p.902). Rpt. AH (p.97).
(60) ibid., (p.101).
(61) The date has been suggested by Elizabeth Heine who pointed out that the essay refers to an exhibition of caricatures by Max Beerbohm which took place in 1908.
(62) The Edwardian Turn of Mind, p.19.
(63) Forster's habit of perceiving in good writing a deeper spiritual level beneath the political surface is also evident from one of his remarks about T.E. Lawrence - "T.E. was intensely patriotic, lived for the Empire ... But the deepest impulse I could ever see in him was not the Empire nor even England, only the desire to write well." T.E. Lawrence by His Friends, ed. A.W. Lawrence (1937; rpt. London: Cape, 1954) pp. 235-9 (p. 237).
(64) Oscar Wilde, 'The Critic as Artist' (Part II) in Plays, Prose Writings and Poems (London: Dent and Sons, 1930) pp. 32-65 (p.60).
(65) 'The Poems of Kipling', King's College Ms., Vol. 15, pp. 52-83 (p.53).
(66) ibid. (p.53).
(67) ibid. (pp.55-6).
(68) ibid. (pp. 56-7).
(69) ibid. (p.58).
(70) ibid. (p.64).
(71) ibid.
(72) ibid. (p.70).
(73) ibid. (p.71). If the paper was indeed written in 1908, Forster seems to have had an emotional or spiritual knowledge of India, derived at least in part from Kipling, which was only confirmed by his actual visits in 1912 and 1921.
(74) ibid. (pp.73-4).
(75) ibid. (p.72). Forster detected this same gift of mysticism in Constance Sitwell, author of Flowers and Elephants, a trivial novel about an English girl's travels in India. The novel merely intersperses local detail with wistful observation, but Forster is so captivated by the writer's sensitivity to the spirit of India that he praises her novel with nearly the same enthusiasm that he shows for Kim. Forster's

undiscriminating praise is probably a consequence of his generous habit of drawing attention to minor and promising novelists. See Forster's 'Foreword' to Flowers and Elephants (London: Cape, 1928).
(76) ibid. (p.73).
(77) ibid. (p.75).
(78) ibid. (pp.77-8).
(79) ibid. (pp.79-80).
(80) ibid. (p.82).
(81) ibid. (p.85).
(82) ibid. (p.83).
(83) 'The Boy Who Never Grew Up', Daily Herald, 9 June 1920, p.7 (p.7).
(84) 'That Job's Done', The Listener, 10 March 1937, Supplement No.33, pp.III-IV. An English translation of Mussolini's Fascism - Doctrine and Institutions, which spells out the Fascist notion of a guild state, had been published in 1935. See Chapter I.
(85) 'Some Books', King's College Ms., 29 April 1942 vol. 22, pp. 142-6 (p.143).
(86) Furbank I, p.164.
(87) Geoffrey Tillotson refutes at great length Forster's notion in Aspects that James's social horizon is too narrow. Tillotson points out that Forster ignores The Princess Casamassima in which James displays a wide social focus. See 'Henry James and His Limitations' in Criticism and the Nineteenth Century (London: Athlone Press, 1951) pp.244-69.
(88) 'Henry James and the Young Men', The Listener, 16 July 1959, p.103, (p.103).
(89) Letter of 29 January 1918, King's College Ms.
(90) 'The Creator as Critic', p.85.
(91) ibid., p.86.
(92) 'Henry James as Art Critic', The Listener, 11 October 1956, p.572, (p.572). Review of James's The Painter's Eye edited by John Sweeney.
(93) ibid. (p.572).
(94) For Forster and D.H. Lawrence see The Cave and the Mountain, pp. 379-87, J.B. Beer's '"The Last Englishman": Lawrence's Appreciation of Forster', and Carl Baron's 'Forster on Lawrence' - both in E.M. Forster - A Human Exploration. For T.E. Lawrence see J. Meyers, 'E.M. Forster & T.E. Lawrence: A Friendship', South Atlantic Quarterly, Spring 1970, vol. LXIX, pp. 205-16. For T.S. Eliot see G.K. Das's 'E.M. Forster, T.S. Eliot and the 'Hymn Before Action' (op.

cit.), for Virginia Woolf see Harish Trivedi, 'Forster and Virginia Woolf: The Critical Friends' (op.cit.).
(95) 'Our Curiosity and Despair' (op.cit.). Rpt. (revised) as 'Proust' in AH.
(96) 'Three Generations', p.196.
(97) ibid., p.204. The essay is comparable with Orwell's celebrated essay 'Inside the Whale' which traces the response of writers to politics between 1900 and 1940 and is more approving of Henry Miller's honestly apolitical attitude than of the immature politics of a writer like Auden.
(98) 'The Book of the Age? James Joyce's Ulysses', New Leader, 12 March 1926, pp.13-14 (p.13).
(99) Culture and Anarchy, p.11.
(100) Letter dated 16 December 1929, King's College Ms.
(101) Letter dated 14 October 1943, King's College Ms.
(102) Letter dated 20 November 1943, King's College Ms.
(103) 'Some Books', dated 24 February 1944, King's College Ms., vol. 22, pp. 300-5 (p.300).
(104) ibid. (p.302).
(105) ibid. (p.303).
(106) ibid. (p.304).
(107) Vyorsty, 2, pp.240-6. Translated as 'Contemporary English Literature' (unpublished) by Gerald S. Smith. This article is unlisted in Kirkpatrick. Quotations are from a personal copy obtained from the translator by Mr.Iain Wright of Queens' College, Cambridge.
(108) See Furbank II, Notes, p.332.
(109) This is probably a reference to Orwell's 'Inside the Whale' (1940).
(110) The Development of English Prose Between 1918-1939, p.23.

CONCLUSION

The notion of the human mind as a principle which creates or imposes order upon a universe that has no objective order of its own may be problematic philosophically, but it has been regularly espoused over the centuries, particularly in periods of social crisis and particularly by those sceptical of religious faith and its promise of cosmic harmony. Marxism, Mysticism, Fascism and Existentialism all represent, in one sense, searches for stabilizing order at the philosophical, social, political and personal levels. Within this broad spectrum Forster's quasi-aestheticist liberal humanist principles have a minor but quirky (and therefore interesting) position. They developed spasmodically out of a polemic with their intellectual and cultural milieu, and representing in themselves an attack upon the life-denying nature of holistic philosophical systems deliberately eschewed the consistency that might have reduced them into a clear-cut doctrine.

Forster's search for order - his system of thought about man, society, politics, art and artists - stemming as it does from an anarchist temperament, has no order of its own. The purpose of this book has hitherto been, by exploring the implications of the term 'order' as they relate to his ideas about literature and society, to provide a thematic coherence to Forster's explorations in his non-fiction, to, as it were, order his search for order by revealing subcurrents that flow through his wide ranging but apparently heterogeneous criticism. I shall now attempt to establish the close links between the socio-cultural context and ideas which germinated and developed within it, the interlinks within the ideas themselves, and wherever possible their present relevance.

Traditional notions of order had to be

CONCLUSION

substantially modified after the cataclysmic social turbulence which followed the relative stability of Edwardian England. It became increasingly difficult in the twenties and thirties to cling to earlier notions of order in the cosmos, in the human personality, in society, and even in works of art. If science can be said to have constructed the coffin for faith in cosmic unity ever since the Renaissance, the stage of hammering down the coffin's lid seems to have been reached when Einsteinian physics proved the absence of universal absolutes and astronomy revealed the earth as a splinter within an unimaginably vast and chaotic universe. Over the same period, but at a microcosmic level, an analogous revolution occurred through the ideas of Freudian and post-Freudian psychology which showed that the inner self of the individual was no more ordered than the cosmos around it. A third revolutionary idea which seriously took root in the English mind only after the First War was the Marxist argument that society is not so much an agglomeration of individuals as a structure comprising conflicting economic classes. Economic regulation and state controlled planning rather than personal moral idealism were therefore the imperative needs. And finally, the completely senseless slaughter of millions of human beings during the First War bred despair both with regard to human nature and in the likelihood of social progress.

Liberal idealism had become entrenched as the English political and cultural orthodoxy until approximately the early twenties. The central premises of this orthodoxy were that individuals possess unique personalities which they must be free to develop and that socio-economic reform is bound to flower by the pluralization of civilized individuals. Disinterested enquiry, intellectual enlightenment, personal relations and aesthetic appreciation were upheld as the values that would foster moral development. But what value did these notions have in a universe which gave room only to relativism and scepticism, where unique individuals massacred others equally unique, where psychology demolished the idea of rational personality by showing an irrational subconscious determining behaviour, where Marxism showed the elitist character of liberal values, and where technological change rapidly rendered archaic the aristocratic old world which equated the pursuit of beauty and truth with civilization? Forster's criticism, which has been read in this book as his own answer to the central liberal dilemma, is valuable even today because in arguing the perennial

CONCLUSION

importance of liberal humanist values it stresses the necessity of individual distinction and art if life is to remain recognizably human. Forster's ideas have a contemporary relevance because they comprise a level headed critique of tendencies within both capitalist and socialist societies: they focus on the limitations of capitalism by exposing the hollowness of aestheticism and ivory tower exclusiveness, and of socialism by their criticism of every dogmatic ideology which, at the other extreme, equates 'order' with 'social order' and thereby prevents personal freedom and creativity. In doing this, Forster's criticism contributes to a better understanding of the nature of order at the personal, social, religious and aesthetic levels, and to some of the ways in which these categories can be made to coexist in harmony with each other.

The argument about the need to preserve 'love', 'freedom' and 'the human spirit', which collectively constitute creative individualism counterpoints with the argument for state planning for the economic needs without which the opportunities for effective expression are confined to an elite minority. Neither the danger to human freedom from state authority nor the threat to state power from an excess of personal freedom has been minimized sufficiently for us to cease regarding as important those critics, such as Forster, who perform a watchdog function so powerfully and conscientiously. It may seem inconsistent for Forster to have championed a liberal compromise late in life, after having extolled the virtues of individual effort earlier on, but the reprehensible - if not despicable - role of both the antagonistic states in the First War has been exposed by the plethora of literature which the War generated. Conversely, state planning was one of the few positive features within the gloom and despair created by the Second War. Hence the compromise, the agreement about the need for planning to achieve equality alongside the demonstration of the poverty of an egalitarian society which is unaware of spiritual needs. This compromise is perhaps indicative of the theoretical limitations of liberalism but is not, in any real sense, compromising. On the contrary it represents the via media upheld as an ideal by Social Democracies today. Forster's ideas about social order seem relevant precisely because they are derived from his notions about the nature and needs of the individual.

Society and the state are not the only kinds of 'order' that restrict freedom of expression and the

CONCLUSION

development of human individuality. Forster's criticism also shows that religious dogma, with its emphasis on blind worship, can be equally repressive. By pointing in the direction of a composite ideal order, Forster's ideas about religion relate indirectly but obviously to those about man, society and art. The central religious principle affirmed is a paradox fundamental to both Plotinus and Hinduism, namely that the individual is both a part of as well as uniquely separate from his universe. Without exaggerating the relevance of these ideas, it scarcely needs to be pointed out that they are likely to seem interesting to any society in which some doubt and others affirm the validity of religion, as well as to individuals who disbelieve and yet need sustenance from a quiet but confident affirmation of human endeavour.

Extended into his aesthetics, Forster's notion of the individual as both part of and unique within his context takes two complementary forms: first, that the work of art is both a product of unique genius and an overflow from a subterranean reservoir or general human consciousness, and second that art is both autonomous and socially indispensable. The conclusions reached from the discussion of Forster's opinions on the etiology of art, the nature of the artist, the structure of the work of art and the nature of aesthetic response collectively reveal a blend of two streams of thought which derive from the traditions of aestheticism and moralism, art as autotelic and moral. The contemporaneity of this position becomes clear if we think of Leavis and Trilling, both of whom adopt a philosophy of criticism which is fundamentally similar.

A further corollary of Forster's weltanschauung and aesthetics seems discernible in his criticism of the novel, where he is less a descriptive critic than a theoretician prescribing (albeit characteristically tentatively) the ways in which fictional universes may be more perfectly ordered than hitherto. New and varying notions about fictional structure had been argued by James, Wells, Woolf, Lawrence and Proust, but Forster, while borrowing some of their ideas, also significantly diverged from them to create a new, personal aesthetic of fiction. In proposing that fiction approaches perfection when it is musically ordered, a correspondence becomes apparent between Forster's ideas about society and art because he weaves into his discussion of the novel the suggestion that only in music can the individual components (the notes and tunes) achieve a sort of

CONCLUSION

spiritual liberation while contributing simultaneously to the larger musical structure of which they are a part. The fundamental idea enunciated once again is the necessity of forging an order in which respect for individuality, uniqueness and autonomy is not at odds with the overall framework within which these must necessarily exist. As a theory of fiction this is probably more idiosyncratically personal than theories of fiction usually are, but perhaps interesting and peripherally valuable for that very reason.

Forster's view of criticism and his methods as a critic stem from and are consistent with his world view and aesthetics, with his view that the arts invite response and enjoyment rather than rational analysis and study. This may make Forster the critic impressionistic, unabashedly subjective, ahistorical and somewhat chaotic, but these drawbacks are more than compensated for by the subtlety, charm, unusual perception and genuine enthusiasm with which he recommends books and authors. The part documentary and part analytic account of Forster's 'practical' criticism (with an emphasis on unpublished writing) has similarly been closely related to the total social, cultural and aesthetic context of which it is a part. My purpose has been to demonstrate precisely how Forster's outlook and art intertwine to produce criticism that is compelling and worthy of wider recognition.

'Expansion, not completion' was Forster's advice to the novelist. The critic, unlike the novelist, seeks not to communicate intimations of the unseen and expansive spiritual reality underlying the surface of things. His inferior task (as Forster might himself have pointed out) being to outline a context, clarify ideas and demonstrate their interrelationship and relevance, 'completion' is the ideal he must hope he has attained.

SELECT BIBLIOGRAPHY:

(a) Books by E.M. Forster (in chronological order):

Egypt (London: Labour Research Dept., 1920).
Alexandria: A History and a Guide (1922; rpt.
    Alexandria: Whitehead Morris, 1938).
Pharos and Pharillon (London: Hogarth, 1923).
A Passage to India (1924), Abinger edn., ed. O.
    Stallybrass (London: Edward Arnold, 1978).
Aspects of the Novel and related writings (1927),
    Abinger edn., ed. O. Stallybrass (London: Edward Arnold, 1974).
Goldsworthy Lowes Dickinson and related writings
    (1934), Abinger edn., ed. O. Stallybrass
    (London: Edward Arnold, 1973).
Abinger Harvest (1936; rpt. Harmondsworth: Penguin
    Books, 1976).
Nordic Twilight (London: Macmillan War Pamphlets,
    No.3, 1940).
The New Disorder (1941; rpt. New York, 1949).
The Development of English Prose Between 1918 and
    1939 (Glasgow: Jackson, Son & Co., 1945).
Two Cheers for Democracy (1951), Abinger edn., ed.
    O. Stallybrass (London: Edward Arnold, 1972).
The Hill of Devi: Being Letters from Dewas State
    Senior (London: Edward Arnold, 1953).
Marianne Thornton: 1797-1887 (London: Edward Arnold,
    1956.
Maurice (1971; rpt. Harmondsworth: Penguin, 1975).
Albergo Empedocle and other writings, ed. George
    Thomson (New York: Liveright, 1971).
Commonplace Book (London: Scolar Press, 1978).
Arctic Summer and other fiction, Abinger edn., ed.
    Elizabeth Heine (London: Edward Arnold, 1980).

SELECT BIBLIOGRAPHY

(b) Forster's published essays, book reviews and letters (in chronological order): (1)

'Our Diversions, Diana's Dilemma', Egyptian Mail, 25 August 1917, p.2.
'Our Diversions, 2: Sunday Music', Egyptian Mail, 2 September 1917, p.2.
'A Musician in Egypt', Egyptian Mail, 21 October 1917, p.2.
'Our Diversions, The Scallies', Egyptian Mail, 18 November 1917, p.2. Rpt. as 'Our Diversions, 1: The Scallies', in AH.
'XXth Century Alexandria: The New Quay', Egyptian Mail, 2 December 1917, p.2.
'Gippo English', Egyptian Mail, 16 December 1917, p.2.
'The Den', Egyptian Mail, 30 December 1917, p.2. Rpt. in Pharos and Pharillon.
'Alexandria Vignettes: Photographic Egypt', Egyptian Mail, 31 January 1918, p.2.
'Alexandria Vignettes: Cotton From The Outside', Egyptian Mail, 3 February 1918, p.2. Rpt. as 'Cotton From The Outside', in Pharos and Pharillon.
'Alexandria Vignettes: The Solitary Place', Egyptian Mail, 10 March 1918, p.2. Rpt. as 'The Solitary Place', in Pharos and Pharillon.
'Alexandria Vignettes: The Higher Aspects', Egyptian Mail, 5 May 1918, p.2.
'Alexandria Vignettes: The Return From Siwa', Egyptian Mail, 14 July 1918, p.2 as 'The Return From Siwa', in Pharos and Pharillon.
'Alexandria Vignettes: Lunch at the Bishop's', Egyptian Mail, 31 July 1918, p.2. Rpt. as 'St. Athanasius', Athenaeum, 16 May 1919, p.327.
'The Modern Sons of the Pharaohs', Egyptian Mail, 18 August 1918, p.2.
'Alexandria Vignettes: Epiphany', Egyptian Mail, 6 October 1918, p.2. Rpt. as 'Epiphany', in Pharos and Pharillon.
'Alexandria Vignettes: Canopus, Menouthis, Aboukir', Egyptian Mail, 29 December 1918, p.2. 'Alexandria Vignettes: Army English', Egyptian Mail, 12 January 1919, p.2.
'Alexandria Vignettes: England's Honour (Being Extracts From the Diary of Mme. Kyriakidis, Ramleh)', Egyptian Mail, 26 January 1919, p.2.
'A First Flight', National Review, March 1919, vol. 73, pp. 118-19.
'A Beresford Novel', Daily News, 19 March 1919, p.6.
'The Trouble in Egypt: Treatment of the Fellahin',

SELECT BIBLIOGRAPHY

Manchester Guardian, 29 March 1919, p.8.
'The Young Pretender', Daily News, 17 April 1919, p. 6.
'A Popular Theatre', Athenaeum, 18 April 1919, pp.216-17.
'The Fiction Factory (By a Novelist)', Daily News, 23 April 1919, p.6. Rpt. in Aspects.
'The Poetry of C.P. Cavafy', Athenaeum, 25 April 1919, pp.247-8. Rpt. (revised) in Pharos and Pharillon.
'From Gay to Grave', Daily News, 1 May 1919, p.6.
'Dual Control', Daily News, 2 May 1919, p.6.
'St. Athanasius (pt. II)', Athenaeum, 23 May 1919, pp. 358-9. Rpt. in Pharos and Pharillon.
'Eight Snakes', Daily Herald, 21 May 1919, p.8.
'Ideals and Realities of Battle', Daily News, 24 May 1919, p.2.
'A Little Bit of All Right', Daily Herald, 28 May 1919, p.8.
'Hawkeritis', Daily Herald, 30 May 1919, p.4.
'Two Egypts', Athenaeum, 30 May 1919, pp. 393-4.
'Breakable Butterflies', Athenaeum, 6 June 1919, pp. 426-7.
'Entertainment', Daily News, 9 June 1919, p.6.
'Painted Reality', Daily News, 10 June 1919, p.2.
'Kill Your Eagle', Daily News, 17 June 1919, p.5.
'The Extreme Case', Athenaeum, 4 July 1919, pp.561-2.
'A Concert of Old Instruments', Athenaeum, 11 July 1919, p.597.
'"Amis and Amilies" at Weybridge', Athenaeum, 25 July 1919, pp. 662-3.
'A Moving Document', Daily Herald, 30 July 1919, p.8
'Visions', Daily News, 31 July 1919, p.2.
'A Flood in the Office', Athenaeum, 8 August 1919, pp. 717-18.
'My Country', Daily News, 15 August 1919, p.6.
'Grip', Athenaeum, 5 September 1919, p.852.
'Maternal Love', Athenaeum, 19 September 1919, pp. 923-4.
'The Temple', Athenaeum, 26 September 1919, p.947.
'Tolstoy at the St. James's', Athenaeum, 10 October 1919, p.1011.
'The End of the Samovar', Daily News, 11 November 1919, p.5.
'The Egyptian Labour Corps.', The Times, 13 November 1919, p.8.
'News From Norway', Daily Herald, 26 November 1919, p.8.
'Sakuntala', Athenaeum, 28 November 1919, p.1267.
'Music in Edinburgh: The Reid Concerts', Athenaeum,

SELECT BIBLIOGRAPHY

26 December 1919, p.1406.
'Literature and History', Athenaeum, 2 January 1920, pp.26-7.
'Frenchmen and France', Daily News, 3 January 1920, p.7.
'Civilization', Daily Herald, 21 January 1920, p.8.
'Songs of Loveliness', Daily News, 27 January 1920, p.5.
'Cousin X', Daily News, 3 February 1920, p.5.
'Notice of Sketches', Athenaeum, 13 February 1920, p.215.
'Where There is Nothing', Athenaeum, 27 February 1920, pp. 270-1.
'The White Devil at Cambridge', New Statesman, 20 March 1920, pp. 708-9.
'Literary Notes', Daily Herald, 14 April 1920, p.8.
'The Golden Peak', Athenaeum, 14 May 1920, pp.631-2.
'The Churning of the Ocean', Athenaeum, 21 May 1920, pp. 667-8.
'The School Feast', Daily News, 28 May 1920, p.4.
'Jehovah, Buddha and the Greeks', Athenaeum, 4 June 1920, pp. 730-1.
'The Boy Who Never Grew Up', Daily Herald, 9 June 1920, p.7.
'Literary Notes', Daily Herald, 9 June 1920, p.7.
'Literary Notes', Daily Herald, 23 June 1920, p.7.
'A Great History', Athenaeum, 2 & 9 July 1920, pp.8-9, pp. 42-3.
'A Cautionary Tale', Nation, London, 9 October 1920, pp. 47-8.
'Missionaries', Athenaeum, 22 October 1920, pp. 545-7.
'Mr. Wells's "Outline"', Athenaeum, 19 November 1920, pp. 690-1.
'The Untidy Gentleman', Nation, London, 4 December 1920, pp.344, 346.
'Breaking-Up Day - New Style', Manchester Guardian, 8 December 1920, p.8.
'The Poetry of Iqbal', Athenaeum, 10 December 1920, pp.803-4.
'In the Temple of Criticism', Nation, London, 8 January 1921, pp. 512, 514.
'Victorian Writers', Athenaeum, 28 January 1921, pp. 93-4.
'Pilgrim's Progress', Daily News, 8 February 1921, p.6.
'Reflections in India, 1: Too Late', Nation and Athenaeum, 21 January 1922, pp. 614-15.
'Reflections in India, 2: The Prince's Progress', Nation and Athenaeum, 28 January 1922, pp. 644-6.

SELECT BIBLIOGRAPHY

'India and the Turk', Nation and Athenaeum, 30
     September 1922, pp. 844-5.
'"Another Little War"', Daily News, 9 October 1922,
     p.6.
'Eliza in Chains', Cornhill Magazine, May 1924, N.S.
     vol. 56, pp.598-609.
'An Eighteenth Century Sailor', Nation and Athenaeum,
     4 October 1924, p.22.
'A Birth in the Desert', Nation and Athenaeum, 8
     November 1924, pp. 210-11.
'The True Joan of Arc: Shaw's or France's?', New
     Leader, 19 June 1925, p.10.
'Indian Caves', Nation and Athenaeum, 11 July 1925,
     p.462.
'Peeping at Elizabeth', Nation and Athenaeum, 8
     August 1925, pp. 568-9.
'Poverty's Challenge: The Terrible Tolstoy', New
     Leader, 4 September 1925, pp.11-12.
'Literature or Life? Henry Nevinson: The Boy Who
     Never Stuck', New Leader, 2 October 1925, p.14.
'The Book of the Age? James Joyce's "Ulysses"', New
     Leader, 12 March 1926, pp.13-14.
'Escaping the House of Common Sense', New Leader,
     16 April 1926, p.11.
'Virgil and Tommy: The Mystery of Dean Inge', New
     Leader, 17 September 1926, p.11.
'Hakluyt', Nation and Athenaeum, 12 November 1927,
     pp.226, 228, 230.
'Ibsen the Romantic', Nation and Athenaeum, 17
     March 1928, pp. 902-3. Rpt. in AH.
'Little Creatures', Nation and Athenaeum, 9 June
     1928, p.333.
'The New Censorship', Nation and Athenaeum, 8
     September 1928, p.726.
'The "Censorship" of Books, 4', Nineteenth Century
     and after, April 1929, vol. 105, pp.444-5.
'Mr. D.H. Lawrence and Lord Brentford', Nation and
     Athenaeum, 11 January 1930, pp.508-9.
'D.H. Lawrence', Nation and Athenaeum, 29 March 1930,
     p.888.
'D.H. Lawrence', The Listener, 30 April 1930, pp.
     753-4.
'A Broadcast Debate', Nation and Athenaeum, 10 May
     1930, p.191.
'The Hat Case', Spectator, 28 June 1930, p.1055.
'The Hat Case', Spectator, 12 July 1930, p.54.
'The Freedom of the B.B.C.', New Statesman and
     Nation, 4 April 1931, pp.209-10.
'The Cult of D.H. Lawrence', Spectator, 18 April
     1931, p.627.
'An Artist's Life', Spectator, 25 April 1931, p.669.

SELECT BIBLIOGRAPHY

'Death of a Poet: Birth of a Critic', The Listener, 26 August 1931, p.333.
'On a Novel That Stands Apart', News Chronicle, 6 November 1931, p.4.
'Are the B.B.C. Too Cautious?', Spectator, 19 December 1931, p.848.
'Napoleon', New Statesman and Nation, 16 January 1932, p.68.
'William Cowper, An Englishman', Spectator,16 January 1932, p.75.
'The Next War', New Statesman and Nation, 23 January 1932, p.90.
'George Crabbe', Spectator, 20 February 1932, pp. 243-5.
'The "Osterley Park" Ballads', Spectator, 19 March 1932, p.420.
'An Approach to Blake', Spectator, 2 April 1932, p.474.
'The Stratford Jubilee of 1769', Spectator, 23 April 1932, p.586. Rpt. in TCD.
'Review', Spectator, 7 May 1932, pp. 659-60.
'Writers At Bay', Spectator, 21 May 1932, p.724.
'Has "It" Broken Down', New Statesman and Nation, 25 June 1932, p.822.
'Affable Hawk', Spectator, 23 July 1932, p.125.
'Mr. G. Lowes Dickinson', The Times, 6 August 1932, p.10.
'Coleridge in His Letters', Spectator, 10 September 1932, pp.309-10.
'Books of the Week', The Listener, 12 October 1932, pp. 536-7.
'D.O.R.A.', New Statesman and Nation, 15 October 1932, p.442.
'Books of the Week', The Listener, 16 November 1932, pp.721-2.
'Side Dishes', The Listener, 30 November 1932, pp. 799-800.
'Tales of Unrest', The Listener, 14 December 1932, pp. 869-70.
'Not New Books', The Listener, 28 December 1932, pp. 951-2.
'The Future of Books', The Listener, 18 January 1933 p.105.
'The University and the Universe', Spectator, 17 March 1933, pp. 368-9.
'The English Eccentrics', Spectator, 19 May 1933, p.716.
'The Barn Door', New Statesman and Nation, 27 May 1933, pp. 690, 692.
'Breaking Up', Spectator, 28 July 1933, p.119.
'Mus in Urbe', Spectator, 17 November 1933, pp.746,

SELECT BIBLIOGRAPHY

748.
'"Seven Days' Hard"', The Listener, 14 March 1934, p.452.
'Our Greatest Benefactor, 4', Spectator, 15 June 1934, p.914.
'Good Society', New Statesman and Nation, 23 June 1934, pp.950, 952.
'Mr. E.M. Forster Replies', Time and Tide, 30 June 1934, p.829.
'Pageant of Trees', The Times, 18 July 1934, p.10.
'The Old School', Spectator, 27 July 1934, p.136.
'Still the Sedition Bill', Time and Tide, 27 October 1934, p.1340.
'English Freedom', Spectator, 23 November 1934, pp. 791-2. Partially incorporated in 'Liberty in England', London Mercury, August 1935, vol. 32, pp. 327-31.
'The Invaders', Now and Then, Winter 1934, No.49, pp. 15-16.
'International Congress of Writers', New Statesman and Nation, 6 July 1935, p.9.
'The Psychology of Monarchy', New Stateman and Nation, 22 February 1936, p.260.
'Ancient and Modern', The Listener, 11 November 1936 pp. 921-2.
'Tolstoy's "War and Peace"', The Listener, 13 January 1937, p.87.
'Church, Community and State', The Listener, 27 January 1937, p.177.
'The Job's Done', The Listener, 10 March 1937, Supplement No.33, pp. III-IV.
'Recollectionism', New Statesman and Nation, 13 March 1937, pp. 405-6.
'Coronation Nightmare', Spectator, 19 March 1937, pp. 509-10.
'Royalty and Loyalty', New Statesman and Nation, 24 April 1937, p.680.
'A Smack for Russia', The Listener, 12 May 1937, p.943.
'Eccentric Englishwomen, 7: Luckie Buchan', Spectator, 28 May 1937, pp. 986-7.
'Books of the Year: From a Broadcast Talk ... on December 30', The Listener, 5 January 1938, pp. 41-2.
'General Knowledge', New Statesman and Nation, 15 January 1938, pp. 78-9.
'Efficiency and Liberty - Great Britain: Discussion Between E.M. Forster and Captain A.M. Ludovici, with Wilson Harris in the Chair', The Listener, 9 March 1938, pp. 497-8, 530-1.
'The Rev. James Gatliff', New Statesman and Nation,

SELECT BIBLIOGRAPHY

       9 April 1938, pp. 620-2.
'Trees and Peace', Manchester Evening News, 15 July 1938, p.12.
'The Feast of Tongues', Spectator, 29 July 1938, pp. 194-5.
'Indians in England', New Statesman and Nation, 27 August 1938, pp. 311-12.
'The Duty of an Editor', The Listener, 20 October 1938, p.850.
'Review', The Listener, 24 November 1938, p.1142.
'The Ivory Tower', London Mercury, December 1938, vol. 39, pp. 119-30.
'The Long Run', New Statesman and Nation, 10 December 1938, pp. 971-2.
'The Books of 1938: Reviewed by E.M. Forster at the Microphone on December 26', The Listener, 29 December 1938, pp. 1422-3.
'Here's Wishing! Messages Broadcast on December 26, 1: E.M.Forster', The Listener, 5 January 1939, p.18.
'Woodlanders on Devi', New Statesman and Nation, 6 May 1939, pp. 679-80.
'Freedom For What', The Listener, 1 June 1939, p.1177.
'Books in General', New Statesman and Nation, 19 August 1939, pp. 282-3.
'Reading as Usual', The Listener, 21 September 1939, pp. 586-7.
'"My Poultry Are Not Officers"', The Listener, 26 October 1939, Supplement No.III.
'Books in 1939', The Listener, 11 January 1940, pp. 85-6.
'The Freedom of the Artist: A Discussion between E.M. Forster and H.V. Hodson', The Listener, 28 March 1940, pp. 636-7.
'Nazism and Morals: Dangers of "Gestapo" Methods', Daily Telegraph and Morning Post, 16 April 1940 p.6.
'These "Lost Leaders"', Spectator, 5 July 1940, p.12.
'English Quislings', Spectator, 19 July 1940, p.63.
'Omega and Apha', New Statesman and Nation, 10 August 1940, pp.140-1.
'Lord Halifax's Broadcast', The Listener, 15 August 1940, p.244.
'A Note on Capturedism', Mermaid, October 1940, vol. 11, No.1, p.15.
'A Bedside Book', The Listener, 7 November 1940, p.675.
'The Individual and His God', The Listener, 5 December 1940, pp.801-2.

SELECT BIBLIOGRAPHY

'Cambridge', New Statesman and Nation, 29 March 1941 pp. 328, 330.
'George Crabbe: The Poet and the Man', The Listener, 29 May 1941, pp. 769-70.
'The C Minor of That Life', Abinger Chronicle, June 1941, vol. 2, pp. 35-9.
'The National Council of Civil Liberties', Time and Tide, 28 June & 5 July 1941, pp. 540, 561.
'Books in 1941', The Listener, 10 July 1941, p.63.
'Indian Broadcasting', New Statesman and Nation, 2 & 16 August 1941, pp. 112, 160.
'The Woman and the Onion', The Listener, 27 November 1941, p.720.
'An Indian on W.B. Yeats', The Listener, 24 December 1942, p.824.
'The Claims of Art', The Listener, 30 December 1943, pp. 742-3.
'A Clash of Authority', The Listener, 22 June 1944, pp. 685-6.
'A Great Indian Poet-Philosopher', The Listener, 23 May 1946, p.174.
'The Edinburgh Festival', Sunday Times, 31 August 1947, p.4.
'Literature in India', London Calling, 11 September 1947, No. 416, p.2.
'The P.E.N. and the Sword', The Listener, 11 December 1947, pp. 1029-30.
'The N.C.C.L.', New Statesman and Nation, 15 May 1948, p.396.
'Civil Liberties', New Statesman and Nation, 5 June 1948, p.460.
'Looking Back on the Aldeburgh Festival', The Listener, 24 June 1948, pp. 1011, 1013.
'The Aldeburgh Festival', The Listener, 8 July 1948, p.61.
'Butler Approached', Spectator, 12 November 1948, p. 634.
'Entrance to an Unwritten Novel', The Listener, 23 December 1948, pp. 975-6.
'Review', The Listener, 27 October 1949, p. 725.
'Bikaner', The Listener, 22 June 1950, p.1065.
'Maurice O'Sullivan', The Listener, 13 July 1950, p.59.
'Review', The Listener, 21 September 1950, p.391.
'The Cambridge Chancellorship', Spectator, 10 November 1950, p.468.
'Nominating the Chancellor', Cambridge Review, 18 November 1950, p.146.
'Andre Gide: A Personal Tribute', The Listener, 1 March 1951, p.343.
'Fifth Anniversay of the Third Programme', The

SELECT BIBLIOGRAPHY

Listener, 4 October 1951, pp. 539-41.
'Audience Research', The Listener, 18 October & 1
    November 1951, pp. 655, 742.
'Voyage of Discovery', Times Literary Supplement,
    8 February 1952, p.103.
'The Chapel of Kings (sic)', The Listener, 29 May
    1952, pp. 885, 887.
'The Legacy of Samuel Butler', The Listener, 12 June
    1952, pp. 955-6.
'Tributes to Sir Desmond MacCarthy', The Listener,
    26 June 1952, p.1031.
'Portraits from Memory', The Listener, 24 July 1952,
    p.142.
'The Possessed', The Listener, 9 October 1952, pp.
    595, 597.
'Toward a Definition of Tolerance', New York Times
    Magazine, 22 February 1953, Section 6, p.13.
'The Art of Fiction, 1: E.M. Forster', Paris Review,
    Spring 1953, vol.1, pp. 28-41.
'Lear in India', The Listener, 26 March 1953, p.519.
'"Lelia: The Life of George Sand"', The Listener,
    18 June 1953, p.1015.
'The Art and Architecture of India', The Listener,
    10 September 1953, pp. 419-21.
'The Birth of Krishna', Observer, 11 October 1953,
    p.9 Rpt. in The Hill of Devi.
'Society and the Homosexual: A Magistrate's Figures',
    New Statesman and Nation, 31 October 1953, pp.
    508-9.
'Dr. Trevelyan's Love of Letters', Cambridge Review,
    13 February 1954, vol. 75, p.292.
'East and West', Observer, 21 February 1954, p.9.
'Tidying India', The Listener, 11 March 1954, pp.
    435-6.
'Review', The Listener, 12 August 1954, p. 253.
'Revolution at Bayreuth', The Listener, 4 November
    1954, pp. 755-7.
'The Law and Obscenity', The Listener, 11 November
    & 23 December 1954, pp.813, 1117.
'The World Mountain', The Listener, 2 December 1954,
    pp. 977-8.
'Books of 1954: A Symposium', Observer, 26 December
    1954, p.7.
'A Letter', Twentieth Century, February 1955, vol.
    157, pp. 99-101.
'Review', The Listener, 10 February 1955, p.257.
'"The Mint" by T.E. Lawrence', The Listener, 17
    February 1955, pp. 279-80.
'Sidling After Crabbe', The Listener, 9 June 1955,
    pp. 1039, 1041.
'A Shrine For Diaghilev', Observer, 25 December

SELECT BIBLIOGRAPHY

> 1955, p.4.
> 'Review', The Listener, 16 February 1956, p.257.
> 'The Swindon Classics', Observer, 11 March 1956, p.17.
> 'Daughter Dear', London Magazine, April 1956, vol. 3, pp.15-19. Rpt. in Marianne Thornton.
> 'Cats and King's', The Listener, 12 April 1956, p.417.
> 'Money for the Arts', Times Literary Supplement, 17 August 1956, p. 487.
> 'A Great Humanist: E.M. Forster on Goldsworthy Lowes Dickinson', The Listener, 11 October 1956, pp. 545-7.
> 'Henry James as Art Critic', The Listener, 11 October 1956, p. 572.
> 'Bloomsbury, an Early Note: February, 1929', Pawn, November 1956, No.3, p.10.
> '"Pygmalion"', The Times, 7 December 1956, p.11.
> 'Books of the Year, 1: Chosen by Eminent Contemporaries', Sunday Times, 23 December 1956, pp. 6, 8.
> 'Tourism v. Thuggism', The Listener, 17 January, 1957, p.124.
> 'Dull Opiate', Observer, 24 February 1957, p.12.
> 'The Blue Boy', The Listener, 14 March 1957, p.444.
> 'The Charm and Strength of Mrs. Gaskell', Sunday Times, 7 April 1957, pp.10-11.
> 'Neglected Spinster', Observer, 25 August 1957, p.12.
> 'Prof. Edward Dent', The Times, 26 August 1957, p.10.
> 'On Remaining an Agnostic', The Listener, 31 October 1957, p.701.
> 'De Senectute', London Magazine, November 1957, vol. 4, pp.15-18.
> 'Review', The Listener, 21 November 1957, pp. 850, 853.
> 'Light on Deoli', The Listener, 5 December 1957, p.951.
> 'Vice Prosecutions', Spectator, 17 January 1958, p.73.
> 'Moving the Statue', The Times, 13 March 1958, p.11.
> 'High Principles and Low Spirits', Spectator, 28 March 1958, p.398.
> 'Wolfenden Report', The Times, 9 May 1958, p.13.
> 'This Worrying World', The Listener, 22 May 1958, p.865.
> 'Review', Library, June 1958, Series 5, vol.13, pp. 142-3.
> 'Review', The Listener, 19 June 1958, p.1027.
> 'A View Without a Room', Observer, 27 July 1958, p. 15.
> 'C.P. Cavafy', Umbrella, October 1958, vol.1, pp. 5-7.

SELECT BIBLIOGRAPHY

'E.K. Bennett (Francis) (1887-1958)', Caian, Michaelmas Term 1958, vol. 55, pp. 123-7.
'Uncle and Niece', The Listener, 4 December 1958, p.949.
'Fog Over Ferney', The Listener, 18 December 1958, pp.1029-30.
'Recollections of Nassenheide', The Listener, 1 January 1959, pp. 12-14.
'Erotic Indian Sculpture', The Listener, 12 March 1959, pp. 469, 471.
'Art Treasures of Cambridge', The Listener, 26 March 1959, p.551.
'Henry James and the Young Men', The Listener, 16 July 1959, p.103.
'A Known Indian', Observer, 16 August 1959, p.14.
'Nuisance Value', Spectator, 2 October 1959, p.431.
'Descent to the Plains', Observer, 14 August 1960, p.20.
'Review', The Listener, 18 August 1960, p.269.
'The Sahib From Bloomsbury', Observer, 5 November 1961, p.29.
'Books of the Year: Contributors to the Observer, name some of the outstanding books they have read in the past year', Observer, 17 December 1961, p.22.
'Indian Entries', Encounter, January 1962, vol.18, pp.20-7.
'A Presidential Address to the Cambridge Humanists - Summer 1959', University Humanist Federation Bulletin, Spring 1963, No.11, pp. 2-8.
'"Where Angels Fear to Tread"', The Times, 12 July 1963, p.11.
'Books of the Year: A Personal Choice', Observer, 22 December 1963, p.15.
'E.M. Forster Points Out - Vice Versa', Cambridge News, 22 February 1964, p.4.
'Moonstruck', Guardian, 7 August 1964, p.8.
'Pylons on the March: Profits That Will be Made', The Times, 5 September 1964, p.9.

(c) Forster's contributions to books by other authors (in chronological order):

Introductory and Terminal Notes in Mrs. Eliza Fay, Original Letters From India, (London: Hogarth, 1925) pp.7-24, 273-85.
Foreword in Constance Sitwell, Flowers and Elephants (London:Cape, 1927) pp.7-11.
'Some Memories', in Gilbert Beith, ed., Edward Carpenter: In Appreciation (London: Allen & Unwin, 1931) pp. 74-81.

SELECT BIBLIOGRAPHY

Introduction to *The Life of George Crabbe by His Son* (London: Oxford Univ. Press, 1933) pp. VII-XIX.

Introductory Note in Maurice Sullivan, *Twenty Years a Growing* (London: Chatto & Windus, 1933) pp. V-VI.

Preface to Mulkraj Anand, *Untouchable* (London: Wishart, 1935) pp. 7-11.

Forward in Alec Craig, *The Banned Books of England* (London: Allen & Unwin, 1937) pp 9-11.

Contribution in A.W. Lawrence, ed., *T.E. Lawrence by His Friends* (1937; rpt. London: Cape, 1954) pp. 235-9.

'Havoc', in J.M. Keynes and others, *Britain and the Beast* (London: Dent, 1937) pp. 44-7.

'Notes for a Reply', in Quentin Bell, ed., *Julian Bell: Essays, Poems and Letters* (London: Hogarth, 1938) pp. 391-2.

Introduction to K.R. Srinivasa Iyengar, *Literature and Authorship in India* (London: Allen & Unwin, 1943) pp. 7-8.

'Edward Gibbon', and 'Tolstoy's Birthday', in George Orwell, ed., *Talking to India* (London: Allen & Unwin, 1943) pp. 11-16, 117-21.

Introduction and Notes in G.L. Dickinson, *Letters from John Chinaman and other essays* (London: Allen & Unwin, 1946) pp. 7-8, 9-10.

Foreward to G.V. Desani, *Hali* (London: Saturn Press, 1950) p. IX.

Introduction to Huthi Singh, *Maura* (London: Constable, 1951) pp. VII-VIII.

Introduction to Peter Townsend, ed., *Cambridge Anthology* (London: Hogarth, 1952) pp. VII-VIII.

Address, in *Forrest Reid Memorial* (Glasgow: 1952) pp. 3-6.

'Forrest Reid (1876-1947)', in Forrest Reid, *Tom Barber, Young Tom, The Retreat, Uncle Stephen* (New York: Pantheon, 1955).

Preface to G.L. Dickinson, *The Greek View of Life* (London: Methuen, 1957) pp. V-IX.

Introduction and Notes in *The Aeneid of Virgil*, trans. Michael Oakley (London: Dent, 1957) pp. V-XII.

Contribution in Philip Toynbee, *The Fearful Choice: A Debate on Nuclear Policy* (London: Gollancz, 1958) pp. 82-3.

Introduction to Donald Windham, *The Warm Country* (London: Hart Davis, 1960) pp. 9-10.

Introduction to Giusseppe di Lampedusa, *Two Stories and a Memory*, trans. Archibald Colquhoun (London: Collins & Harvill, 1962) pp. 5-8.

SELECT BIBLIOGRAPHY

(d) <u>Forster's unpublished essays and B.B.C. broadcasts in the Forster Archives at King's College Cambridge (in chronological order): (2)</u>

'The Relation of Dryden to Milton and Pope', c.1897, vol. 21.
'The Novelists of the Eighteenth Century and their influence on those of the nineteenth', October 1899, vol.15.
'Pagus Quidam', c. 1906-7, vol.15.
'The Poems of Kipling', c. 1908, vol.15.
'The Feminine Note in Literature', December 1910, vol.15.
'Pornography and Sentimentality', c.1911, Miscellaneous Fragments.
'The Enjoyment of English Literature', 3 March 1913, vol.15.
'Samuel Butler', December 1913, vol.16.
'Literature and the War', c. 1914-15, vol.16.
'The Great Frost', 15 February 1929, unbound B.B.C. broadcast.
'Books', 13 August 1931, vol.22. (Volumes 22 and 23 consist entirely of typescripts, carbon copies and photo copies of Forster's B.B.C. broadcasts.)
'The Creator as Critic', six lectures, Lent Term 1931, volume titled <u>Miscellaneous</u>.
'Book Talk: I', 24 October 1932, vol.22.
'Books of the Week', 7 November 1932, vol. 22.
'Bookshelf', 26 December 1938, vol.22.
'Three Generations', 28 January 1939, vol.16.
'Beethoven's Piano Sonatas', c. 1939-40. Unclassified.
'Books of 1939', 5 January 1940, vol.22.
'New Year's Greetings', 6 January 1942, vol.22.
'Masterpieces of English Literature', 24 February 1942, vol.22.
'Books and the Writer', 3 July 1942. vol.22
'Books and the People', 20 July 1942, vol.22.
'My Debt to India', 13 August 1942, vol.22.
'New Books', 11 November 1942, vol.22.
'Tolstoy's Short Stories', 11 March 1943, vol. 22.
'Book Talk: II', 25 September 1944, vol.22.
'The Short Story', 15 December 1944, vol.22.
'Does Writing Pay', 12 November 1945, vol. 23.
'A Roman "Society"', 1946, vol.16.
'Some Books' - B.B.C. broadcasts with this title (in vol.22) are dated:

15 October 1941, 15 November 1941, 10 December 1941, 4 March 1942, 1 April 1942, 29 April 1942,

SELECT BIBLIOGRAPHY

    27 May 1942, 24 June 1942, 19 August 1942, 16 September 1942, 14 October 1942, 3 February 1943, 3 March 1943, 28 April 1943, 26 May 1943, 20 June 1943, 18 July 1943, 15 August 1943, 12 September 1943, 3 October 1943, 10 October 1943, 4 November 1943, 30 December 1943.

'Some Books' - broadcasts with this title (in vol. 23) are dated:

    27 January 1944, 24 February 1944, 23 March 1944, 11 April 1944, 9 May 1944, 4 July 1944, 1 August 1944, 29 August 1944, 26 September 1944, 24 October 1944, 21 November 1944, 19 December 1944, 13 February 1945, 9 May 1945, 5 June 1945, 3 July 1945, 31 July 1945, August 1945, July 1946, August 1946, 20 November 1946, 12 March 1947.

'Message to India', 15 August 1947, vol.23.
'Books: Talk for Sixth Forms', 24 September 1947, vol.22.
'Mahatma Gandhi', c. 1948, vol. 21.
'It's Good English', 13 April 1948, vol.23.
'I Speak For Myself', 11 January 1949, vol.23.
'Portrait of Forrest Reid', 25 January 1952, vol. 23.
'Founder's Day Speech', 6 December 1952, vol.15.
'England, Italy and India', 16 November 1959, vol. 23.
'Birthday Luncheon', 9 January 1959, vol.21.
'George Crabbe', 24 Janauary 1960, vol.23.
'Billy Budd', 12 November 1960, vol. 23.
Essays which have not been dated are:
'The Bugiale', vol.21.
'Cornaro', vol.15.
'Death of a Clock', vol.16.
'The English Character', vol.16.
'English Literature since the War', vol.16.
'Guide Books', vol.21.
'Happy v . Sad Endings', vol.15.
'The Lost Guide', vol.21.
'Modern Writing', <u>Indian Book</u>.
'Prophecy', unclassified.

(e)   <u>Forster's Letters in King's College</u>.

(I)   Letters from Forster to:

J.R. Ackerley, Florence Barger, The B.B.C., Edward Carpenter, C.P. Cavafy, E.J. Dent, Goldsworthy

SELECT BIBLIOGRAPHY

  Lowes Dickinson, T.S. Eliot, Roger Fry, Helen Gardner, Edward Garnett, John Hampson, Hsio Chi'en, T.E. Lawrence, Rosamund Lehmann, Percy Lubbock, G.H. Ludolf, Syed Ross Masood, Charles Mauron, W.J.H. Sprott, Robert C. Trevelyan.

(II) Letters to Forster from:

A.C. Benson, Wildrid S. Blunt, Robert Bridges, The B.B.C., Benjamin Britten, R.J. Buckingham, Edward Carpenter, C.P. Cavafy, E.J. Dent, Goldsworthy Lowes Dickinson, Norman Douglas, Mohammad El-Adl, T.S. Eliot, John Galsworthy, Andre Gide, John Hampson, Thomas Hardy, Gerald Heard, Aldous Huxley, Ernest Jones, H. Festing Jones, D.H. Lawrence, T.E. Lawrence, Sinclair Lewis, Percy Lubbock, Thomas Mann, Syed Ross Masood, C.F.G. Masterman, G.E. Moore, J. Middleton Murry, H.W. Nevinson, Marmaduke Pickthall, William Plomer, Forrest Reid, Bertrand Russell, Siegfried Sassoon, Edith Sitwell, Osbert Sitwell, W.J.H. Sprott, Lytton Strachey, Marianne Thornton, Arnold Toynbee, G.M. Trevelyan, Robert C. Trevelyan, Frank Vicary, Hugh Walpole, Beatrice Webb, H.G. Wells, Edith Wharton, Leonard Woolf, W.B. Yeats.

(f) <u>Secondary Material</u>:

Abrams, M.H.	<u>The Mirror and the Lamp: Romantic Theory and the Critical Tradition</u> (1953; rpt. New York: Oxford U.P. 1974).
Ackerley, J.R.	<u>E.M. Forster: A Portrait</u> (London: Ian McKelvie, 1970). <u>Hindoo Holiday: An Indian Journal</u> (London: Chatto & Windus, 1932).
Allen, C.K.	<u>Bureaucracy Triumphant</u> (London: Oxford U.P., 1931).
Allen, Glen O.	'Structure, Symbol and Theme in <u>A Passage to India</u>', P.M.L.A., December 1955, vol. LXX, pp.934-54.
Annan, Noel	'Forster's Self Discovery', <u>The Listener</u>, 4 August 1977, pp. 155-6. 'The Intellectual Aristocracy', in <u>Studies in Social History: A Tribute to G.M. Trevelyan</u>, ed. J.H. Plumb (London: Longmans, Green & Co., 1955) pp. 241-287.

SELECT BIBLIOGRAPHY

	Leslie Stephen: His Thought and Character in Relation to His Time (London: MacGibbon & Kee, 1951).
Arlott, John	'Forster and Broadcasting', in Aspects of E.M. Forster: essays and recollections written for his ninetieth birthday, ed. O. Stallybrass (London: Edward Arnold, 1969) pp. 87-92.
Arnold, Matthew	Culture and Society: An Essay in Social and Political Criticism (1869), intro. J. Dover Wilson (London: Macmillan, 1938). 'Literature and Science' (1882), in The Complete Prose Works of Matthew Arnold: Philistinism in England and America, ed. R.H. Super (Ann Arbor: Univ. of Michigan Press, 1974) vol. X, pp. 53-73.
Baron, Carl	'Forster on Lawrence', in E.M. Forster: A Human Exploration, ed. G.K. Das & John Beer (London: Macmillan, 1979) pp. 186-195.
Beer, John	The Achievement of E.M. Forster (London: Chatto & Windus, 1962). Blake's Humanism (Manchester: Manchester U.P., 1968). 'Introduction: The Elusive Forster', in E.M. Forster: A Human Exploration, ed. Das & Beer (op. cit.) pp.1-10. '"The Last Englishman": Lawrence's Appreciation of Forster', in A Human Exploration, pp.245-68.
Bell, Clive	Art (London: Chatto & Windus, 1914). Civilization: An Essay (London: Chatto & Windus, 1928). Old Friends: Personal Recollections (London: Chatto & Windus, 1956). Proust (London: Hogarth, 1928).
Bell, Julian	'War and Peace: Open Letter to E.M. Forster', in Essays, Poems and Letters, ed. Quentin Bell (London: Hogarth, 1938) pp. 335-90.
Bell, Quentin	Bloomsbury (London: Weidenfeld & Nicolson, 1968).
Belloc, Hilaire	Europe and the Faith (1920; rpt.

SELECT BIBLIOGRAPHY

Bentley, Michael
London: Constable, 1924).
The Liberal Mind, 1914-29 (Cambridge: Cambridge U.P.,1977).
'The Liberal Response to Socialism, 1918-29', in Essays in Anti-Labour History: Responses to the Rise of Labour in Britain, ed. Kenneth D. Brown (London: Macmillan, 1974) pp. 42-73.

Beresford, J.D.
'E.M. Forster and the Anarchist', in New Adelphi, June 1928, vol.I, pp. 366-7.

Bergson, Henri
Matter and Memory, trans. N.M. Paul & W.S. Palmer (1911; rpt. London: Allen & Unwin, 1962).
Time and Free Will: An Essay on the Immediate Data of Consciousness, trans. F.L. Pogson (1889; rpt. London: Swan Sonnenschein, 1910).

Berland, A
'James and Forster: The Morality of Class', Cambridge Journal, February 1953, vol. VI, pp. 259-80.

Besant, Walter
'The Art of Fiction' (1884), in Realism and Romanticism in Fiction: An Approach to the Novel, ed. E. Current Garcia & W.R. Patrick (Chicago: Scott Foresman, 1962) pp. 68-85.

Birje-Patil, J.
'Forster and Dewas', in A Human Exploration, ed. Das & Beer (op. cit.) pp. 102-8.

Booth, Wayne C.
'The Ironist's Voice: E.M. Forster as Essayist', in A Rhetoric of Irony (Chicago: Chicago U.P. 1974) pp.185-90.
The Rhetoric of Fiction (Chicago: Chicago U.P., 1961).

Bowra, C.M.
'Beauty in Bloomsbury', Yale Review, March 1955, vol. XLIV, pp. 461-4.

Bradbury, Malcolm
'An Approach through Structure', in Towards a Poetics of Fiction, ed. Mark Spilka (Bloomington: Indiana U.P., 1977) pp. 3-10.

- ed.
Forster: A Collection of Critical Essays (New Jersey: Prentice Hall, 1966).
The Social Context of Modern English Literature (Oxford:

SELECT BIBLIOGRAPHY

	Blackwell, 1971).
	'Two Passages to India: Forster as Victorian and Modern', in *Aspects of E.M. Forster*, ed. O. Stallybrass (op.cit.) pp. 123-42.
Bradley, A.C.	'Poetry for Poetry's Sake', in *Oxford Lectures on Poetry* (1909; rpt. London: Macmillan, 1959) pp. 3-34.
Branson, Noreen	*Britain in the Nineteen Twenties* (London: Weidenfeld & Nicolson, 1975).
- & Margot Heinemann	*Britain in the Nineteen Thirties* (1971; rpt. St. Albans: Panther Books, 1973).
Brenan, Gerald	*The Face of Spain* (London: Turnstile Press, 1950).
Briggs, Asa	*History of Broadcasting in the United Kingdom: The Golden Age of the Wireless* (London: Oxford U.P., 1965), vol. II.
Britten, Benjamin	'Some Notes on Forster and Music' in *Aspects of E.M. Forster*, ed. Stallybrass, (op.cit.) pp. 81-6.
Brown, E.K.	'The Revival of E.M. Forster', in *Forms of Modern Fiction: essays collected in honour of J.W. Beach*, ed. William van O'Connor (Minneapolis; Univ. of Minnesota Press, 1948) pp. 161-74.
	Rhythm in the Novel (Toronto: Toronto U.P., 1950).
	'Two Formulas for Fiction: Henry James and H.G. Wells', *College English*, October 1946, vol. 8. No.1, pp.7-17.
Burkill, T.A.	*The Evolution of Christian Thought* (Ithaca: Cornell U.P., 1971).
Burra, Peter	'Introduction' to the Everyman edn. of *A Passage to India*, rpt. as Appendix 'B' in *A Passage to India*, pp. 315-27.
Caudwell, Christopher	*Studies in a Dying Culture*, Intro. John Strachey (London: Bodley Head, 1938).
Cavaliero, Glen	*A Reading of E.M. Forster*

SELECT BIBLIOGRAPHY

Cecil, David
(London: Macmillan, 1979).
'E.M. Forster', in Poets and Storytellers: A Book of Critical Essays (London: Constable, 1949) pp. 181-201.

Chesterton, G.K.
The New Jerusalem (London: Hodder and Stoughton, 1920).

Clark, Jon, & others, ed.
Culture and Crisis in Britain in the Thirties (London: Lawrence & Wishart, 1979).

Colmer, John
'Criticism and Biography', and 'Essays, Lectures, and Broadcasts', in E.M. Forster: The Personal Voice (London: Routledge and Kegan Paul, 1975) pp. 173-92, 193-218.
'Form and Design in the Novel', in Approaches to the Novel, ed. John Colmer (London: Oliver & Boyd, 1966) pp. 1-17.

Cook, Chris
A Short History of the Liberal Party: 1900-1976 (London: Macmillan, 1976).

Cox, C.B.
The Free Spirit: A Study of Liberal Humanism in the Novels of George Eliot, Henry James, E.M. Forster, Virginia Woolf, and Angus Wilson (London: Oxford U.P., 1963).

Crane, R.S.
'The Concept of Plot and the Plot of Tom Jones', in Critics & Criticism: Ancient and Modern, ed. R.S. Crane (Chicago: Univ. of Chicago Press, 1952) pp. 616-47.

Cranston, Maurice
'Book Reviews', London Magazine, September 1954, vol.I, pp.77-81.

Crews, Frederick C.
E.M. Forster: The Perils of Humanism (Princeton: Princeton U.P., 1962).

Daiches, David
Some Late Victorian Attitudes (London: Andre Deutsch, 1969).

Dangerfield, George
The Strange Death of Liberal England (1935; rpt. New York: Capricorn, 1961).

Das, G.K. & John Beer, ed.
E.M. Forster: A Human Exploration (London: Macmillan, 1979).

Das, G.K.
E.M. Forster's India (London: Macmillan, 1979).

SELECT BIBLIOGRAPHY

David, Edward
: 'E.M. Forster, T.S. Eliot and the 'Hymn Before Action', in A Human Exploration, pp. 208-15.
'The New Liberalism of C.F.G. Masterman, 1873-1927', in Essays in Anti-Labour History, ed. Kenneth D. Brown, pp. 17-41.

Dean, Dennis
: 'The Character of the Early Labour Party', in The Edwardian Age: Conflict and Stability: 1900-1914. ed. Alan O'Day (London: Macmillan, 1979) pp. 97-112.

Dickinson, G.L.
: After 2000 Years: A Dialogue between Plato and a Modern Young Man (London: Allen & Unwin, 1930).
The Autobiography of Goldsworthy Lowes Dickinson and other unpublished writings, ed. Dennis Proctor (London: Duckworth, 1973).
'The Emergence of a Latent Memory Under Hypnosis', Proceedings of the Society for Psychical Research, August 1911, vol. 25, pp. 455-67.
The Greek View of Life (1896), preface by E.M. Forster (London: Methuen, 1957).
Letters from John Chinaman & other essays, intro. E.M. Forster (London: Allen and Unwin, 1946).
The Magic Flute: A Fantasia (London: Allen & Unwin, 1920).
The Meaning of Good: A Dialogue (Glasgow: Maclehouse, 1901).
A Modern Symposium (London: Brimley Johnson, 1905).

Dobree, Bonamy
: 'E.M. Forster', in The Lamp and The Lute: Studies in Six Modern Authors (Oxford: Clarendon, 1929) pp. 66-85.

Donoghue, Denis
: 'An Ear for Fiction', in T.L.S. 31 January 1975, p.103.

Drew, John
: 'A Passage via Alexandria?', in A Human Exploration, pp. 89-101.

Dworkin, Ronald
: 'Liberalism', in Private and Public Morality, ed. Stuart Hampshire (Cambridge: Cambridge U.P., 1978) pp. 113-43.

SELECT BIBLIOGRAPHY

Edel, Leon — *Bloomsbury: A House of Lions* (London: Hogarth, 1979).

- & G.N. Ray — *Henry James and H.G. Wells: A Record of their Friendship, their Debate on the Art of Fiction, and their Quarrel* (London: Hart Davis, 1958).

Fishman, Solomon — *The Interpretation of Art: Essays on the Art Criticism of John Ruskin, Walter Pater, Clive Bell, Roger Fry and Herbert Read* (Berkeley: Univ. of California Press, 1963).

Ford, Ford Madox — *The English Novel: From the Earliest Times to the Death of Joseph Conrad,* (London: Constable, 1930).

Friedman, Alan — 'E.M. Forster: Expansion Not Completion', in *The Turn of the Novel: The Transition to Modern Fiction* (New York: Oxford U.P., 1966) pp. 106-29.

Friedman, Norman — 'Forms of Plot', in *The Theory of the Novel*, ed. Philip Stevick (New York: Free Press, 1969) pp. 145-66.
'Point of View in Fiction: The Development of a Critical Concept', in *The Theory of the Novel* (ibid.) pp. 108-38.

Fry, Roger — *Architectural Heresies of a Painter* (London: Chatto & Windus, 1921).
'Art History as an Academic Study', in *Last Lectures*, ed. Kenneth Clark (Cambridge: Cambridge U.P., 1939) pp. 1-21.
The Artist and Psycho-Analysis (London: Hogarth, 1924).
'An Essay in Aesthetics', in *Vision and Design* (London: Chatto & Windus, 1920) pp. 11-25.
'Some Questions in Esthetics', in *Transformations: critical and speculative essays on Art* (London: Chatto & Windus, 1926) pp. 1-43.

Furbank, P.N. — *E.M. Forster: A Life* (1978 & 1979; rpt. London: Oxford U.P., 1979) vol. I & vol. II.
'Forster and Bloomsbury Prose',

SELECT BIBLIOGRAPHY

	in A Human Exploration, pp. 161-6.
	'The Personality of E.M.Forster', Encounter, November 1970, vol. 35, No.5, pp. 61-8.
Gardner, Philip ed.	E.M. Forster: The Critical Heritage (London, Routledge & Kegan Paul, 1973).
Garnett, David	'Forster and Bloomsbury', in Aspects of E.M. Forster, pp. 29-36.
Gay, Penelope	'E.M. Forster and John Ruskin: The Ambivalent Connection', Southern Review, 1978, vol. XI, No.3, pp. 283-95.
Geismar, M.	'The Higher and Higher Criticism' Nation (New York), 10 November 1956, pp. 407-10.
Gide, André	Back From the U.S.S.R., trans. Dorothy Bussy (London: Secker & Warburg, 1937).
Goldman, Mark	The Reader's Art: Virginia Woolf as Literary Critic (The Hague: Mouton, 1976).
Gordon, David	D.H. Lawrence as a Literary Critic (New Haven: Yale U.P., 1966).
Gransden, Karl W.	E.M. Forster (London: Oliver and Boyd, 1962).
	'E.M. Forster at Eighty', Encounter, January 1959, vol. XII, pp. 77-81.
Graves, Robert	'Poetry and Politics', in The Common Asphodel: Collected Essays on Poetry - 1922-1949) (London: Hamish Hamilton, 1949) pp. 273-84.
- & Alan Hodge	The Long Week-End: A Social History of Great Britain, 1918-1939 (London: Faber, 1940).
Grubb, Frederick	'Homage to E.M. Forster', Contemporary Review, January 1959, vol. CXLV, pp. 20-3.
Hamilton, Clayton	The Materials and Methods of Fiction (London: Grant Richards, 1909).
Hampshire, Stuart	'E.M. Forster', in Modern Writers and other essays (1952; rpt. London: Chatto and Windus, 1969) pp.47-55.
Hannay, Howard	'Roger Fry's Theory of Art', in

SELECT BIBLIOGRAPHY

	Roger Fry & other essays (London: Allen and Unwin, 1937) pp. 15-51.
Hanquart, Evelyne	'Forster on Contemporary English Literature', The Aligarh Journal of Studies (1980), vol.V No.1, pp. 102-10.
Havighurst, A.J.	Radical Journalist: H.W. Massingham: 1860-1924 (Cambridge: Cambridge U.P., 1974).
Heard, Henry Fitzgerald ('Gerald')	Man the Master (London: Faber, 1944).
	Pain, Sex and Time: A New Hypothesis of Evolution (London: Cassell, 1939).
	'The Significance of the New Pacifism', in The New Pacifism, by Heard & others (London: Allenson & Co., 1936) pp.13-22.
	The Social Substance of Religion: An Essay on the Evolution of Religion (London: Allen & Unwin, 1931).
	The Source of Civilization (London: Cape, 1935).
Henderson, Philip	'Bloomsbury: Virginia Woolf, E.M. Forster', in The Novel Today: Studies in Contemporary Attitudes (London: John Lane, 1936) pp. 87-96.
Hobhouse, L.T.	Liberalism, intro. Alan P.Grimes (1911; rpt. New York: Oxford U.P., 1964).
Holroyd, Michael	'Bloomsbury: The Legend and the Myth', in Lytton Strachey and the Bloomsbury Group: His Work, Their Influence (1967; rpt. Harmondsworth, Penguin, 1971) pp. 17-54.
Holt, Lee Elbert	'E.M. Forster and Samuel Butler', P.M.L.A., September 1946, vol. LXI, pp.804-19.
Hough, Graham	'Ruskin and Roger Fry: Two Aesthetic Theories', in Image and Experience: Studies in a Literary Revolution (London: Duckworth, 1960) pp. 160-76.
Howe, Irving	'The Pleasures of Cultivation', New Republic, 10 December 1951, vol. CXXV, pp. 16-17.

SELECT BIBLIOGRAPHY

Hyams, Edward — The New Statesman: The History of the First Fifty Years - 1913-1963, (London: Longmans, Green & Co., 1963).

Hynes, Samuel — The Auden Generation: Literature and Politics in England in the 1930s (London: Bodley Head, 1976).
The Edwardian Turn of Mind (London: Oxford U.P., 1968).
'The Old Man at King's: Forster at 85', in Edwardian Occasions: Essays on English Writing in the Early Twentieth Century (London: Routledge & Kegan Paul, 1972), pp.104-11.
'The Whole Contention Between Mr. Bennett and Mrs. Woolf', in Edwardian Occasions (ibid.), pp. 24-38.

Isherwood, Christopher — 'Mr. Forster Tidies Up', in The Listener, 25 March 1936, vol.XV, p. 603.
Lions and Shadows (London: Hogarth, 1938).

Jack, P.M. — 'E.M. Forster's Delightful Essays', New York Times Book Review, 24 May 1936, p.2.

James, Henry — 'The Art of Fiction', (1884), in The Art of Fiction and other essays, ed. Morris Roberts (New York: Oxford U.P., 1948) pp. 3-23.
Theory of Fiction: Henry James, ed. James E. Miller (Lincoln: Univ. of Nebraska Press, 1972).

Johnson, Lesley — The Cultural Critics: From Matthew Arnold to Raymond Williams (London: Routledge & Kegan Paul, 1979).

Johnstone, J.K. — The Bloomsbury Group: A Study of E.M. Forster, Lytton Strachey, Virginia Woolf and their circle (London: Secker and Warburg, 1954).

Jones, David — 'E.M. Forster on his Life and his Books: An Interview Recorded for Television', The Listener, 1 January 1959, pp. 11-12.

Joseph, David I. — The Art of Rearrangement: E.M.

SELECT BIBLIOGRAPHY

Kelvin, Norman
: Forster's 'Abinger Harvest' (New Haven: Yale Univ. Press, 1964).
'Literature, the Past and the Present', in E.M. Forster (Carbondale and Edwardsville: Southern Illinois Univ. Press, 1967) pp. 143-74.

Kemp, Harry & Laura Riding
: The Left Heresy in Literature and Life (London: Methuen, 1939).

Kermode, Frank
: 'Forster', The Listener, 18 June 1970, p.833.
'Mr. E.M. Forster as a Symbolist', The Listener, 2 January 1958, pp. 17-18, Rpt. in Forster: A Collection of Critical Essays, ed. M. Bradbury pp. 90-5.

Keynes, J.M.
: 'My Early Beliefs', in Two Memoirs (London: Hart Davis, 1949) pp. 75-103.

Kirkpatrick, B.J.
: A Bibliography of E.M. Forster (1965; rpt. London: Hart Davis, 1968).

Klingopoulos, G.D.
: 'E.M. Forster's Sense of History and Cavafy', Essays in Criticism, April 1958, vol. VIII, pp. 156-65.
'Mr. Forster's Good Influence', in The Modern Age, pp. 263-74.

Kronenberger, Louis
: 'Mr. Forster's Harvest', Nation (New York), 17 June 1936, vol. CXLII, pp. 780-1.

Kumar, Shiv K.
: Bergson and the Stream of Consciousness Novel (London: Blackie, 1962).

Lamont, Corliss
: Humanism as a Philosophy (London: Watts & Co., 1952).

Laski, Harold
: The Decline of Liberalism (Hobhouse Memorial Lecture, 1940) (London: Oxford U.P., 1940).
The Rise of European Liberalism (London: Allen & Unwin, 1936).

Lawrence, D.H.
: Letters, ed. Aldous Huxley (London: Heinemann, 1932).
Selected Literary Criticism, ed. Anthony Beal (London: Heinemann, 1955).

SELECT BIBLIOGRAPHY

Lazarus, H.P.   'The Slighter Gestures of E.M. Forster', Nation (New York), 29 November 1947, vol. CLXV, pp. 598-600.

Leavis, F.R.   'E.M. Forster', in The Common Pursuit (1962; rpt. Harmondsworth: Penguin, 1978) pp. 261-77.
'Keynes, Lawrence and Cambridge', in The Common Pursuit, pp. 255-60.
Mass Civilization and Minority Culture (Minority Pamphlet I) (Cambridge: Minority Press, 1930).
'Meet Mr. Forster', Scrutiny, Autumn 1944, vol. 12, No.4, pp. 308-9.
Two Cultures? The Significance of C.P. Snow (London: Chatto & Windus, 1962).

Leavis, Q.D.   Fiction and the Reading Public (London: Chatto & Windus, 1932).
'Mr. E.M. Forster', in A Selection From Scrutiny, ed. F.R. Leavis (Cambridge: Cambridge U.P., 1968) vol.I, pp. 134-8.

Liddell, Robert   Cavafy: A Critical Biography (London: Duckworth, 1974).

Littell, P.   'E.M. Forster', New Republic, 8 July 1936, vol. LXXXVII, pp. 273-4.

Lubbock, Percy   The Craft of Fiction (London: Cape, 1921).

Lynes, Carlos Jr.   'Andre Gide and the Problem of Form in the Novel', in Forms of Modern Fiction, ed. O'Connor (op.cit.) pp. 175-88.

Macaulay, Rose   The Writings of E.M. Forster (London: Hogarth, 1938).

Macpherson, C.B.   'Natural Rights in Hobbes and Locke', in Political Theory and the Rights of Man, ed. D.D. Raphael (London: Macmillan, 1967), pp.1-15.

Marcuse, Herbert   The Aesthetic Dimension (London: Macmillan Papermac, 1979).

Martin, R.   The Love That Failed: Ideal and Reality in the writings of E.M. Forster (The Hague: Mouton &

SELECT BIBLIOGRAPHY

	Co., 1974).
Masterman, C.F.G.	The New Liberalism (London: Leonard Parsons, 1920).
Mauron, Charles	Aesthetics and Psychology, trans. Roger Fry & Katherine John (London: Hogarth, 1935).
	The Nature of Beauty in Art and Literature, preface & translation by Roger Fry (London: Hogarth, 1927).
McCallum, Pamela M.	'The Cultural Theory of I.A. Richards, T.S. Eliot and F.R. Leavis' (Unpublished Ph.D. dissertation, Cambridge University, 1978).
McConkey, James	The Novels of E.M. Forster (Ithaca: University of Iowa, 1957).
McDowell, F.P.W.	E.M. Forster: An Annotated Bibliography of Writings About Him (Illinois: Northern Illinois U.P., 1976).
	'E.M. Forster's Conception of the Critic', Tennessee Studies in English Literature (1965), vol. X, pp. 93-100.
	'E.M. Forster and G.L. Dickinson', Studies in the Novel, Winter 1973, vol. V, pp. 441-56.
	'"Unexplored Riches and Unused Methods of Release": Nonfictional Prose and General Estimate', in E.M. Forster (New York: Twayne Publishers) pp. 125-40.
Meyers, J.	'E.M. Forster and T.E. Lawrence: A Friendship', South Atlantic Quarterly, Spring 1970, vol. LXIX, pp. 205-16.
Mill, John Stuart	'Civilization' (1836), in Mill's Essays on Literature and Society, ed. J.B. Schneewind (New York: Collier Books, 1965) pp. 148-82.
	Mill on Bentham and Coleridge, intro. F.R. Leavis (London: Chatto & Windus, 1962).
	On Liberty (1859), intro. Gertrude Himmelfarb (Harmondsworth, Penguin, 1974).
	'What is Poetry' (1833), in Mill's Essays, ed. J.B. Schneewind (op.cit.) pp. 102-17.

SELECT BIBLIOGRAPHY

Moore, G.	'The Significance of Bloomsbury', <u>Kenyon Review</u> Winter 1955, vol. XVII, pp. 119-29.
Moore, G.E.	<u>Principia Ethica</u> (1903; rpt. Cambridge: Cambridge Univ. Press, 1971).
Muir, Edwin	<u>The Structure of the Novel</u> (London: Hogarth, 1928).
O'Connor, William van	'A Visit With E.M. Forster', <u>Western Review</u>, Spring 1955, vol. XIX, pp. 215-19. 'Samuel Butler and Bloomsbury', in <u>From Jane Austen to Joseph Conrad: Essays collected in memory of James T. Hillhouse</u>, ed. R.C. Rathburn & M. Steinmann (Minneapolis: Univ. of Minnesota Press, 1958) pp. 257-73.
O'Faolain, Sean	'E.M. Forster', <u>London Mercury</u> April 1938, vol. XXXVII, pp. 643-44.
Orwell, George	'Inside the Whale', (1940), in <u>Collected Essays</u> (London: Secker & Warburg, 1961) pp. 118-159. 'Wells, Hitler and the World State' (1941), in <u>Collected Essays</u>, pp. 160-6.
Parrinder, Patrick	<u>Authors and Authority: A Study of English Literary Criticism and Its Relation to Culture</u> (London: Routledge & Kegan Paul, 1977).
Parry, Benita	'E.M. Forster: <u>A Passage to India</u>', in <u>Delusions and Discoveries: Studies on India in the British Imagination 1880-1930</u> (London: Allen Lane, 1972) pp. 260-320.
Peel, Robert M.	'Plot: Pattern or Power', <u>Books and Bookmen</u>, January 1973, vol. XVIII, pp. 34-7.
Pelling, Henry	<u>Popular Politics and Society in Late Victorian Britain</u> (London: Macmillan, 1968).
Pellew, J.D.C.	'The Beliefs of E.M. Forster', <u>Theology</u>, April 1940, vol. XV, pp. 278-85.
Pinchin, Jane L.	'The Bridge: E.M. Forster in Alexandria', in <u>Alexandria Still:</u>

SELECT BIBLIOGRAPHY

	Forster, Durrell and Cavafy (Princeton: Princeton U.P., 1977) pp. 82-158.
Plomer, William	'Books in General', New Statesman and Nation, 17 October 1953, vol. XLVI, pp. 457-8.
Proust, Marcel	Swann's Way, trans. C.K. Scott Moncrieff (London: Chatto & Windus, 1922).
	Swann in Love, trans. C.K. Scott Moncrieff (London: Chatto & Windus, 1922).
Ransom, John Crowe	'Editorial Notes: E.M. Forster', Kenyon Review, Autumn 1943, vol. V, pp. 618-23.
	'Gestures of Dissent', Yale Review, September 1936, No. XXVI, pp. 181-3.
Reed, Walter L.	'The Problem with a Poetics of the Novel', in Towards a Poetics of Fiction, ed. Mark Spilka (op.cit.) pp. 62-74.
Reid, Forrest	'E.M. Forster', in Spectator, 25 March 1938, vol. CLX, pp. 532, 534.
Rolph, C.H.	Books in the Dock (London: Andre Deutsch, 1969).
Rosenbaum, S.P. ed.	The Bloomsbury Group: A Collection of Memoirs, Commentary and Criticism (London: Croom Helm, 1975).
	'E.M. Forster and George Meredith', P.M.L.A., October 1971, vol. LXXXVI, pp. 1037-8.
Ruskin, John	'The Mountain Glory', in Modern Painters (1857; rpt. London: Smith, Elder & Co., 1873) pp. 353-93.
Sen, Ela	'A Room With a View: E.M. Forster Talks to Ela Sen', Envoy July 1956, vol. 1, No.9, p.12.
Shaheen, M.	'Forster and Proust', T.L.S., 21 February 1975, p.197.
	'Forster on Meredith, Review of English Studies, May 1973, vol. 24, No. 94, pp. 185-91.
Singh, Brijraj	The Development of a Critical Tradition: From Pater to Yeats (Delhi: Macmillan, 1978).
Smith, H.A.	'Forster's Humanism and the Nineteenth Century', in Forster:

SELECT BIBLIOGRAPHY

Spender, Stephen	A Collection of Critical Essays, ed. M. Bradbury, pp. 106-16.
The Destructive Element: A Study of Modern Writers and Beliefs (London: Cape, 1935).
'E.M. Forster (1879-1970)', New York Review of Books, 23 July 1970, p.4.
Forward From Liberalism (London: Gollancz, 1937).
'Personal Relations and Public Powers', in The Creative Element: A Study of Vision, Despair and Orthodoxy among some modern writers (London: Hamish Hamilton, 1953) pp. 77-91.
The Thirties and After: Poetry, Politics, People (1933-75) (Glasgow: Fontana, 1978).
World Within World (London: Hamish Hamilton, 1951).
Spilka, Mark	'Henry James and Walter Besant: The Art of Fiction Controversy', in Towards a Poetics of Fiction, ed. Mark Spilka (Bloomington: Indiana U.P., 1977) pp. 190-210.
Sprott, W.J.H.	'Forster as a humanist', in Aspects of E.M. Forster. ed. O. Stallybrass, pp. 73-80.
Stallybrass, Oliver J., ed.	Aspects of E.M. Forster: essays and recollections written for his ninetieth birthday (London: Edward Arnold, 1969).
Stevenson, R.L.	'A Humble Remonstrance' (1884) in Realism and Romanticism in Fiction, ed. E. Current Garcia & W.R. Patrick (op. cit.) pp. 109-18.
Stone, Wilfred	The Cave and the Mountain: A Study of E.M. Forster (1966; rpt. Stanford. Stanford U.P., 1969).
'Forster on Love and Money', in Aspects of E.M. Forster, ed. Stallybrass, pp. 107-21.
'Forster on Profit and Loss', in A Human Exploration, ed. Das & Beer, pp. 69-78.
'Overleaping Class: Forster's Problem in Connection', Modern

SELECT BIBLIOGRAPHY

	Language Quarterly, December 1978, vol. 39, pp. 386-404.
Symons, Julian	The Thirties: A Dream Revolved (London: Cresset Press, 1960).
Thomson, George H.	'E.M. Forster, Gerald Heard and Bloomsbury', English Literature in Transition (1969), vol. 12, No.2, pp. 87-91.
	'E.M. Forster and Howard Sturgis', Texas Studies in Modern Language and Literature, Fall 1968, pp. 423-33.
	The Fiction of E.M. Forster (Detroit: Wayne State U.P., 1962).
	'A Forster Miscellany: Thoughts on the Uncollected Writings', in Aspects of E.M. Forster, ed. Stallybrass, pp. 155-76.
Tillotson, Geoffrey	'Henry James and His Limitations', in Criticism and the Nineteenth Century (London: Athlone Press, 1951) pp. 244-69.
Trevelyan, G.M.	'Mr. E.M.Forster on Scott', in A Layman's Love of Letters (London: Longmans, Green & Co., 1954) pp. 96-105.
Trilling, Lionel	'Dr. Leavis and the Moral Tradition', in A Gathering of Fugitives (1956; rpt. London: Secker & Warburg, 1957) pp. 101-6.
	E.M. Forster: A Study (1944; rpt. London: Hogarth, 1967).
	'Freud and Literature', in The Liberal Imagination: Essays on Literature and Society (1948; rpt. London: Secker & Warburg, 1951) pp. 34-57.
	'The Great Aunt of Mr. Forster', in A Gathering of Fugitives (op.cit.), pp. 1-11.
	'Kipling', in The Liberal Imagination (ibid.), pp. 118-128.
	Matthew Arnold (New York: Norton & Co., 1939).
	'The Primal Curse', New Republic, 5 October 1938, vol. XCVI, p. 247.
	'The Snow-Leavis Controversy',

SELECT BIBLIOGRAPHY

	in <u>Beyond Culture: Essays on Literature and Learning</u> (1955; rpt. London: Secker & Warburg, 1966) pp. 145-77.
Trivedi, Harish	'Forster and Virginia Woolf: The Critical Friends', in <u>A Human Exploration</u>, ed. Das & Beer (op.cit.), pp. 216-30.
Truitt, Willis	'Thematic and Symbolic Ideology in the Works of E.M. Forster', <u>The Journal of Aesthetics and Art Criticism</u>, Fall 1971, pp. 101-9.
Warner, Rex	<u>E.M. Forster</u> (London: Longmans, Green and Co., 1950).
Warren, Austin	'E.M. Forster', in <u>Rage For Order: Essays in Criticism</u> (Chicago: Univ. of Chicago Press, 1948) pp. 119-41.
Watson, George G.	<u>The Literary Critics: A Study of English Descriptive Criticism</u> (1964; rpt. London: Chatto & Windus, 1973).
	<u>Politics and Literature in Modern Britain</u> (London: Macmillan, 1977).
Watt, Donald	'G.E. Moore and the Bloomsbury Group', <u>English Literature in Transition</u>, vol. 12, No.3, pp. 119-34.
Wellek, René	'Kant and Schiller', in <u>A History of Modern Criticism</u> (London: Cape, 1955), vol. I, pp. 227-55.
	'August Wilhelm Schlegel', in <u>A History of Modern Criticism</u> (London: Cape, 1955), vol. II, pp. 36-73.
	'Stephane Mallarmé', in <u>A History of Modern Criticism</u> (1965; rpt. London: Cape, 1966), vol. IV, pp. 452-63.
	'Walter Pater', in <u>A History of Modern Criticism</u> (ibid.) pp. 381-99.
Wells, H.G.	<u>After Democracy: Address and Papers on the Present World Situation</u> (London: Watts & Co., 1932).
	<u>Boon, The Mind of the Race, The Wild Asses of the Devil, and The</u>

SELECT BIBLIOGRAPHY

	Last Trump (London: Fisher & Unwin, 1915).
	The Open Conspiracy: Blueprints for a World Revolution (London: Gollancz, 1928).
	'My Point of View', in Points of View: A Series of Broadcast Addresses (London: Allen & Unwin, 1930) pp. 49-69.
Wilde, Alan	Art and Order: A Study of E.M. Forster (London: Peter Owen, 1964).
Wilde, Oscar	'The Critic as Artist' (in two parts), in Plays, Prose Writings and Poems (London: Dent, 1930) pp. 1-31, 32-66.
Williams, Orlo	'Recent Books', Criterion, February 1928, vol. VII, pp. 176-9.
Williams, Francis	Dangerous Estate: The Anatomy of Newspapers (London: Longmans, Green & Co., 1957).
Williams, Raymond	Culture and Society, 1780-1950 (1958; rpt. Harmondsworth: Penguin, 1976).
	'The Bloomsbury Fraction', in Problems in Culture and Materialism (London: Verso, 1980) pp. 148-69.
Wilson, Angus	'A Conversation with E.M. Forster', Encounter, November 1957, vol. IX, pp. 17-18.
Wilson, Edmund	Axel's Castle: A Study in the imaginative literature of 1870-1930 (New York: Charles Scribner's Sons, 1931).
Woolf, Leonard	Sowing: An Autobiography of the Years 1880-1904 (London: Hogarth, 1960).
	Growing: An Autobiography of the Years 1904-1911 (London: Hogarth, 1961).
	Beginning Again: An Autobiography of the Years 1911-1918 (London: Hogarth, 1964).
	Downhill All the Way: An Autobiography of the Years 1918-1939. (London: Hogarth, 1967).
	The Journey Not the Arrival Matters: An Autobiography of the Years 1939-1969 (London:

SELECT BIBLIOGRAPHY

	Hogarth, 1969). 'Samuel Butler', in <u>Essays on Literature, History, Politics</u> etc. (London: Hogarth, 1927) pp. 44-56.
Woolf, Virginia	'The Anatomy of Fiction', in <u>Granite and Rainbow</u> (London: Hogarth, 1932) pp. 51-8. 'The Leaning Tower', in <u>Collected Essays</u> (London: Hogarth, 1966) vol. IV, pp. 162-81. 'Modern Fiction', in <u>Collected Essays</u> (ibid.), vol. I, pp. 103-10. 'Mr. Bennett and Mrs. Brown', in <u>Collected Essays</u> (ibid.), vol. II, pp. 319-37. 'The Narrow Bridge of Art', in <u>Granite and Rainbow</u> (see above) pp. 11-23. 'The Novels of E.M. Forster', in <u>The Death of the Moth and other essays</u> (London: Hogarth, 1942) pp. 104-12. 'Robinson Crusoe', in <u>The Common Reader</u>, 2nd series (London: Hogarth, 1932) pp. 51-8. <u>Roger Fry: A Biography</u> (London: Hogarth, 1940).
Wright, Iain	'F.R. Leavis, the 'Scrutiny' Movement and the Crisis', in <u>Culture and Crisis in Britain in the Thirties</u> (London: Lawrence and Wishart, 1979) pp. 37-65.

NOTES

(1) I have usually not listed those articles by Forster that have been anthologized. For a full bibliography, see Kirkpatrick.
(2) I have not given page numbers because much of this material is still in the process of proper classification.

INDEX

Abinger Harvest, 12, 15-16, 114, 164, 174, 175, 182, 184, 186
Abrams, M.H. (The Mirror and the Lamp), 100, 104, 123
aestheticism, see art for art's sake
Alexandria/Alexandria: A History and a Guide, 12, 78-82, 86, 195
Allen, C.K. (Bureaucracy Triumphant), 58
'Anonymity: An Enquiry', 98, 101
A Passage to India, 1-2, 3, 10-11, 17, 25, 46, 173
Arnold, Matthew, 3, 4, 10, 61-3, 94, 103, 108-10, 116, 157, 161, 165, 184-5, 198
Arius (of Alexandria), 81-2
art/artists, 37, 46, 55, 63-5, 67, 85, 92-116, 123, 131-2, 134, 142-4, 152-6, 161-2, 174, 196
art for art's sake ('Art for Art's Sake'), 15, 65, 103-4, 107, 116, 161, 188
Aspects of the Novel, 12, 15, 98, 107, 125-7, 130-3, 140, 145, 152, 157, 158, 165, 178, 181, 195, 198
Asquith, 15
Athenaeum, 4
Atlee, 60
Auden, W.H., 25, 115, 179
Austen, Jane, 124, 164, 177-8, 186

Baker, Ernest (History of the English Novel), 159
Balzac, 128
Banerjee, G.N. (Hellenism in Ancient India), 78
B.B.C., 15, 74, 114
Beach, J., 128
Beethoven, 42, 88, 127, 157
Bell, Clive, 96, 105, 115, 154, 161
Bell, Julian, 25; 'War and Peace: Open Letter to E.M. Forster', 42, 64
Belloc, Hilaire, 76, 81-2
Benn, Sir Ernest (Modern Government), 58
Bennett, Arnold, 128
Bentley, Eric (The Cult of the Superman), 40
Bentley, Michael, 6, 10

249

INDEX

Bentwich, Norman (<u>Hellenism</u>), 78
Bergson, Henri, 96-7, 124, 140-1
Bernal, J.D., 28
Beveridge Report, 60
Bloomsbury Group, 3, 14, 67, 106-7, 194
Blake, William, 57, 99-100, 181, 183, 186
Bodkin, Maud (<u>Archetypal Patterns in Poetry</u>), 97
'Books That Influenced Me', 180-1
Booth, Wayne C., 129
Bradley, A.C., 94, 103-4, 106, 116
Brailsford, Henry, 13
Branson, Noreen, 8; -- and Margot Heinemann, 24
Brentford, Lord (<u>Do We Need a Censor</u>), 114
British Union of Fascists, 25
Brock, A. Clutton (<u>Essay on Books</u>), 158
Bryce, Lord, 6
Butler, Samuel (<u>Erewhon</u>), 40, 175, 177, 179-80

Cambridge: scientists (Eddington and Jeans), 23; Humanists, 75, 82
Carlyle, Thomas (<u>Of Heroes, Hero-Worship and the Heroic in History</u>), 40, 162, 181
Carpenter, Edward, 57
Carroll, Lewis, 140
Caudwell, Christopher (<u>Studies in a Dying Culture</u>), 25, 36-7, 38-9, 64, 66, 158
Cavafy, C.P., 186
'The Challenge of Our Time', 60, 63-4
Chekhov, Anton, 162, 186
Chesterton, G.K. (<u>The New Jerusalem</u>), 76
Christ/Christian/Christianity, 17, 30, 39, 42-5, 58, 74-82, 86-8, 174
Clark, Kenneth (<u>The Nude</u>), 43, 99
Clement (of Alexandria), 68, 80-1
Coleridge, S.T., 10, 93, 95, 100, 102, 143, 155, 162, 182, 184, 186
<u>Commonplace Book</u> (Forster's), 13, 23, 40, 43, 73, 77, 126
communism/communist, 41
Conrad, Joseph, 164, 186
Crabbe, George, 170, 182-3
'The Creator as Critic', 95-6, 175-6, 195
Crews, Frederick, 4
critic/criticism, 67, 92, 96, 108-9, 113, 152-65, 168-202

<u>Daily Herald</u>, 14-15
<u>Daily News</u>, 15
Dante, 45, 157, 161, 162-3, 168-9, 170, 174, 196, 199
de la Mare, Walter, 14, 201
Deimel, Theodor (<u>Carlyle und der Nationalsozialismus</u>), 40
democracy, 57-60
<u>The Development of English Prose Between 1918-1939</u>, 201-2
Dickinson, Goldsworthy Lowes, 3-4, 11, 13, 53, 68, 86, 201; disillusionment after 1914, 6; and the League of Nations, 6; idea of Good, 30; humanism in <u>The Magic Flute</u>, 88-9; 'The Emergence of a Latent Memory Under Hypnosis',

INDEX

95; view of art, 107
Donne, John, 173
Dostoevsky, 144, 164
Dryden, John, 176-7
'The Duty of Society to the artist', 98, 113
Dworkin, Ronald, 38-9, 67

Eddington, 23
Ede, H.S. (<u>A Life of Gaudier-Brzeska</u>), 43
<u>Egyptian Mail</u>, 171
Einstein, Albert, 8-9, 202
Eliot, T.S., 24, 98, 155, 158, 162-3, 194 196, 201
Elizabethan age, 172-3, 185-6
Empson, William, 160

Faith, 53-5, 72-3, 77-8
Fascism, 15-16, 24-5, 27, 30, 40-2, 46, 55, 64; Fascist, 26-7, 34, 40-1, 58-9, 194
'The Fiction Factory', 159
Firbank, Ronald, 140
First World War, <u>see</u> War
Flaubert, 128
Ford, Ford Madox, 128, 158-9
freedom, 26-8, 34-9, 41-2, 46-7, 53-4, 58, 60-1, 63, 65
Freeman, John, 14
Freud, Sigmund, 8-9, 97, 124, 161, 202; ideas of, 33, 54, 96
Fry, Roger (<u>see also</u> 'Roger Fry'), 67, 94, 97, 103, 105, 107, 112, 137-8, 145, 161
'The Function of Literature in War Time',

110-11
Furbank, P.N., 2, 17, 160-1, 165

Galsworthy, John, 128
'The Game of Life', 34-5
Gaskell, Elizabeth, 178
George, Stefan, 40
Gibbon, Edward, 67, 175, 177
Gide, Andre (<u>Back from the USSR</u>, trans. Dorothy Bussy), 36; <u>Les Faux Monayeurs</u>, 136
Graves, Robert, 65
Green, T.H., 62
Gurdjieff, 29

Haldane, J.B.S., 28
Hall, Radclyffe (<u>The Well of Loneliness</u>), 113
Hamilton, Clayton (<u>The Materials and Methods of Fiction</u>), 132, 159
Hammond, J.L., 13
Hanley, James (<u>Boy</u>), 114
Hardy, Thomas, 128, 157, 178, 181-2, 190
Hayek, F.A., 30
Hazlitt, William, 16
Heard, Henry Fitzgerald ('Gerald'), 29, 31-4, 42, 65, 175
Hegel/Hegelian, 28
Heinemann, Margot, <u>see</u> Branson
Hewart, Lord (The New Despotism), 58-9
<u>The Hill of Devi</u>, 13, 82
Hinduism, 17, 74, 82-6, 152
Hitler, 24, 25, 36, 40, 58
Hobhouse, L.T., 13, 55-6, 62-3
<u>Howards End</u>, 1-2, 46
'How I Listen to Music', 125
Hoyle, Fred, 23
humanism, <u>see</u> liberal
Huxley, Aldous, 14, 29,

251

INDEX

32, 124, 175
Huxley, Julian, 23
Huysmans, J.K., 24
'Hymn Before Action', 83-4
Hynes, Samuel, 57, 187

Ibsen, Henrik, 162-3, 164, 179, 186-7
imagination, 54, 94-9, 146, 156
<u>Independent Review</u>, 3-4, 6, 13
Independent Labour Party, 14
'Inspiration', 94
'In the Temple of Criticism', 158
Isherwood, Christopher, 29, 31
Islam, 17, 74, 84, 86-7
ivory tower ('The Ivory Tower'), 64-6, 84, 85, 96, 107-8, 186

James, Henry, 128-9, 137-8, 145-6, 164, 165, 186, 194-6, 198
James, William, 124
Jeans, 23
'Jehovah, Buddha and the Greeks', 78
'Jew Consciousness', 40
Joad, C.E.M., 31
Jones, David, 3
Joyce, James, 124, 157, 164, 165, 179, 198-9, 200, 201
Jung, C.G., 95-7, 139

Kant, 115
Keats, John, 92
Kemp, Harry and Laura Riding (<u>The Left Heresy in Literature and Life</u>), 56
Keynes, J.M., 13
Kipling, Rudyard, 5, 54, 75, 158, 162-3, 169, 186, 187-94, 199

Kirkpatrick, B.J., 12
Kramrisch, Stella, 85, 102
Krishna, 68, 74, 82-6
Krishnamurthy, J., 29

Labour Party, 6, 7, 14
Laski, Harold, 4, 30, 59-60, 175
Lawrence, D.H., 40, 114, 128, 157, 158, 161, 165, 179, 186, 195, 196, 200, 201
Lawrence, T.E., 86, 186, 196, 198
League of Nations, 6, 13
Leavis, F.R. and Q.D., 112-13, 116, 161, 163-5
Lenin/Leninist, 36-7
Lewis, C. Day, 25, 114
liberal/liberalism:
  decline of, 2, 197;
  Edwardian, 3;
  journals, 3; 'new', 4;
  and Fabians, 5, 13;
  after 1914, 5-7, 8-12;
  intelligentsia, 10;
  philosophy/philosophical, 12, 62;
  newspaper, 15;
  democracy, 15, 25, 85;
  humanism, 17, 38, 42-3, 59, 78, 170;
  notion of freedom, 34, 37-8; creed, 55;
  Laski on, 59-60;
  in the thirties, 64;
  view of society, 67;
  view of culture, 112
Liberal Party, 6, 7-12, 13
liberty, 30, 38-42, 60
'Liberty in England', 15-16, 39, 58, 114
Lindsay, Jack (<u>A Handbook of Freedom</u>), 35, 38-9
Lips, Eva (<u>What Hitler Did To Us</u>), 40
<u>The Listener</u>, 15
love, 26-7, 31-4, 39-42,

252

INDEX

46-7, 53-5, 57-8, 99, 102
Lowes, John Livingstone (The Road to Xanadu), 95, 97
Lubbock, Percy (The Craft of Fiction), 128-30, 158
Lynd, Robert (The Art of Letters), 158

Macaulay, Rose, 14
MacCarthy, Desmond, 14
MacNeice, Louis, 25
'Macolnia Shops', 16
Mallarmé, Stefan, 124
Mann, Thomas, 126
Marcuse, Herbert, 66
Martin, Kingsley, 14
Marx, Karl, 37, 39, 161; Marxism, 4, 11, 30, 41, 45-6, 62, 64, 66; Marxist, 26, 28, 34-6, 65, 66, 107
Masood, Syed Ross, 86
Massingham, H.W., 9, 13
Masterman, C.F.G., 13
Mauron, Charles, 94, 97, 127, 154
Melville, Herman, 164, 165, 195
'The Menace to Freedom', 25, 29-31, 33, 35, 37
Meredith, George, 73, 164, 178-9
Mill, John Stuart, 3, 4, 35, 41, 55-6, 58-9, 61, 63; Millite liberalism, 93, 133
Milton, John, 35, 66, 92, 114, 168-9, 174
'The Mind of the Indian Native State', 15
Moore, G.E., 3, 4, 75
Mosley, Oswald, 25
Mortimer, Raymond, 14
Murray, Gilbert, 6
Murry, John Middleton, 13, 29, 158

music, 123-32, 140, 142-5, 199
Mussolini, 25, 40
mystics/mysticism, 30, 72-3, 79, 93
'My Wood', 43-6

Nation, 3-4, 9, 13-14
Nation and Athenaeum, 13-15
National Council of Civil Liberties, 25
Nevinson, Henry, 14
'The New disorder', 29, 33, 72, 92-3
Nietzsche, 40
Nordic Twilight, 40
'Notes on the English Character', 15, 43, 180, 185
'Not Looking at Pictures' 106
New Statesman, 13-14
New Statesman and Nation, 14-15

Origen (Of Alexandria), 68, 80-1
Orwell, George, 28, 161, 186
Ouida, 77
'Our Greatest Benefactor', 87
Ouspensky, 29

Parrinder, Patrick, 162-3
Pater, Walter, 156, 161
'Peeping at Elizabeth', 172-4, 185
personal relations, 53-4, 56, 177
Pharos and Pharillon, 12
Philo (of Alexandria), 79-80
Plotinus/Plotinian, 68, 79-81, 93, 99, 101, 133
Proust/Proustian, 8, 95-6, 124, 162, 164, 172, 177, 186, 196-8, 199, 201;

INDEX

A La Recherche du Temps Perdu, 96, 140-2, 196-7

'Racial Exercise', 40
Radhakrishnan, S., 29
'The Raison d'Etre of Criticism in the Arts', 94-5, 108, 125-6, 153, 157
Reid, Forrest, 162-3
religion, see Hinduism, Islam and Christianity
Renan, 75
Richards, I.A., 105, 159-60, 161
Rickword, Edgell (A Handbook of Freedom), 35-6, 38-9
Riding, Laura, see Kemp
Robeson, Paul, 99
'Roger Fry', 16, 22
Romantic/Romanticism, 12, 93-5, 100, 115, 123, 124, 157, 163, 178, 182; poets, 3, 16, 116, 123, 182, 193; and Rousseau, 27
Rousseau, 28, 37
Ruskin, John, 163
Russell, Bertrand, 23, 78
Russia/Russian, 162; -- Revolution, 24-5, 41; and the Beaverbrook-Rothermere press, 24; artists in, 36-7

scepticism, 6, 24, 46
Schlegel, A.W., 145-6
scientists/scientific ideas, 23, 28-9, 67
Scott, Sir Walter, 164, 165
Second World War, see War
Shakespeare, 163, 165, 168, 170-2, 173-4, 175, 176;

Richard II, 59,
Macbeth, 104, 156;
Othello, 110-11;
Hamlet, 156;
Julius Caesar, 168-74;
Antony and Cleopatra, 169-72
Sharp, Clifford, 14
Shaw, George Bernard, 14, 179, 186
Shelley, P.B., 57, 100, 131-2, 182
Sheppard, Canon 'Dick', 32
Simpson, James, 87
Skelton, Robert, 162, 168-9, 174
socialism/socialist; Christian, 11, 45-6; Scientific, 11, 30, 34; -- and the Labour Party, 14; co-operation, 38; liberal, 62; philosophy, 63
society/social order, 53-4, 64-8, 72, 101, 108, 111-12, 113-15, 142-3, 153-4
The Spectator, 15
Spender, Stephen, 11, 25, 64
Spengler, Oswald, 42
spirit/spiritualism/human spirit, 39, 42-5, 61, 63, 72-3, 93, 98, 101-2, 110, 131, 133-4, 136, 142, 144-5, 154, 161, 162
Stalin, 25, 42
Stallybrass, O.J., 158
Stein, Gertrude, 133
Stephen, Leslie, 3, 162
Stone, Wilfred, 4, 10-11, 17, 68
Strachey, John (The Coming Struggle for Power), 41, 64
Strachey, Lytton, 68, 186, 200
Swinburne, A.C., 103

254

INDEX

Swift, Jonathan, 139, 165, 179, 181, 198
Symons, Julian, 64

Thornton, Henry ('Henry Thornton'), 42
'Three Anti-Nazi Broadcasts', 40
'Three Generations', 178-9, 193, 197, 200, 201
tolerance, 57-8, 64, 72, 78, 84, 93
Tolstoy, Leo, 162, 164, 186; What, Then, Must We Do, 44-5; on art, 103, 108-9; War and Peace, 129, 143
Toynbee, Arnold, 31, 42, 47
Trilling, Lionel, 109-10, 161, 163-5
Two Cheers for Democracy, 12, 15-16
Tyndale-Biscoe, C.E., 77

Virgil, 22-3, 191-2
Voltaire, 28, 67, 68, 86, 88, 175-6, 177, 181

Wagner/Wagnerian, 28, 40, 124-5, 127, 140, 172
War: First World War, 3-12, 23-4, 30, 171-2;
Second World War, 5, 29, 60, 111, 175, 199
Warren, Austin (Rage for Order), 42, 102-3
Webbs, Beatrice and Sidney, 14, 169
Wellek, Rene, 115, 145
Wells, H.G., 8, 28, 31, 37, 128, 137-8, 145-6, 186
'What I Believe', 16, 22, 24, 26-7, 29-31, 42, 53, 54-5, 61, 63-4, 68, 72, 107
Whitman, Walt, 57
Wilde, Oscar, 75, 103, 155-6, 161
Williams, Raymond, 10, 67, 185
Woolf, Leonard, 4-7, 14, 180-1, 186
Woolf, Virginia, 106, 124, 128, 132, 134, 137-8, 143, 145-6, 161, 164, 165, 196, 200, 201
Wordsworth, 61, 66, 95, 100, 108, 162-3, 182, 183-4, 186

Yeats, W.B., 201

Zola, Emil, 128